Groves Monographs on Marriage and Family

Series Editor: Brian Paul Masciadrelli

# Groves Monographs on Marriage and Family

*Groves Monographs on Marriage and Family is an edited book series based on the annual meetings of the Groves Conference on Marriage and Family, an interdisciplinary, interprofessional organization of limited invited membership founded in 1934. Groves Monographs publishes work on the leading edges of theory development and empirical research in the field of family studies. Individual volumes are edited by the chairs of the annual Groves Conferences and include peer-reviewed chapters by the conference presenters and invited authors. Topics are timely and provocative with diverse themes.*

Groves Monographs on Marriage and Family
Volume 5

# Gender, Sexual Identity, and Families:
# The Personal Is Political

## Kevin P. Lyness
*Antioch University New England*

## Judith L. Fischer
*Texas Tech University*

*Volume Editors*

Michigan Publishing
*University of Michigan Library*
*Ann Arbor, Michigan*
*2019*

*For information:*
Groves Conference on Marriage and Family
P.O. Box 1011, Forest Lake, MN 55025
*grovesmanager@yahoo.com*
*www.grovesconference.org*


Groves Monographs on Marriage & Family, Volume 5
Gender, sexual identity, and families: The personal *is* political
[edited by] Kevin P. Lyness, Judith L. Fischer

ISBN: 978-1-60785-596-5

Michigan Publishing
University of Michigan Library
Ann Arbor, Michigan
2019

# Gender, Sexual Identity, and Families: The Personal Is Political

# Contents

*Introduction*

**Gender, Sexual Identity, and Families:**

**The Personal *is* Political**

*Kevin P. Lyness*

*Antioch University New England*

As I write this in the Autumn of 2018 issues of gender are again taking front stage in our politics in the US. Dr. Christine Blasey Ford and Judge Brett Kavanaugh just testified in front of the US Senate subcommittee regarding Judge Kavanaugh's nomination to the US Supreme Court and her accusations of drunken sexual assault (amid other accusations). At the core, this has been about gender and power and we see gender politics playing out in extreme ways—just one example is that Dr. Ford was compelled to be nice, helpful, and responsive, while Judge Kavanaugh was free to be angry, evasive, and nonresponsive. The media is full of analyses of these dynamics (e.g., Fisher, 2018; Lithwick, 2018; Nilson, 2018) and the controversy has opened further our national discussion about sexual violence against women built on the #MeToo movement and other related movements that have brought these issues to the forefront of popular culture. Similarly, at the forefront of our political discourse, there have been political shifts from condemnation to favorable judicial rulings on same-sex marriage and see-sawing political efforts to ban and accept transgender people in the military and other arenas of communities.

Of course, these gender dynamics are nothing new, and whole books could be (and have been written) on how gender and sexuality have been used to marginalize and oppress. In 1988, Virginia Goldner said "Gender … is not a secondary, mediating variable like race, class, or ethnicity, but, rather, a fundamental, organizing principle of all family systems" (p. 17). She goes on to say "gender and generation are best understood as the two fundamental, organizing principles of family life"

(p. 18, italics added). Gender is clearly a key piece of understanding family relationships, and in this volume we add some pieces to the puzzle of understanding the roles that gender and the intersection of gender with sexuality play in families. The Groves Conference on Marriage and Family has long promoted progressive values and takes a social justice approach to looking at family relationships. In the summer of 2016, in Denver, Colorado, we held our Annual Conference to talk about these issues in the variety of ways that they fit with the interdisciplinary nature of Groves. We have articles here that were inspired by the conference or discussed at the conference and that cover a wide range of topics related to gender, sexual identity, and families, covering the lifespan and exploring a range of topics on this issue.

This volume has several important themes. The first is that, unsurprisingly, gender and the role of gender in the power dynamics of families takes center stage in most of these articles. The monograph starts with an exploration of gender polarization over time using the Bem Sex Role Inventory. The research demonstrates that gender polarization increased over the 25-year span of this longitudinal study. Another important theme of this volume is how gender intersects with sexual orientation, explored in a series of chapters looking at shifts in attitudes and treatment of lesbian, gay, bisexual, and transgender populations. Authors explore the role of the Defense of Marriage Act (DOMA) and its repeal, the increasing recognition for transgender individuals in couples and families, as well as the situations of older transgender women in family relationships. Another chapter takes a look at how a church community treats its LGBT members from the perspective of those members, and still another chapter explores alternative relationship paradigms. An overriding theme from these chapters concerns the struggles and the successes of social justice advancement. A theme that connects several chapters is the contextualizing of sexuality and gender issues through a developmental approach. Two chapters explore the role of gender in sexual decision making in youth, a third highlights the use of dance to interpret cultural messages about gender and family, and two others explore later life issues (the aforementioned chapter on older transgender women in families along with a chapter on elder financial exploitation and the role gender plays). Midlife issues are examined by family professionals reflecting on their experiences with gender and work life.

This monograph will appeal to family scientists and to clinicians working with families, and who seek a multidisciplinary approach. There are results from qualitative inquiries as well quantitative studies. Moreover, the contributors are clinicians, researchers, and university administrators working to advance understanding of gender and sexuality in families. The final chapter is a selective glossary — an introduction to concepts of gender and sexuality and a primer on contemporary best practices in language that many will find helpful. As current events and these chapters illuminate, understandings of gender and sexuality and identity continue to unfold in nonlinear and even frustrating fashion, yet the social justice impetus behind these chapters reflects the importance of persistence in our endeavors.

## References

Fisher, M. (2018, September). Analysis: Kavanaugh hearing an epic struggle over trust, gender, politics. *The Press Herald*. Retrieved from www.pressherald.com.

Goldner, V. (1988). Generation and gender: Normative and covert hierarchies. *Family Process, 27*, 17-31.

Lithwick, D. (2018, September). Jurisprudence: Fear a Justice Brett Kavanaugh. *Slate*. Retrieved from www.slate.com.

Nilson, E. (2018, September). "This brings back so much pain": Why so many women saw themselves in Christine Blasey Ford's story of sexual assault. *Vox*. Retrieved from www.vox.com.

## Chapter 1

**The War on Gender Equality is Working:**

**The Bem Sex Role Inventory Across 25 Years**

*Judith L Fischer*

*Texas Tech University*

*Cheryl A. Juergens*

*Gallatin City-County Health Department (MT)*

Acknowledgements: This project was supported in part by Grant No. R01 HD 18864 "Network Supports and Coping in Adult Transitions" from NICHD to Judith Fischer & Donna Sollie. The authors declare that they have no conflicts of interest. We thank many people past and present who worked on this project.

*The enculturated-lens theory of individual gender formation…situate[s] the individual from birth to death in a social and historical context containing the lenses of androcentrism and gender polarization (Bem, 1993, p. 138).*

Decades ago the women's movement provided encouragement that institutional barriers to gender equality were falling (Bem, 1993). But Bem's 1993 writings also described the entrenched U.S. social world as one that was structured by white heterosexual men to maintain and defend male privilege. In such a patriarchy, men could not cross gender boundaries without heavy stigmatization; thus, for secure gender identity, "real" men had to suppress tendencies toward femininity within themselves. Although the majority of US men were not themselves powerful in society, Bem argued that they were able to avoid feeling emasculated by seeing themselves as more powerful than women and gay men. In support of this theorizing, Cheryan, Cameron Schwartz, Katagiri, and Monin (2015) reported that, compared to controls, men who felt threatened responded by increasing their self-reported masculinity and decreasing their femininity. As well, an androcentric societal structure meant that women worked rigorously to live up to the ideal of the "real" woman as someone who was sexually attractive to men (Bem, 1993). Men who threaten women in the context of relationships also regulate and contest women's autonomy (DeShong, 2015). Furthermore, unchanging workplace constraints that reflect the policies of gendered institutions overrule individual desires (Pedulla & Thébaud, 2015).

When under perceived threat, it is unsurprising that powerful societal institutions and psychological processes push back (Wood & Eagly, 2002). The gender equality gains of the 1960s and 1970s challenged the security of the gender identities of men and women (Bem, 1993), and were met with backlash (Bem, 1993; Faludi, 1991). By 2010, the gender revolution was described by a scholar as "uneven and stalled" (England, 2010, p. 149) in that women were not moving up in their jobs and careers and women's traditional jobs continued to be devalued and unattractive to men. To be a feminist became equated with being anti-men (Robnett, Anderson, & Hunter, 2012). Fueled in part by patriarchal beliefs, the New Right (Ruth, 1983), composed of people and organizations from the Radical Religious Right, Moral Majority, and New Conservatism, became a counter movement to gender equality. Concomitant with this patriarchal thrust were intensified restrictions on women's reproductive choices (Finlay, 2006). The backlash of the late 1980s and early 1990s was reflected in the political and cultural successes of the New Right. Fitting into this context, the events of September 11, 2001 (9/11) provided a pretext for a pervasive, intense mainstream backlash (Anderson, 2015; Faludi, 2007; Lorber, 2005). As Faludi described in detail in her 2007 book The Terror Dream, the U.S. responded to a threat to the homeland by transforming it into a threat to the domestic home, an excuse to erase the gains of gender equality and restore real men to their purported "rightful" positions. Faludi described this 9/11 response as rooted in androcentric myths and delusions that conformed to a long tradition of such U.S. responses to real threats. Gilligan (2011) identified tensions surrounding femininity: in a democracy, to be caring is to be human, but in a patriarchy to be caring is dismissed as feminine.

This study was conducted to identify historical shifts in gender role identity. It is bookended by earlier times that saw increasing promotion of gender equality and later times that saw increasing pressures to reverse these gains through the revival of long-standing cultural identifications with patriarchy, androcentrism, and gender polarization. At its heart, if the war on gender equality is working it should reveal itself at a personal level. That is, self-identifications of masculinity and femininity would differ in ways reflecting greater polarization in recent times compared to earlier times. There are a variety of ways to index gender equality, such as work force participation, wages, and shared home tasks. We chose to consider gendered identifications because of the important personal and relational consequences to individuals in a world ordered by gender (Starr & Zurbriggen, 2016) and by binary conceptualizations of gender.

There are several explanations that could explain the changes/differences in masculinity and femininity in different time periods. First, is an historical times explanation. In this study, the term historical times refers to the year or time of measurement; it is shorthand for the cultural and societal themes evident at that time. According to Bem (1993), people in different historical times will differ based on the historical events and accompanying cultural expectations and norms of the time. She asserted that "the assignment of women and men to different and unequal positions in the social structure" accounted for conventional gendering of women and men and not childhood socialization (Bem, 1993, p. 135). Between 1982 and 2007 there were many important social changes such as increased: national average age of first marriage (U.S. Census Bureau, 2015), parents' age of first birth (Kirmeyer & Hamilton, 2011), participation of women in the workforce (Wood & Eagly, 2002), and time span between high school and the assumption of adult responsibilities (Arnett, 2000). As well, the events of 9/11 were seared in public consciousness (Faludi, 2007). At the time of measurement in the spring of 2007, these events were less than six years in the past and, as a result, the country was still at war. Thus, time of measurement is the focus of this research.

A second explanation for gender role changes is to consider cohort changes/differences. Birth cohorts are people defined by their year of birth or a span of years such as decade of birth. Birth cohorts are sometimes identified with names associated with particular generations even though exact years may vary from study to study (Parry & Urwin, 2011; Sessa, Kabacoff, Deal, & Brown, 2007). Grouping people into generations reflects the belief that each cohort "share[s] a different set of values and attitudes, as a result of shared events and experiences" (Parry & Urwin, 2011, p. 80), that they share cohort-defining events (that could be modified by parental practices, Stewart & Healy, 1989) or formative experiences when coming of age (Twenge, 1997). When college students are studied, time of coming of age and time of measurement can refer to the same thing. Thus, explanations based on formative experiences (Twenge, 1997) cannot be disentangled from historical time of measurement. However, when adults are studied longitudinally there is a period of separation between formative experiences and later ones.

Comparing two cohorts at one point in time and finding differences does not necessarily support a cohort explanation because members of these cohorts also differ in age. So, in addition to historical times and cohort/formative experiences as explanations of change/difference, there is a third explanation, that refers to age or maturation effects (Parry & Urwin, 2011). Younger selves differ from older selves based on their physical and psychosocial stages of development and accumulations of life experiences. A single design cannot disentangle explanations based on age, historical times, or cohort/formative years.

## Study Design Issues

The disentanglement of time of measurement, cohort, and age requires a multifaceted design. Schaie (1965) formulated procedures to study changes and differences and his explication of most efficient designs informs this study. As illustrated in Table 1, we chose three of Schaie's designs: longitudinal, cross-sectional, and time lag. There are two historical time periods of measurement, 1982 and 2007, and two cohorts, late baby boomers (BB) and Generation Y (GY). Two ages are represented: college senior emerging adults (CS) and midlife adults (ML). The longitudinal component (row) is of a late baby boomer 1958-1962 birth cohort studied in 1982 and 2007 when they were approximately 22 and 47 years old (CS and ML). The cross-sectional (same historical time of measurement) component (column) includes the BB cohort and the GY cohort studied in 2007 when baby boomers were approximately 47 (ML) and the Generation Y group members were approximately 22 years old (birth year 1983 – 1987). The time lag component (diagonal) includes the BB cohort in 1982 compared with the GY cohort in 2007 with both groups approximately 22 years old (CS) at the differing times of measurement.

In the longitudinal design, the time of measurement differs but so do the ages of the participants. Thus, any within-cohort changes could be because of time or age. In the cross-sectional design, two or more groups of people from different birth cohorts participate at the same time, with time of measurement a constant but with varying birth cohorts and ages. Differences between cohorts could be because of cohort membership or age. Finally, when two groups of same-age people, but from different cohorts and different times of measurement (time lag) are assessed, the between-cohort differences could be due to cohort membership or time of measurement. The comparison of patterns of results from these three designs (longitudinal, cross-sectional, time lag) allows inferences about likely loci of changes/differences (Schaie, 1965). The pattern that would reflect the effects of time of measurement would include differences between $BB_{CS}$ and $BB_{ML}$ and between $BB_{CS}$ and $GY_{CS}$ in predicted directions. This brief introduction to research design and to historical developments over the past several decades sets the stage for this study.

| Year of Birth | Ages | |
|---|---|---|
| 1983-1987 Generation Y (GY) | | 20-24; $M$ = 22 years College Seniors Group $GY_{CS}$ |
| 1958-1962 Late Baby Boomers (BB) | 20-24; $M$ = 22 years College Seniors Group $BB_{CS}$ | 45-49; $M$ = 47 years Midlife Adults Group $BB_{ML}$ |
| Time of measurement | 1982 | 2007 |

*Note.* GY = Generation Y; BB = later Baby Boomers; CS = College Seniors; ML = Midlife Adults;
*Longitudinal* (row) design compares *Group $BB_{CS}$* with *Group $BB_{ML}$*;
*Time Lag* (diagonal) design compares *Group $BB_{CS}$* with *Group $GY_{CS}$*;
*Cross-sectional* (column) design compares *Group $BB_{ML}$* with *Group $GY_{CS}$*.

*Table 1. Design of Study: Longitudinal, Cross Sectional, and Time Lag*

## Development of Gender Role Identity in Social Contexts

Gender involves a number of dimensions such as the activities people like to do, their attitudes, and their personal-social attributes (Di-Donato & Berenbaum, 2011). Bem's (1981a) gender schema approach (as expressed in the opening quote from 1993) is very different from earlier conceptualizations of masculinity and femininity as a bipolar construct representing "relatively enduring traits which are more or less rooted in anatomy, physiology, and early experience" (Constantinople, 1973, p. 390). In the late 1960s, Bakan (1966) described two dimensions he termed agency (associated with men) and communion (associated with women). Furthermore, masculinity and femininity could be measured separately (Constantinople, 1973). The BSRI established that women and men could endorse positive characteristics of femininity and masculinity using items that were also freed from the requirement that they distinguish females from males (Bem, 1974). The idea of androgyny, that one person could endorse characteristics approved of for both men and women, provided a conceptual and measurement basis for revised thinking about what was appropriate for all individuals and what constituted a flexible gender role identity (Bem, 1977). Compared to 1982, by the year 2007 there were a number of forces pushing for greater gender polarization (Faludi, 2007). Greater polarization is recognized in a number of ways: men and women changing from their younger selves; men and women of the same age varying when measured at different times. The polarization we are interested in involves (a) men changing/different on femininity through declines/lower scores over time; (b) women changing/different on masculinity through declines/lower scores over time; and (c) declines/lower scores on androgynous expressions of self-identity.

## Changes and Differences on BSRI Masculinity and Femininity Scale Scores

This section considers studies that used time lag, cross-sectional, and longitudinal designs from the 1980s to the mid-2000s. These studies included the BSRI masculinity and femininity scales with continuous scores (Bem, 1974). The purpose of this selective review is to weigh evidence for or against the proposition that self-endorsements of gender roles reflect the time of measurement and to gauge support for alternative explanations such as formative experiences or age-related changes. Generally excluded are the articles covered in the Twenge meta-analysis study (1997) described below. The participants in the reviewed research were in the U.S. and almost all were European American. Although our study is based in the U.S., these same struggles, with equality of men and women and of developing a culture free from androcentric views and patriarchal structures, are persistent and occur in many cultures.

Time Lag Designs

Twenge's (1997) meta-analysis is a good starting point for time lag designs and for understanding differences across time in femininity and masculinity among college students. Twenge's time lag design covered twenty-one years of BSRI administration to college students beginning in 1973 where "effects of the women's movement were only beginning to be felt" (p. 305) to 1994 where many social changes toward equality had occurred. The earliest birth cohorts were 1949-1955 (early Baby Boomers) whereas the latest were 1970-1976 (early Generation X). In correlations of BSRI scores with year of administration, Twenge reported increased BSRI masculinity scores among women and men across time. There was also a suggestion that men's femininity scores increased over time. Furthermore, men and women in the most recent years covered did not differ on masculinity, reflecting convergence, but there remained significant differences between men and women on femininity.

Twenge (1997) interpreted her results as reflecting differences in cohort experiences in formative years associated with different historical times. However, these findings are also congruent with an historical times interpretation. More recently, Donnelly and Twenge (2016) conducted meta-analyses on studies from 1993 to 2012 on masculinity, femininity, and androgyny. From 1993 to 2012, only women's femininity scores decreased. The Donnelly and Twenge meta-analysis primarily embraced the years of backlash (Faludi, 1991) when not many changes over time would be expected. The decline in femininity among women is inconsistent with what might be expected.

## Cross-Sectional Designs

In cross-sectional studies there are same time comparisons of people of different ages who also belong to different generations and represent varying experiences with historical events. For older birth cohorts, the women's movement may have occurred too late to have an impact on the emerging adult socialization of gender roles (Strough, Leszczynski, Neely, Flinn, & Margrett, 2007). Among other cohorts the salience of the women's movement would have been occurring at the same time as the development of identity and for still others (presumably younger) the women's movement would have been the status quo or been under attack.

Age differences reflect not just cohort differences but also any differences that accrue due to the experiences of the maturing individual. The maturity principle predicts that people become more communal and more agentic as they take on adult roles (McAdams & Olson, 2010). Traditionally, agency is a match for work roles and communion a match for family/caregiving roles. When men perform work roles and women perform family roles, then agency would increase in men and communion would increase in women as they progress in these roles. But to the extent that men and women are in similar roles they would demonstrate similar agency and/or communion. But, if even "similar" roles are polarized (Suh, Moskowitz, Fournier, & Zuroff, 2004) men and women performing the same roles would still find men becoming more agentic and women more communion oriented. Hypothesizing from a different basis that presumes lessening of parental and procreation needs with increased age, Guttman's parental imperative approach (1975) predicted a cross-over in gender roles. Older men would score higher on femininity than younger men and older women would score higher on masculinity than younger women.

Lemaster, Delaney, and Strough (2015) research compared three age groups in 2013 and found no differences in masculinity, femininity, or androgyny. With no age group or cohort differences, these results could provide support for an historical times explanation. But, without comparisons to earlier times, they shed no light on changes in gender polarization. Two cross-sectional studies of women (Erdwins, Tyer, & Mellinger, 1983; Mellinger & Erdwins, 1985) representing different ages/cohorts provided some support for the self-endorsement of gender roles consistent with the expectations for their cohort. Because time of measurement is constant, these cross-sectional studies shed light on age/cohort differences but not on time of measurement effects.

Using data collected two decades after the Erdwins et al. (1983) study, Strough et al. (2007) compared both men and women on BSRI masculinity and femininity in six age groups At their time of measurement in the mid-2000s, women's masculinity scores varied by age: younger millennials and boomers were higher than the older preboomers, explained as a function of historical times when coming of age (Strough et al., 2007). These findings support the role of the gender equality movement of the 1960s and 1970s in framing gender role endorsement. However, it is also possible that there are age-related aspects at play such as role involvements in work and family at play (Erdwins et al., 1983; Mellinger & Erdwins, 1985). These cross-sectional studies do not allow conclusions about time of measurement.

## Longitudinal Designs

A third approach to understanding gender roles that allows examination of time of measurement and age-related phenomenon is the longitudinal design where the same cohort(s) are studied over time. In this type of design, changes in scores on masculinity and femininity scales may be associated with (a) aging, (b) current life experiences (career, family, etc.), and/or (c) time of measurement. Yanico (1985) followed first-year college women from 1976 to 1980 and found no across-time differences on masculinity or femininity scores -- as might be expected in this pre-backlash time. Across a 10-year time span encompassing the 1980s (a largely pre-backlash time period), Hyde, Krajnki, and Skuldt-Niederberger (1991) also found no across time differences in gender role categories. There are too few longitudinal studies to draw conclusions about effects across changing historical times.

In sum, the commentaries reviewed about the effects of the earlier movement toward gender equality and the effects of the more recent backlash presented compelling arguments. The research supported the idea that historical times represented by cultural messages at time of measurement were influences on self-endorsement of femininity and masculinity. Furthermore, cultural messages when coming of age, as well as age-related social roles, were also described as important to women's and men's self-reports of masculinity and femininity. Although there was strong support for the influences of historical times in earlier decades (Twenge, 1997) these results could be interpreted as time of measurement or time of coming of age (the explanation preferred by Twenge, 1997). And the studies that could shed light on effects of historical times were subject to alternative explanations. Taken together, there was tentative support for the idea that in post 9/11 times there would be gender conformity and polarization. But as noted in the review, a study with only a single design results in an inability to disentangle effects of time of measurement from birth cohort from age of participants. There are other limitations in the literature: (a) reliance on women in studies that included assessment of social roles of work and family; (b) use of nondiverse samples; (c) lack of assessment of the invariance of the measures across birth cohorts, time, and age; (d) heavy use of cross-sectional designs that were reviewed together in an overall time lag meta-analysis on college students from the mid-1970s to the mid-1990s (Twenge, 1997) and beyond (Donnelly & Twenge, 2016); (e) a scarcity of studies with measurements in more recent times; and (f) few studies of gender roles among the members of the millennial generation, many of whom came of age post 9/11.

## Current Study and Hypotheses

Bem's theory of gender schema (1981a, 1993) highlighted the importance of culture to the development and expression of gender role identity. Our primary interest is in demonstrating the impact of the war on equality during the recent backlash years on gender polarization. When the historical times encourage heightened awareness of and endorsement of traditional gender roles, there should be greater gender polarization compared to times that support gender equality. This study incorporates three designs, longitudinal, time lag, and cross-sectional, that allows inferences to be made about the impact of changes in society between two times of measurement (1982 and 2007). As well, the overall design allows checking the validity of the conclusions about time of measurement effects by consideration of alternative explanations based on either time period when growing up or age-related social roles. There are a number of advances in this study over previous research. For example, previous research did not use gender schema theory and many were atheoretical. We used the BSRI original, long form (Bem, 1974) as this has been used in most of the research. There is evidence that a short form has superior measurement qualities (Campbell, Gillaspy, & Thompson, 1997) and we come back to this in the discussion on measurement invariance. Our times of measurement span 25 years and reflect gender equality support (1982) and the post-9/11 backlash (2007). We included a sample from Generation Y (millennials) and later Baby Boomers. We included men as well as women to overcome the limitation of a number of studies that included only women.

Gender polarization is considered in two hypotheses about scores on masculinity, femininity, and androgyny: Hypothesis 1a, longitudinally, across time, compared to an earlier time period that encouraged gender equality, the more recent time period that discouraged gender equality would demonstrate decreased masculinity scores among baby boomer women and decreased femininity scores among baby boomer men; Hypothesis 1b, there would be decreases among baby boomers across time in androgyny. Hypothesis 2a predicts across time lags, college senior men would score lower on femininity and college senior women would score lower on masculinity in more recent times than in earlier times; and, Hypothesis 2b, androgyny would be lower in more recent times than in earlier times. Androgyny reflects a balanced and higher endorsement of masculine and feminine roles (Heilbrun & Pitman, 1979).

Because our samples are from two different cohorts assessed at two different times, there are a number of demographic characteristics that may distinguish these groups beyond the associations with work and family social roles noted in the literature review. We compare groups on demographics, such as ethnicity (see Harris, 1994, who questioned the validity of the BSRI for non-European American groups), religion, religiosity (Thompson & Remmes, 2002, who predicated their study on examining the notion that "masculinity thwarts people from embracing spirituality, whereas femininity promotes religious experience", p. 521), and financial status (Mulholland, 1996, who associated entrepreneurialism with masculinity), and use these items as control variables in preliminary analyses.

## Method

### Participants and Procedures

The participants came from the same large Texas university in the southwestern U.S. Twenty-five years following the initial sampling of college seniors in 1982, the members of the 1982 cohort were invited to return in 2007. For analysis purposes, college seniors were restricted in age to 20-24 years, thereby including those who were more homogenous in age and who underwent college experiences at similar ages. Procedures in each recruitment period were approved by the institutional review board for the protection of human subjects; recruitment techniques depended upon year. All recruitment and data collection took place in spring and summer.

Participants recruited in 1982 understood that they were part of a longitudinal study, with five waves of measurement in 1982, 1983, 1984, 1990, and 2007. Only the 1982 and 2007 waves were used in this analysis (no comparable new group of college seniors was recruited until 2007). In 1982, random stratified sampling was used to include equivalent numbers of men and women. After letter and phone contact, participants met with project staff, filled out the questionnaire with the BSRI, were interviewed, and were paid $5.00.

In 2007, these participants were followed-up via letters and mailed surveys that included the long form BSRI (or for some, a short survey with no BSRI) with postage paid return envelopes. They were offered opportunities to enroll in drawings for cash rewards of $100 via a separate postage paid postcard. In all, 43% of the original participants in the larger study returned surveys. From these 180 returnees, participants were eliminated from this particular study if they were not part of the 1982 college senior group, if they had returned only the short survey (that omitted the BSRI), and if they were older or younger than the 18-24 age cut-offs used in this analysis. After these eliminations, there were 33 men and 29 women (n = 62) representing a late baby boomer cohort termed Group BB and designated as $BB_{CS}$ in 1982 and $BB_{ML}$ in 2007.

In 2007, college undergraduates, including college seniors, were solicited via university emailed announcements, the university electronic announcement board, and in-person announcements in classes to complete a paper and pencil survey which included the BSRI among other measures. This approach meant almost every student had an equal opportunity to volunteer for the study. Rewards included random drawings for prizes donated by local businesses as well as drawings for monetary awards of $100. Recruitment of college seniors was monitored and data collection continued until similar numbers of men and women to those in the earlier longitudinal study were recruited. From a larger sample of 2007 responding college seniors, participants were selected randomly within the constraints of having a sample similar in number and gender distribution to that of the baby boomer group. In 2007 there were 35 men and 30 women (n = 68) college seniors representing Generation Y termed Group $GY_{CS}$. Groups $BB_{CS}$ and $GY_{CS}$ did not differ significantly in gender composition. In general, participants were European American and affiliated with Catholic/Protestant/Christian religions. College senior participants were less partnered than midlife adults and were less involved in full-time employment.

## Measures

Dependent measures. The dependent variables were gender role measures from the 60-item Bem Sex Role Inventory (Bem, 1974). Sample masculinity items are: Defends own beliefs, Independent, Assertive. Sample femininity items were: Cheerful, Affectionate, Sympathetic. Items were answered on the original 7-point scale ranging from 1 = never or almost never true to 7 = always or almost always true in response to the prompt "Describe yourself". The mean scale score was calculated and could range from 1 to 7. Measures of Cronbach's alpha internal consistency reliability were acceptable, ranging from .66 to .92. Androgyny was calculated by the Heilbrun and Pitman (1979) procedure: (Masculinity+Femininity) – (|Masculinity-Femininity|).

To assess possible attrition effects, 2007 returnees from the baby boomer group were compared to nonreturnees on 1982 demographic characteristics and masculinity and femininity scale scores. There were no statistically significant differences between those who continued with the study and those who did not. When possible, analyses were conducted with and without covariates of ethnicity, religiosity, financial status, and relationships status. These preliminary analyses found nonsignificant covariates and patterns of significance and nonsignificance did not change across analyses. Therefore, the results reported are based on analyses without covariates.

## Results

### Testing Hypotheses

Table 2 includes means and standard deviations of masculinity and femininity by cohort group, year of measurement, and gender. As well, Cronbach's alpha measures of internal consistency are also listed in Table 2. Due to societal backlash and stalled support for gender equality, the overall hypothesis is that the femininity, masculinity, and androgyny scores of those in 2007 would reflect greater polarization compared to those in 1982. In order to support this time of measurement hypothesis, the findings must fit a pattern that there are longitudinal differences (Hypothesis 1a; Hypothesis 1b) as well as time lag differences (Hypothesis 2a; Hypothesis 2b). Support for each hypothesis was examined in the context of multivariate analyses of variance and follow-ups. Figures 1 – 4 graph the results with longitudinal results in Figure 1, time-lag results in Figure 2, and cross-sectional results in Figure 3. Androgyny scores are plotted in Figure 4 for longitudinal, time-lag, and cross-sectional designs.

Hypothesis 1. Hypothesis 1a called for longitudinal differences across time among baby boomers. Time (1982 and 2007) and gender role scores (masculinity and femininity) were repeated measures and gender was a between-groups factor in the multivariate analyses (MANOVA). A main effect of time was expected and was found (Wilks $\lambda = .76$, $p < .001$, $\eta^2 = .24$). The main effect of time was unmodified by interactions with BSRI, gender, or both. Overall, BSRI scores declined from 4.98 to 4.74.

Based on our specific hypothesis of declines in men's femininity and women's masculinity scores, follow-up tests were conducted. Within-gender analyses with paired t-tests of particular BSRI scores were calculated (see Figure 1). Across time, women's masculinity scores declined (t(28) = 2.12, p < .05) from a mean of 4.93 to 4.70. Although women's masculinity scores and femininity scores declined in similar magnitudes, the decline in femininity scores among women was not significant (4.97, 4.74). Among men, femininity scores declined (t(32) = 3.97, p < .001) from a mean of 4.72 to a mean of 4.35, but men's masculinity scores did not decline significantly (5.31, 5.16). These patterns support the hypothesis of greater polarization over time periods from greater to lesser support for gender equality.

The Hypothesis 1b prediction, of a decline in androgyny scores over time, was supported (Wilks $\lambda$ = .77, p < .001, $\eta^2$ = .23). Androgyny scores were higher in 1982 than in 2007 (9.07 > 8.48), true for both men and women. In sum, the longitudinal design results supported greater gender polarization in more recent times than in more distant times.

Hypothesis 2. Hypothesis 2a called for time lag comparisons that would support greater gender polarization among college seniors in 2007 than in 1982 ($GY_{CS}$, $BB_{CS}$). The BSRI scores were treated as repeated measures, time of measurement and gender were treated as between group factors. There was a significant three-way interaction (Wilks $\lambda$ = .94, p < .01, $\eta^2$ = .06). The follow-up findings (see Figure 2) to this three-way interaction demonstrated, as predicted, men's scores on femininity were significantly higher in 1982 than in 2007 (4. 72 > 4.32) (F(1,66) = 8.14, p < .01, $\eta^2$ = .11), and women's scores on masculinity were higher in 1982 than in 2007 (4.93 > 4.56) (F(1,57) = 4.26, p < .05, $\eta^2$ = .07). As expected, there were no significant differences on women's scores on femininity or men's scores on masculinity by time of measurement.

With respect to the within person polarization prediction of Hypothesis 2b, there was marginal support (F(1,123) = 3.79, p = .05, $\eta^2$ = .03). As predicted, androgyny scores were higher in 1982 than in 2007 (9.07 > 8.72), true for both men and women. Taken together, the time-lag findings support the hypothesis that there would be greater gender polarization in 2007 than in 1982.

Alternatives. As hypothesized, the longitudinal and time lag results provided support for gender polarization across a 25-year time span. But significant cross-sectional differences could compromise this interpretation. Therefore, we examined scores in the cross-sectional design in 2007 where time of measurement was constant with a MANOVA where cohort ($BB_{ML}$ and $GY_{CS}$) and gender were between group factors and BSRI measures were repeated. There were no cohort effects either as a main effect or in interaction with BSRI or gender. There was a weak three-way interaction of cohort by BSRI by gender (Wilks $\lambda$ = .97, p = .045, $\eta^2$ = .03). Follow-ups within gender indicated there were no significant effects when comparing groups by BSRI scores (for means see

Table 2 and Figure 3). Finally, androgyny scores did not differ by cohort ($F(1,60) = 1.28$, ns, $\eta^2 = .01$), gender ($F < 1.00$), or cohort by gender ($F < 1.00$). That is, the overall score on androgyny of midlife adults in 2007 ($M = 8.48$) was similar to the overall androgyny score of college seniors in 2007 ($M = 8.72$), true for men and women. Taken together, cross-sectional comparisons between midlife adults and college seniors in 2007 pose no challenges to the conclusions of the longitudinal and time-lagged results that there was greater gender polarization in 2007 than in 1982.

| | | Year 1982 | | Year 2007 | | | |
| | | Group BB$_{CS}$ College Seniors (n = 62) | | Group BB$_{ML}$ Midlife Adults (n = 62) | | Group GY$_{CS}$ College Seniors (n = 65) | |
| | | Men (n = 33) | Women (n = 29) | Men (n = 33) | Women (n = 29) | Men (n = 35) | Women (n = 30) |
|---|---|---|---|---|---|---|---|
| *Femininity* | | | | | | | |
| | Mean | 4.72 | 4.97 | 4.35 | 4.74 | 4.32 | 5.06 |
| | SD | .45 | .53 | .59 | .66 | .67 | .60 |
| Cronbach's α | | .71 | .75 | .79 | .86 | .80 | .75 |
| *Masculinity* | | | | | | | |
| | Mean | 5.31 | 4.93 | 5.16 | 4.70 | 5.39 | 4.56 |
| | SD | .69 | .81 | .66 | .83 | .66 | .56 |
| Cronbach's α | | .90 | .91 | .88 | .91 | .86 | .72 |
| *Androgyny* | | | | | | | |
| | Mean | 9.16 | 8.98 | 8.53 | 8.44 | 8.57 | 8.87 |
| | SD | .78 | 1.01 | 1.00 | 1.14 | 1.29 | 1.03 |

Table 2. Means, Standard Deviations, and Cronbach's Alpha of 20-item BSRI Femininity, Masculinity, Androgyny Scale Scores By Time of Measurement, Group, and Gender

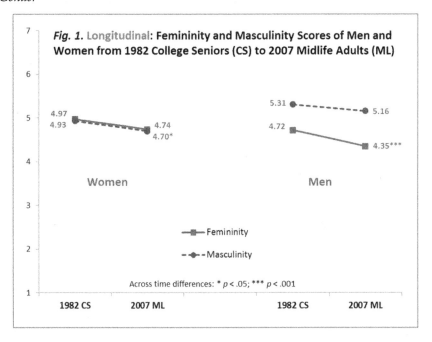

Fig. 1. Longitudinal: Femininity and Masculinity Scores of Men and Women from 1982 College Seniors (CS) to 2007 Midlife Adults (ML)

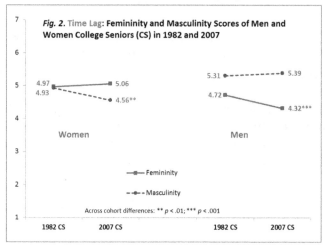

Fig. 2. Time Lag: Femininity and Masculinity Scores of Men and Women College Seniors (CS) in 1982 and 2007

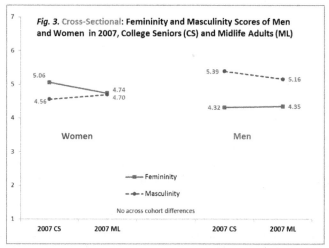

Fig. 3. Cross-Sectional: Femininity and Masculinity Scores of Men and Women in 2007, College Seniors (CS) and Midlife Adults (ML)

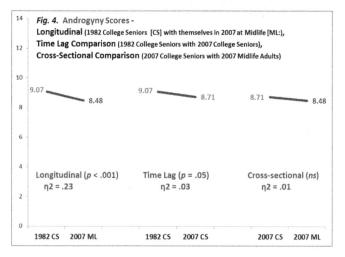

Fig. 4. Androgyny Scores - Longitudinal (1982 College Seniors [CS] with themselves in 2007 at Midlife [ML:), Time Lag Comparison (1982 College Seniors with 2007 College Seniors), Cross-Sectional Comparison (2007 College Seniors with 2007 Midlife Adults)

## Discussion

The past fifty decades demonstrate fluctuations in support for gender equality. The 1960s and early 1970s saw the rise of a movement for gender equality (Bem, 1993; England, 2010). By the late 1980s and early 1990s this movement was countered by the New Right backlash (England, 2010; Faludi, 1991). And into this emergent backlash, the events of September 11, 2001, were fashioned into a potent push for traditional gender roles, for the reemergence of the gender polarization patterns characteristic of androcentric and patriarchal cultures (Faludi, 2007; Lorber, 2005). Bem's (1981a, 1993) gender schema theory of gender role development argued that the adoption of conventional gender roles was more a product of the assigned roles in the social structure than of childhood socialization. In the language of this study, 1982 and 2007 represented two time periods characterized by different views of the roles of women and men. In 1982, gender equality was more culturally accepted, but in 2007, gender polarization was more strongly promoted. This study was designed to test the hypothesis that time of measurement would be a factor in the self-endorsed gender role scores of women and men, that the war on gender equality would be evident in such personal arenas as self-descriptions on masculine and feminine characteristics.

Because past research was characterized by designs that could not disentangle time of measurement from experiences growing up or from experiences as an adult, we incorporated three designs in this study (Schaie, 1965). The first design was longitudinal, comparing the same cohort from 1982 to 2007. Initially, these late baby boomers were all college seniors but, by 2007, they were midlife adults. The second design was time lag, comparing a cohort of college seniors in 1982 (the late baby boomers) with a cohort of college seniors in 2007 (Generation Y), groups who participated in different historical times and who came of age in markedly different times. The third design was cross-sectional with two groups measured in 2007. In this third design, one group was the GY cohort of college seniors and the other was of the baby boomer midlife adults. Each group measured in 2007 came of age in different times. They were also of differing ages with varying engagements in social roles of career and partnering.

Through triangulation of the resulting patterns across these designs, support for a time of measurement hypothesis was apparent. Such support is seen if, in both the longitudinal and time lag designs, there were expected differences between those assessed in 2007 from those assessed in 1982. Greater polarization was found (lower scores on femininity among men, lower scores on masculinity among women, and lower scores on androgyny among men and women). Furthermore, alternative explanations of age/maturation/imperatives were ruled out as there were no contradictory findings in the cross-sectional design analyses. The results extended the Twenge (1997) findings of increases in gender roles when her time frame began at the stirrings of the women's movement to a period of greater support for gender equality (1974 to 1994). Although Twenge (1997) favored a coming of age explanation, our findings reinterpret her results as reflecting a time of measurement effect. Gender polarization had decreased over the time frame she analyzed compared to the time frame of this study which saw an increase in polarization. With respect to gender role scores, we conclude that changes in historical times affect people regardless of when they came of age.

The effect of time of measurement would appear to rest on women demonstrating differences or changes in masculinity and men demonstrating differences or changes in femininity, changes in the characteristics generally considered more evident in the other gender, at least when considered through a binary lens. Neither men nor women in this study showed increases or decreases on characteristics generally considered more evident in the same gender. However, in the more recent meta-analysis, Donnelly and Twenge (2016) reported that women's femininity scores decreased from 1993 to 2012, a nineteen-year span that was generally within the backlash years. Because of the time span covered it is difficult to interpret these findings. By contrast, Twenge's (1997) earlier analysis and ours spanned changing historical times. Generally, it appeared that over the past several decades, the effect of the war on gender equality is to suppress expression of roles more closely associated with the other gender than with the same gender. In times of gender equality backlash and when under threat, men suppress the feminine (Cheryan et al., 2015). In times of support for gender equality, the way people become more gender equal is for men to acknowledge more feminine qualities and women to acknowledge more masculine qualities.

As we look at the cross-sectional findings that compared college seniors and midlife adults in 2007, there were no cohort differences on masculinity, femininity, or androgyny despite the considerable differences in age and in social roles of career involvement and partnering. Thus, both cohorts "got" the gender polarization message of the times. These findings are consistent with the study by Lemaster el al. (2015), which compared three age cohorts in 2013 and found no differences on masculinity, femininity, or androgyny. The cross-sectional and longitudinal findings could have provided support for a maturity hypothesis (McAdams & Olson, 2010) had older men demonstrated higher scores on masculinity and older women demonstrated higher scores on femininity than younger men and women. There was no support for such an age-related hypothesis. Nor was there support for the parental imperative theorizing of Guttman (1975) that there would be a cross-over effect with men becoming more feminine and women becoming more masculine with age.

Writing in 1987, Helson and Moane speculated that midlife adults might find themselves more similar to current college seniors than to themselves when they had been college seniors. Indeed, results of this study provide support for this time of measurement prediction. As well, our findings offer the opportunity to more fully parse meanings behind the historical times perspective. Birth cohorts have been identified by generational groupings that provide a short hand to describe those who experience similar events and cultural and societal expectations. These generations develop their identities, gender roles and other perceptions of self as they come of age. However, the study's lack of differences between midlife adults in 2007 compared to emerging adults in 2007 failed to confirm the importance of experiences when growing up. In support of Bem's (1993) theorizing, current cultural contexts, regardless of generations, seemed to be strong enough to override variations in experiences growing up. For example, the midlife adults and college seniors in 2007 all shared the larger post 9/11 cultural context which Faludi (1991), Finlay (2006), and Lorber (2005) described. Indeed, history is marked by events that are turning points for many in the society, not just a particular cohort. If the commentaries we cited about the effects of recent history are correct, the attacks of 9/11, coming in the midst of a rising cultural backlash against the advances of women, may have been one of those periods of time that affected people regardless of generation. Thus, it becomes important to consider that what appear to be coming of age experiences or age-related roles instead may be more reflective of the contexts in which people are situated (Bem, 1993).

Of interest in these findings is the lack of effects (in analyses of covariance) of social role differences in such areas as marriage/partnering and career as an explanation for differences in gender roles. In the literature, studies that looked at social role involvements and gender roles were primarily cross-sectional and involved women only (e.g., Erdwins et al., 1983; Mellinger & Erdwins, 1985). By contrast, our study included men and women. A major difference between the samples used in these studies and ours was that most of the previous literature included birth cohorts that ended with late baby boomers. Our study included late boomers and millennials.

In a different time, with men and women equally involved in work and careers, with supportive social policies that allow and encourage such equality (Bem, 1993), gender polarization should disappear. However, Bem (1993) encouraged broader thinking on the subject. In order to dismantle gender polarization, she argued that androcentrism must be taken apart as well. Americans should "reconstruct their social institutions to be so inclusive of both male and female experience that neither gender is automatically advantaged or disadvantaged by the social structure" (Bem, 1993, p. 186). In such a world, concepts of masculinity and femininity and androgyny, among others, would be banished from the "cultural consciousness" (p. 192-193). For example, as Ferree (2010) noted, workplaces, such as law firms, may demand overwork that currently finds more women than men opting out. As well, some careers, such as those in information technology, allow men to retain typical gender schemas but women in the field adopt atypical gender schemas (Lemons & Parzinger, 2007). The movements of the 1960s for peace, civil rights, women's rights, gay liberation (as these movements were called) were all challenges to patriarchy and to an androcentric and gender polarized world. At this writing, post-2016 Presidential election, the backlash dream of a patriarchal, androcentric, gender polarized atmosphere is reflected in the 45th president, the cabinet, and advisory appointments. As well, there is a notable resurgence of women and men who reject such arrangements. The day after the 2017 U.S. inauguration, women's marches around the world brought over a million protesters together to assert the importance of human rights (Stein, Hendrix, & Hauslohner, 2017).

## Limitations and Strengths

Although the study enjoyed a number of strengths, such as, different cohorts, different time periods, a prospective longitudinal design, and use of the 20-item BSRI scales to allow comparison with other research, there were some limitations. Effect sizes were generally small to moderate. We used binary categories: men and women; femininity and masculinity. As well, the study lacked diversity in ethnicity, social class, religious affiliation, and geography. Almost all participants were European American, all went to college, and recruitment was from only one university in one state in the U.S. These characteristics of our study limit generalizability to other experiences and regions of the country (Konrad & Harris, 2002) or to other countries (e.g., Colley, Mulhern, Maltby, & Wood, 2009). Gender intersects with race, class, ethnicity, and culture (Ferree, 2010; Stewart, Winter, Henderson-King, Henderson-King, 2015) but the lack of variability in our study precluded investigation of intersectionality. Goldberg, Kelly, Matthews, Kang, and Sumaroka's (2012) research on college students of diverse ethnicities in 1988 and 2010 examined views on work-care benefits and costs. Such research is a reminder of the importance of including diverse samples in research on attitudes about gender roles, and by extension, on self-perceptions of gender roles. In this study, a preliminary analysis on the more diverse 2007 sample of college seniors indicated that ethnicity was not a significant predictor of gender role self-endorsements. However, the numbers of participants in our study precluded identifying possible differences among non-European American participants.

Although groups in this study differed as expected on social roles and age, we did not study people across their own life transitions which could help to tease out if and how these variables are associated with masculinity and femininity (McHugh & Frieze, 1997). The study was not experimental in that participants were not randomly assigned to groups in which societal or personal messages were manipulated. Nonetheless, the experimental study results of the Cheryan et al. (2015) experiment, in which men's experiences were manipulated, supported the idea that men's self-endorsement of femininity was responsive to threat.

Because our design allowed disentangling coming of age from time of measurement, we were able to comment on timing of socialization effects. Socialization effects during childhood and coming of age were not supported. But socialization effects may have been present in different contexts, with different areas of development beyond the exclusive focus in this study on gender roles. As noted by others (e.g., Donnelly & Twenge, 2016), the items on the BSRI could have different meanings in different decades, that is, they might not have demonstrated invariance over time. With 20 items per scale, our sample size was too small to test for invariance. However, the 10-item per scale BSRI (trimmed from the 20-item per scale measure) (Bem, 1981b) was testable for invariance. When we analyzed the 10-item version for metric and scalar invariance, these were acceptable in longitudinal, time-lagged, and cross-sectional analyses (Fischer & Juergens, 2015). As well, parallel analyses of the 10-item scales produced results that were similar to those reported here for the 20-item version. Thus, we conclude that the comparisons in this study were based on similar meanings of items across the 25 years.

In the future, use of such scales will be valuable in documenting continuity and discontinuity in the self-endorsements of gender roles as historical times change. Research will be able to track for whom and under what circumstances there are changes in gender polarization. When the future embraces the dismantling of androcentrism and gender polarization, then such measurements will no longer be needed.

## Compliance with Ethical Standards
The authors declare that they have no conflicts of interest. All research

was approved by the university's institutional review board. Informed consent procedures were followed.

## References

Anderson, K. J. (2015). *Modern misogyny: Anti-feminism in a post-feminist era.* New York, NY: Oxford University Press.

Arnett, J. J. (2000). Emerging adulthood: A theory of development from the late teens through the twenties. *American Psychologist, 55,* 469-480. doi: 10.1037/0003-066X.55.5.469

Bakan, D. (1966). *The duality of human existence: An essay on psychology and religion.* Oxford, England: Rand McNally.

Bem, S. L. (1974). The measurement of psychological androgyny. *Journal of Counseling and Clinical Psychology, 42*(2), 155-162. doi:10.1037/h0036215

Bem, S. L. (1977). On the utility of alternative procedures for assessing psychological androgyny. *Journal of Consulting and Clinical Psychology, 45*(2), 196-205. doi:10.1037/0022-006X.45.2.196

Bem, S. L. (1981a). Gender schema theory: A cognitive account of sex typing. *Psychological Review, 88*(4), 354-364. doi:10.1037/0033-295X.88.4.354

Bem, S. L. (1981b). *The Bem Sex-Role Inventory: A professional manual.* Palo Alto, CA: Consulting Psychologists Press.

Bem, S. L. (1993). *The lenses of gender: Transforming the debate on sexual inequality.* New Haven, CT: Yale University Press.

Campbell, T., Gillaspy, J. J., & Thompson, B. (1997). The factor structure of the Bem Sex-Role Inventory (BSRI): Confirmatory analysis of long and short forms. *Educational and Psychological Measurement, 57*(1), 118-124. doi:10.1177/0013164497057001008

Cheryan, S., Schwartz Cameron, J., Katagiri, Z., & Monin, B. (2015). Manning up: Threatened men compensate by disavowing feminine preferences and embracing masculine attributes. *Social Psychology, 46*(4), 218-227. doi:10.1027/1864-9335/a000239

Colley, A., Mulhern, G., Maltby, J., & Wood, A. M. (2009). The short form BSRI: Instrumentality, expressiveness and gender associations among a United Kingdom sample. *Personality and Individual Differences, 46*(3), 384-387. doi:10.1016/j.paid.2008.11.005

Constantinople, A. (1973). Masculinity-femininity: An exception to a famous dictum?. *Psychological Bulletin, 80*(5), 389-407. doi:10.1037/h0035334

DeShong, H. F. (2015). Policing femininity, affirming masculinity: Relationship violence, control and spatial limitation. *Journal of Gender Studies, 24*(1), 85-103. doi:10.1080/09589236.2013.833087

DiDonato, M. D., & Berenbaum, S. A. (2011). The benefits and drawbacks of gender typing: How different dimensions are related to psychological adjustment. *Archives of Sexual Behavior, 40*(2), April, 457-463. doi:10.1007/s10508-010-9620-5

Donnelly, K., & Twenge, J. M. (2016). Masculine and feminine traits on the Bem Sex-Role Inventory, 1993-2012: A cross-temporal meta-analysis. *Sex Roles*, online. doi: 10.1007/s11199-016-0625-y

England, P. (2010). The gender revolution: Uneven and stalled. *Gender & Society, 24*(2), 149-166. doi:10.1177/0891243210361475

Erdwins, C. J., Tyer, Z. E., & Mellinger, J. C.(1983). A comparison of sex role and related personality traits in young, middle-aged, and older women. *International Journal of Aging and Human Development, 17*(2), 141-152. doi:10.2190/6YQQ-EDQ3-KFAR-03Q3

Faludi, S. (1991). *Backlash: the undeclared war against American women*. New York, NY: Crown.

Faludi, S. (2007). *The terror dream: myth and misogyny in an insecure America*. New York, NY: Henry Holt & Co.

Ferree, M. M. (2010). Filling the glass: Gender perspectives on families. *Journal of Marriage and Family, 72*(3), 420-439. doi:10.1111/j.1741-3737.2010.00711.x

Finlay, B. (2006). *George W. Bush and the war on women: Turning back the clock on progress*. London: Zed Books.

Fischer, J. L., & Juergens, C. A. (2015). *Bem Sex Role Inventory: Differences between men and women across 25 years.* National Council on Family Relations Annual Meeting, November, Vancouver, British Columbia.

Gilligan, C. (2011). *Joining the resistance.* Oxford, England: Polity Press.

Goldberg, W. A., Kelly, E., Matthews, N. L., Kang, H., Li, W., & Sumaroka, M. (2012). The more things change, the more they stay the same: Gender, culture, and college students' views about work and family. *Journal of Social Issues, 68*(4), 814-837. doi:10.1111/j.1540-4560.2012.01777.x

Guttman, D. L. (1975). Parenthood: Key to the comparative psychology of life? In N. Datan & L. Ginsberg (Eds.) *Life-span developmental psychology: Normative life crises* (pp. 98- 119). San Diego, CA: Academic Press.

Harris, A. C. (1994). Ethnicity as a determinant of sex role identity: A replication study of item selection for the Bem Sex Role Inventory. *Sex Roles, 31*(3-4), 241-273. doi:10.1007/BF01547717

Heilbrun, A. B., & Pitman, D. (1979). Testing some basic assumptions about psychological androgyny. *Journal of Genetic Psychology, 135,* 175-188. doi: 10.1080//00221325.1979.10534069

Helson, R., & Moane, G. (1987). Personality change in women from college to midlife. *Journal of Personality and Social Psychology, 53*(1), July, 176-186. doi:10.1037/0022-3514.53.1.176

Hyde, J. S., Krajnik, M., & Skuldt-Niederberger, K. (1991). Androgyny across the life span: A replication and longitudinal follow-up. *Developmental Psychology, 27,* 516-519. doi:10.1037/0012-1649.27.3.516

Kirmeyer, S. E., & Hamilton, B. E. (2011). *Childbearing differences among three generations of U.S. women. NCHS data brief, no 68.* Hyattsville, MD: National Center for Health Statistics.

Konrad, A. M., & Harris, C. (2002). Desirability of the Bem Sex-Role Inventory items for women and men: A comparison between African Americans and European Americans. *Sex Roles, 47*(5/6), 250-271.

doi.10.1023/A:1021386727269

Lemaster, P., Delaney, R., & Strough, J. (2015). Crossover, degendering, or…? A multidimensional approach to life-span gender development. *Sex Roles*, doi:10.1007/s11199-015-0563-0

Lemons, M. A., & Parzinger, M. (2007). Gender schemas: A cognitive explanation of discrimination of women in technology. *Journal of Business and Psychology, 22*(1), 91-98. doi:10.1007/s10869-007-9050-0

Lorber, J. (2005). Breaking the bonds: *Degendering and feminist change*. New York, NY: W. W. Norton.

McAdams, D. P., & Olson, B. D. (2010). Personality development: Continuity and change over the life course. *Annual Review Of Psychology, 61*, 517-542. doi:10.1146/annurev.psych.093008.100507

McHugh, M. C., & Frieze, I. H. (1997). The measurement of gender-role attitudes: A review and commentary. *Psychology of Women Quarterly, 21*, 1-16. doi:10.1111/j.1471-6402.1997.tb00097.x

Mellinger, J. C., & Erdwins, C. J. (1985). Personality correlates of age and life roles in adult women. *Psychology Of Women Quarterly, 9*(4), 503-514. doi:10.1111/j.1471-6402.1985.tb00899.x

Mulholland, K. (1996). Entrepreneurialism, masculinities and the self-made man. In D. L. Collinson, J. Hearn, D. L. Collinson, J. Hearn (Eds.) *Men as managers, managers as men: Critical perspectives on men, masculinities and managements* (pp. 123-149). Thousand Oaks, CA, US: Sage Publications, Inc.

Parry, E., & Urwin, P. (2011). Generational differences in work values: A review of theory and evidence. *International Journal of Management Reviews, 13*(1), 79-96. doi:10.1111/j.1468-2370.2010.00285.x

Pedulla, D. S., & Thébaud, S. (2015). Can we finish the revolution? Gender, work-family ideals, and institutional constraint. *American Sociological Review, 80*(1), 116-139. doi:10.1177/0003122414564008

Robnett, R. D., Anderson, K. J., & Hunter, L. E. (2012). Predicting feminist identity: Associations between gender-traditional attitudes, feminist stereotyping, and ethnicity. *Sex Roles, 67*(3-4), 143-157.

doi:10.1007/s11199-012-0170-2

Ruth, S. (1983). A feminist analysis of the New Right. *Women's Studies International Forum, 6*(4), 345-351. doi:10.1016/0277-5395(83)90026-2

Schaie, K. W. (1965). A general model for the study of developmental problems. *Psychological Bulletin, 64*(2), 92-107. doi:10.1037/h0022371

Sessa, V. I., Kabacoff, R. I., Deal, J., & Brown, H. (2007). Generational differences in leader values and leadership behaviors. *The Psychologist-Manager Journal, 10*(1), 47-74. doi:10.1080/10887150709336612

Starr, C. R., & Zurbriggen, E. L. (2016). Sandra Bem's gender schema theory after 34 years: A review of its reach and impact. *Sex Roles,* doi:10.1007/s11199-016-0591-4

Stein, P., Hendrix, S., & Hauslohner, A. (2017, January 22). Women's marches: More than one million protesters vow to resist President Trump. *The Washington Post.* Retrieved from http://www.washingtonpost.com

Stewart, A. J., & Healy, J. M. (1989). Linking individual development and social changes. *American Psychologist, 44*(1), 30-42. doi:10.1037/0003-066X.44.1.30

Stewart, A. J., Winter, D. G., Henderson-King, D., & Henderson-King, E. (2015). How politics become personal: Sociohistorical events and their meanings in people's lives. *Journal of Social Issues, 71*(2), 294-308. doi:10.1111/josi.12111

Strough, J., Leszczynski, J. P., Neely, T. L., Flinn, J. A., & Margrett, J. (2007). From adolescence to later adulthood: Femininity, masculinity, and androgyny in six age groups. *Sex Roles, 57*(5-6), 385-396. doi:10.1007/s11199-007-9282-5

Suh, E. J., Moskowitz, D. S., Fournier, M. A., & Zuroff, D. C. (2004). Gender and relationships: Influences on agentic and communal behaviors. *Personal Relationships, 11*(1), 41-59. doi:10.1111/j.1475-

Thompson, E. J., & Remmes, K. R. (2002). Does masculinity thwart being religious? An examination of older men's religiousness. *Journal for the Scientific Study of Religion, 41*(3), 521-532. doi:10.1111/1468-5906.00135

Twenge, J. M. (1997). Changes in masculine and feminine traits over time: A meta-analysis. *Sex Roles, 36*(5-6), 305-325. doi:10.1007/BF02766650

U.S. Census Bureau (2015). *Current population survey, March and annual social and economic supplements, 2014 and earlier.* Downloaded from: http://www.census.gov/hhes/families/files/ms2.csv.

Wood, W., & Eagly, A. H. (2002). A cross-cultural analysis of the behavior of women and men: Implications for the origins of sex differences. *Psychological Bulletin, 128*(5), 699-727. doi:10.1037/0033-2909.128.5.699

Yanico, B. J. (1985). BSRI scores: Stability over four years for college women. *Psychology of Women Quarterly, 9*(2), 277-283. doi:10.1111/j.1471-6402.1985.tb00878.x

*Chapter 2*

## After DOMA: Same-Sex Couples and the

## Shifting Road to Equality

*Alicia Bosley*

*Hofstra University*

### Introduction

On June 26, 2013, the United States Supreme Court ruled that Section Three of the Defense of Marriage Act (DOMA), which defined marriage as between a man and a woman, was unconstitutional (Freedom to Marry, 2013; Human Rights Campaign, 2013; Reilly & Siddiqui, 2013). Section Three of the Defense of Marriage Act defined marriage as being between a man and a woman only, and prevented the federal government from acknowledging any same-sex marriages for the purpose of federal programs or laws, even those recognized by states (GLAAD, 2013). Under DOMA, married gay and lesbian couples were denied important protections and rights, such as social security benefits, family and medical leave, the ability to pool resources without heightened taxation, military family benefits, and hospital visitation rights (Andryszewski, 2008; Freedom to Marry, 2013; GLAAD, 2013; Goldberg, 2009; Mathy & Lehmann, 2004). Thus, the Supreme Court's decision upheld that all married couples deserve equal treatment and respect under the law, and marked the end of the denial of over 1,100 federal protections and benefits of marriage to same-sex couples (Drescher, 2012; Freedom to Marry, 2013; Human Rights Campaign, 2013; Killian, 2010; Mathy, Kerr, & Lehmann, 2004; Pelts, 2014; Steingass, 2012). These privileges of legal married status had previously been available to all other married people, and thus the repeal of Section Three of DOMA was a major victory for marriage equality in the United States (Barnes, 2013; Freedom to Marry, 2013; GLAAD, 2013; Human Rights Campaign, 2013; Reilly & Siddiqui, 2013).

The purpose of this study was to capture the essence of the lived experiences of same-sex couples during this unique and fleeting time period, as a significant event in the marriage equality movement was taking effect

## Literature Review

To date, the existing literature on the repeal of the Defense of Marriage Act is sparse, with most available studies (Aoun, 2016; Dominguez, 2015) focusing on other aspects of same-sex relationships and only including DOMA as one of many considerations. The exception to this is an article (Pelts, 2014) discussing the effects of the June 2013 ruling repealing DOMA. This article discussed the history and current state of same-sex marriage but did not include interviews with, or voices of, same-sex couples. However, a broader examination of literature related to same-sex marriage and DOMA may be helpful in orienting readers to this study.

The Supreme Court's ruling came after nearly 17 years of DOMA being in effect, during which time Section Three had been hotly debated and ruled unconstitutional ten times at the district court, U.S. Bankruptcy Court, and U.S. Court of Appeals levels (Barnes, 2013; Drescher, 2012; Freedom to Marry, 2013; GLAAD, 2013; Human Rights Campaign, 2013; Reilly & Siddiqui, 2013; Rimmerman, 2008). The ruling took effect on July 21, 2013, 25 days after the decision was made (Freedom to Marry, 2013). Married same-sex couples living in 13 states and the District of Columbia, had their marriages federally sanctioned and were eligible for the same federal responsibilities and protections of marriage for the first time in U.S. history (Barnes, 2013; Freedom to Marry, 2013).

However, only Section Three had been ruled unconstitutional (Barnes, 2013; Freedom to Marry, 2013; GLAAD, 2013; Human Rights Campaign, 2013). The remaining significant section of DOMA, Section Two, maintained that individual states were not required to acknowledge the marriages of same-sex couples who were married in another state (Barnes, 2013; GLAAD, 2013; Freedom to Marry, 2013; Human Rights Campaign, 2013). Thus, couples living in states that did not recognize their marriages often had difficulty accessing federal marriage benefits (Freedom to Marry, 2013; Human Rights Campaign, 2013). Due to this inequality in state recognitions, the experiences of same-sex couples had the potential to be drastically different from one state to the next.

The differences did not end in the legal sphere, however. Several political figures spoke out in support of the Supreme Court's decision, while others defended the Act: supporters insisted that it was morally correct, necessary to protect children, and biblically sanctioned (Barnes, 2013; Drescher, 2012; Reilly & Siddiqui, 2013; Rimmerman, 2008). This debate extended to all echelons of U.S. society--deliberations on the subject occurred across social media, periodicals, and websites of educational and political organizations. It was in this sociopolitical climate of heightened scrutiny and uncertainty that same-sex couples had to navigate their relationships and lives. The aim of this study was to explore the lived experiences of same-sex couples across the country, as well as to identify differences in experience based on states and related legal status.

## Method

In order to best address the aims of this study, a mixed-method, convergent parallel design was utilized to attain complementary data on the topic (Morse, 1994). A data validation variant was used in order to allow the qualitative data to corroborate and elaborate upon the results of the quantitative data, as discussed by Creswell and Plano Clark (2011). Following approval by Nova Southeastern University's IRB board, participants were recruited online via a social media site (Facebook); ads were placed on the Facebook pages of the Human Rights Campaign and PFLAG chapters, with permission obtained before posting. Interested participants followed a link to a 25-question survey comprised of open- and closed-ended questions. Survey methodology was used to obtain responses from people across the country, providing a more representative sample of the larger national LGB population than would be feasible via in-person interviewing methods.

Through the quantitative paradigm utilized in this study, the relationship between state of residence (and local marriage laws) and perceptions of Section Three's repeal was sought and assessed. State of residence was divided between three domains: equal marriage protections and recognition; some protections and/or recognition; and no protections or recognition. This study attempted to ascertain a correlational relationship between variables only, as many confounding variables precluded assessing for a causal relationship, and further analysis was beyond the scope and intention of this study.

Through the qualitative methodology utilized in this study, participants were asked to describe their experiences related to the repeal. To remain as close as possible to the research participants' words and truths following the Section Three repeal, the transcendental approach to phenomenology was used, which focuses more on participants' descriptions of their experiences rather than on the researcher's interpretations (Moustakas, 1994), was used. Following data collection, content areas present in both data sets were identified and transferred as needed to facilitate relating the two data types.

| Variables | n | % | Variables | n | % |
|---|---|---|---|---|---|
| **Age Range** | | | **Gender** | | |
| 26-35 | 11 | 42.31 | Male | 18 | 69.23 |
| 36-45 | 5 | 19.23 | Female | 7 | 26.92 |
| 46-55 | 7 | 26.92 | Transgender | 1 | 3.85 |
| 56-65 | 2 | 7.69 | Total | 26 | 100 |
| 66-75 | 1 | 3.85 | | | |
| Total | 26 | 100 | | | |
| **Sexual Orientation** | | | **Ethnicity** | | |
| Gay | 19 | 73.08 | African American | 1 | 3.85 |
| Lesbian | 5 | 19.23 | Asian American | 1 | 3.85 |
| Bisexual | 1 | 3.85 | Caucasian | 20 | 76.92 |
| Queer | 1 | 3.85 | Hispanic or Latino | 2 | 7.69 |
| Total | 26 | 100 | Native American | 1 | 3.85 |
| | | | Mixed Race | 1 | 3.85 |
| | | | Total | 26 | 100 |
| **State of Residence** | | | | | |
| Arizona | 1 | 3.85 | North Carolina | 2 | 7.69 |
| Colorado | 6 | 23.08 | Oregon | 1 | 3.85 |
| Connecticut | 1 | 3.85 | Texas | 2 | 7.69 |
| Florida | 3 | 11.54 | Washington | 2 | 7.69 |
| Michigan | 1 | 3.85 | Wisconsin | 5 | 19.23 |
| New York | 2 | 7.69 | Total | 26 | 100 |
| **Committed Relationship Status *** | | | **Same-gender partner** | | |
| Yes | 26 | 100 | Yes | 25 | 96.15 |
| No | 0 | 0 | No** | 1 | 3.85 |
| Total | 26 | 100 | Total | 26 | 100 |
| **Level of Involvement in LGBTQ Rights Advocacy** | | | | | |
| Not at all active | | | | 4 | 15.38 |
| Not very active | | | | 8 | 30.77 |
| Somewhat active | | | | 11 | 42.31 |
| Very active | | | | 2 | 7.69 |
| Extremely active | | | | 1 | 3.85 |
| Total | | | | 26 | 100 |

* In a committed relationship for at least one year. For the purposes of this study, defined as romantically and emotionally committed to one another.
** This participant was in two relationships; one was a male-female relationship and the other was male-male. As the participant was involved in a same-sex relationship, he was included in the survey despite answering "no" to this question.

*Table 1. Particpant Demographics*

**Participants**

For this study, a sample size of 26 participants was utilized. This sample size is larger than a typical sample size for phenomenological studies, which generally include around 10 participants (Creswell, 1998), but smaller than a typical sample for quantitative studies, generally between 50-85 participants (Collins, Onwuegbuzie, & Jiao, 2007). This sample size was chosen in order to allow for the creation of a rich description of participants' experiences; even if saturation was reached early on in the analysis, this provides added validity to the findings. Second, although many mixed-methods studies utilize separate samples for the quantitative and qualitative portions, this number allows for the utilization of the same sample for both, creating a more integrated and valid study. Participant demographics are available in Table 1. Thirty-one total people responded to the study, however, only those meeting study criteria (over the age of 18; residing in the United States, District of Columbia, or Puerto Rico; and self-identifying as being in a same-sex relationship for at least one year) were included in the analysis. Qualitative results will be discussed first, followed by quantitative results.

## Results

**Commonly Shared Experiences**

Several experiences regarding the Section Three repeal were discussed by multiple participants. These experiences provide a glimpse into the lived experience of respondents and reveal the essence of this event. Four shared themes emerged: Marry or Not?, Support or Not?, Impact or Not?, and Progress or Not?

**Marry or Not?**

As DOMA and its Section Three both concern the definition of legal marriage in the United States, it is perhaps unsurprising that a central theme arising from participants was that involving marriage and their related decisions, or inability to make decisions. This theme was divided into the subthemes We Do!, Still Deciding, and Not Now.

*We do!* Participants within this theme had decided to get married, and most had already done so. Several indicated the importance of the repeal in giving them the ability to get married; one respondent stated that "We are [now] legally married in Washington because we were registered domestic partners. Our partnership turned into marriage. We are very happy." Whereas many of these participants had gotten married in their own states, others had done so in others: a man from North Carolina indicated, "My state doesn't allow same-sex marriage. We married in D.C. instead."

*Still deciding.* The decision to get married was not as simple for some respondents as it was for others. People in this group had extenuating circumstances to consider, specifically, many had medical conditions that made marriage financially difficult. As one man explained, "For us, getting married might not be a good thing. One of us lives with AIDS, and being married would screw up his needs-based medical care."

These responses indicated the high impact finances have on couples' decisions to marry, not unlike in many heterosexual relationships. However, these also highlight the disproportionate burden and stigma placed on gay male couples by AIDS.

*Not now.* Other respondents indicated that marriage was not currently for them and their relationships. Many respondents indicated that they were simply not ready. One man living in Washington explained, "We have only been together for one and a half years - not yet ready to commit to a lifetime together. That said, we are very happy together and both believe marriage and children are possibilities for the future." Another rationale was disagreement with marriage as an institution. An Oregon woman explained, "We have decided not to get married…we both think marriage is a capitalist institution that historically has been used as an excuse to keep women subjugated."

## Support or Not?

Respondents reported varying levels of support for their relationships. Support, as defined by participants in this category, fell under two subcategories. The first, Legal Support, involved legal benefits supporting same-sex couples after the repeal. These included benefits such as hospital visitation for a partner, the right to buy and own a home together, partner inclusion on work-provided insurance, and tax benefits. The second, Social Support, included support from families, friends, and communities.

**Legal support.** Only six of the twenty-six respondents reported legal support following the repeal, primarily in the form of sharing property and tax benefits. This low percentage could be seen as an indication of the newness of the extension of benefits to same-sex couples, the limited number of LGBTQ people who actually have access to these benefits, and work still needed to extend benefits to same-sex couples.

*We've got benefits!* Six respondents replied that they had received benefits as a result of the repeal, and indicated that these were very helpful. A male respondent from Wisconsin expressed, "Being able to share health insurance when we marry is huge. It will give us so much more flexibility and, honestly, a better, fairer quality of life."

***Still Fighting.*** The majority of respondents reported that they had not received benefits following the repeal, often because of respective state laws. Some reported increased discrimination following the repeal: A Colorado man explained,

> Weirdly, my partner's human resources department has become more hard-nosed against us since we don't have legal status...Before there were legal options, they just quietly looked the other way in those situations.

These experiences support the literature regarding the backlash against LGBTQ groups following legal progress (Freedom to Marry, 2013).

**Social support.** Respondents reported levels of support from families, friends, and community members varied greatly. Many respondents indicated they had received positive social backing, others reported mixed support, and a few reported continued discrimination and a lack of social support.

***Positive.*** Many respondents reported that family members, friends, and other people in their lives had been supportive. A man in Washington summed up the experiences of many participants, stating that significant others had been "All positive and supporting," and a woman in Colorado revealed that "My community is very open and accepting and I feel blessed to have moved here."

***Mixed.*** Others reported mixed responses from significant others. Variations were often seen as unsurprising; as a Colorado man summarized, "Varied, of course!"

***Negative.*** Despite the majority of respondents reporting positive reactions from social contacts, some respondents reported negative responses. Often, this came from acquaintances rather than close friends or family members: A Colorado man reported,

> I do feel that the debate has caused some of the community who oppose marriage equality to increase their level of opposition. Only in the past few years have I really felt strongly discriminated against...prior to the current climate of debate about marriage equality they just pretty much left me alone.

**Impact or not?**

A major issue discussed by respondents was the impact of the repeal and related social responses on their individual and relationship well-being and functioning. Generally, participants felt that the repeal had positive effects on themselves and their relationships, but a few spoke of ways that it increased pressure on them. Responses in this category fell under two subcategories, Relationship Impacts and Individual Impacts.

**Relationship impacts.** Most of the impacts reported by respondents were related to their couple relationships. Responses within this theme were further divided into two subthemes, We've Been Affected, in which participants perceived relationship impacts from the repeal, and Still the Same, in which participants felt unaffected by the repeal.

*We've been affected.* One of the most commonly reported impacts was that of social support benefitting respondents' couple relationships. A Wisconsin man wrote that the responses of family and friends had been "Nearly 100% positive and supportive. Their support and love has helped our relationship grow and mature." Other respondents reported that the legal changes had positively impacted their relationships. A Wisconsin resident wrote that "I feel we have more of an opportunity for long term success as a couple by having some federal (and maybe state) recognition if we get married." Finally, many reported feeling safer following the repeal. A New York man wrote, "Although we still are harassed for being gay and together it happens much less frequently."

Unfortunately, not all effects were positive. Several respondents reported feeling increased pressure to get married. For example, a Wisconsin man felt that the repeal had

> Actually made [our relationship status] a bit more insecure. We do not live together, and it's caused questions of commitment to come up. Now that we *can* get married in certain states, will we? If not, what is our relationship all about and where is it leading? (emphasis in original).

*Still the same.* Although many respondents felt their relationships had been impacted by the repeal, others felt unaffected. A Colorado woman explained "Our relationship is rock solid. Increased legal and/or social recognition is just the icing on the cake. We deserve equality and are glad it is happening but did not expect to see it in my lifetime."

**Individual impacts.** Most respondents reported that impacts of the repeal were primarily on their relationships rather than on them personally. However, as the law targeted the LGBTQ population, some respondents felt individual impacts. This subcategory was separated into the themes I've Been Affected and Still the Same.

***I've been affected.*** Respondents discussing this theme spoke of feeling safer following the repeal, this time in an individual sense. A Wisconsin man explained, "I'm happy that opinions are changing, it makes me feel safer, physically and emotionally."

***Still the same.*** Other respondents felt that the repeal and related social responses hadn't impacted them as an individual. A North Carolina resident explained that "My other family members haven't said much about the issue, but that's okay with me, because I've learned to not need their support so much. I continue on with my life anyway."

### Progress or not?

***Overall assessment.*** In the final category, participants gave their overall opinions of the repeal. Views of the repeal were solidly positive, labeling the repeal as a major event in the movement for LGBTQ rights and the morally right decision. This theme was divided into four subthemes: Major Event, Right Decision, About Time, and Next Steps.

***Major event.*** Many participants felt that the repeal was an important, even historical, event. One man from New York elaborated, "It is a major domino falling that signifies the beginning of the downfall to marriage inequality throughout the country." Another man from Colorado went beyond the repeal's immediate implications: "I feel the repeal has meaning far beyond marriage and deals more with basic human dignity."

***Right decision.*** Many participants also spoke of the repeal in an ethical context, expressing their feelings that the right decision had been made. As a New York man stated, "It was the right decision, morally and legally."

***About time!*** Several made statements to the effect that it was "high time" for the repeal. This theme was highly saturated in the data, with several respondents using the phrase, "it's about time" or "it was about time" to describe their feelings about the repeal.

***Next steps.*** Although participants were nearly unanimous in their feelings that the repeal was a significant step forward for marriage equality, they also felt there was more to be done. Some stressed the importance of societal education and acceptance: a New York man wrote, "It will be a long time before it is accepted throughout the nation in more than a legal sense." Respondents also discussed the importance of changing other laws to reach true equality for same sex couples. An Oregon resident discussed hopes that

> Maybe some of the groups listed above (LGBTQ) as well as the money going towards these groups will now hopefully be used to address bigger issues in the community, like homelessness, ac-

cess to healthcare, violence perpetrated against Trans individuals particularly Trans women of color. There are so many things that need attention and this marriage crap is taking all center stage when it's not the most pressing issue to be fighting.

## State Comparisons

In addition to the themes found across all respondents, several themes specific to geographic legal groups emerged. Responses were divided into three categories:

1) Respondents living in states with constitutional bans (Arizona, North Carolina) ($n = 3$)
2) Respondents living in states without full legal marriage but some rights (Colorado, Florida, Michigan, Texas, and Wisconsin) ($n = 17$)
3) States with legal same-sex marriage (Connecticut, New York, Oregon, and Washington) ($n = 6$)

Survey responses were analyzed using descriptive statistics and a one-way ANOVA with a Tukey post-hoc test, as a more complex analysis was beyond the intent and scope of the study, and was precluded by small response rates in some groups. Although most differences were not statistically significant, distinct themes within groups and differences between groups were identified. For visual representations of state differences, refer to Figures 1- 7.

**Participants in States with Legal Same-Sex Marriage.** This group of respondents had state recognition of their marriages prior to the repeal; however, these marriages were being federally recognized for the first time. They tended to live in more socially progressive areas; their relationships were more supported than other groups' and generally were not seen as "a big deal", as an Oregon respondent put it.

Respondents in states with legal same-sex marriage gave written responses reflecting a higher level of relationship freedoms and choices than the other groups. This group contained more married respondents than the other groups; as well as the only participant who indicated an active choice not to get married, rather than deciding due to financial or legal barriers or not feeling ready. Additionally, respondents in this group discussed "moving forward" following the repeal more than the other groups.

**Participants in States with Rulings for Same-Sex Marriage Currently in Appeals.** These respondents were living in rapidly changing political and social climates. Although their states had struck down bans on, or ruled for legalization of, same-sex marriage, all had subsequently seen

**State Differences**
(Statistically significant differences denoted by *)

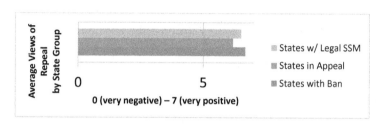

*Figure 1*: Views of DOMA Repeal. Group means: Legal SSM: 6.50, States in Appeal: 6.18, States with Ban: 6.67

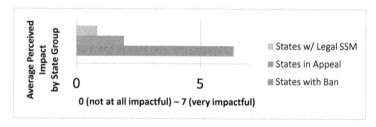

*Figure 2*: Impacts of Benefits Received Following Repeal*. Group means: States with Legal SSM: 0.83*, States in Appeal: 1.92#, States with Ban: 6.33*# (Groups with matching symbols are significantly different from one another)

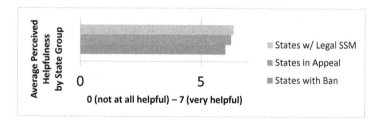

*Figure 3*: Expected Helpfulness of Repeal in Accessing Benefits. Group means: States with Legal SSM: 6.33, States in Appeal: 6.24, States with Ban: 6.0

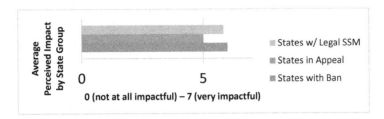

*Figure 4*: Impact of Laws on Couple Relationship. Group means: States with Legal SSM: 5.83, States in Appeal: 5.00, States with Ban: 6.00

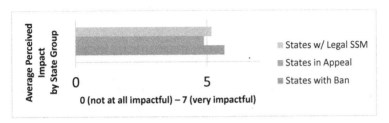

Figure 5: Impact of Social and Public Approval on Couple Relationship. Group means: States with Legal SSM: 5.17, States in Appeal: 4.88, States with Ban: 5.67

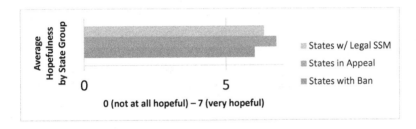

Figure 6: Hopefulness for National Marriage Equality. Group means: States with Legal SSM: 6.33, States in Appeal: 6.76, States with Ban: 6.00

Figure 7: Level of Activity in LGBTQ Rights Advocacy*. Group means: States with Legal SSM: 2.33*, States in Appeal: 2.82#, States with Ban: 1.33*#

appeals on these laws, leaving same-sex couples residing in those states in legal limbo. Many of these states were undergoing legal proceedings, increased advocacy efforts, and increased protests of same-sex marriage.

Respondents in this group showed higher levels of frustration with the legal proceedings, social debates, and instability involving their relationships and legal standing in their written responses. They reported higher levels of political action than the other groups, as well as high levels of optimism for future change. Reflected in the statistical analyses, respondents in this group appeared less vulnerable to changes in legal and social climate in that they reported the least impact of the change in law, perhaps because appeals put their status in limbo in these states. Furthermore, in their written responses, they comprised all reports of increased social discrimination post-repeal. This group also reported more shifts in their couple relationships following the shifts in social and legal contexts.

**Participants in States with Constitutional Bans on Same-Sex Marriage.** Respondents in this group lived in areas in which their relationships were devalued and often openly discriminated against, based on written comments. They had fewer legal rights and protections than respondents from other states, and some had no options for state-recognized unions. These state laws were often mirrored, and fueled, by local public opinion. These conditions provide a context for participant responses from this group of states.

Respondents living in states with constitutional bans gave written responses indicating resiliency and finding ways to thrive despite the lack of state support. They also showed high levels of optimism for eventual marriage equality, despite their current legal situation. However, their written responses indicated higher levels of vulnerability to legal and social situations and reported finding comfort in the new federal benefits extended to them.

In terms of statistically significant differences between groups, participants in states with constitutional bans reported experiencing more impacts on their lives and couple relationships than couples in the other two groups. Additionally, participants differed in their levels of activity in LGBTQ rights advocacy. Specifically, participants living in states with rulings for same-sex marriage in appeals showed significantly higher levels of advocacy than both of the other groups, whereas participants in states with bans against same-sex marriage reported lower levels of activeness than the other groups. Other differences were not statistically significant.

## Discussion

In combining the results of the qualitative and quantitative analysis, several patterns in participants' responses were elucidated. First, both qualitative and quantitative results revealed that overall, participants across groups viewed the Section Three repeal as a positive and important event. Furthermore, participants in all states reported beliefs that the repeal would be helpful in providing same-sex couples access to the privileges and benefits of marriage, as well as supporting the marriage equality movement. Finally, very few participants in any group had received any benefits following the repeal, indicating that more must be done to attain full marriage equality in the United States.

In addition, results highlighted important differences between groups. Despite minimal findings of statistical significance between groups, both qualitative and quantitative results indicated that participants in states with bans on same-sex marriage felt that legal status and social opinion had more impact on their couple relationships than did participants in other states. Further, although very few participants in any group reported receiving benefits following the repeal, based on their written commentary to the questions, participants in states with bans on same-sex marriage reported the fewest received benefits, and also indicated these benefits were more helpful to them than did other groups. This finding highlights an important discrepancy between need and actual support provided to participants in states with bans. Additionally, participants in states undergoing appeals processes regarding same-sex marriage reported significantly higher levels of advocacy in LGBTQ rights advocacy, which may suggest a connection between legal processes and advocacy efforts.

The narratives of this study indicate that the repeal was an important event for LGBTQ rights, with far-reaching implications for marriage and human rights within the United States. However, these narratives also reveal that the fight for marriage equality was not over; that there was still much to be done. The subsequent Supreme Court ruling on June 26, 2015 struck down Section Two of DOMA and thus established nationwide marriage equality, regardless of previous state laws (Liptak, 2016). However, many states responded to the 2013 and 2015 repeals by introducing bills allowing religious exemptions for providing service to LGBTQ clients, restricting adoption by same-sex couples, and allowing for the refusal to grant marriage licenses (ACLU.org, 2017; Blinder & Perez-Pena, 2015; Harris, 2017; Pizer, 2016). Follow-up research would be helpful in assessing the ongoing state of same-sex couples. This may be especially pertinent considering the rarity of participants in this study receiving benefits they were purported to get post-repeal. According to phenomenological theory, the truth of history lies in the experiences of those most intimately connected to the event. It is therefore our role as couple and family researchers and therapists to listen and to assist where we are able.

## Limitations of the Study

Study participants were predominantly male, cisgender, Caucasian, and identified as gay; therefore, results may not apply to all LGBTQ individuals. Second, although Facebook is a popular social media site, particularly in the LGBTQ community, the study was limited to people who were literate and had computer access and Facebook accounts. Other social media sites (e.g., Instagram, Twitter) were not utilized, which may systematically impact the sample. The numbers of people in the state category analyses were very small in some groups. This means that the power to detect differences was low; larger sample sizes in the state categories might have identified differences. Overall, the findings of this study represent the experiences of study participants, and cannot be generalized to all same-sex couples post-repeal. Additional research would contribute valuable information and understanding of the experiences of same-sex couples following the repeal of DOMA's Section Three.

## References

American Civil Liberties Union. (2017). *Past anti-LGBT religious exemption legislation across the country.* Retrieved from https://www.aclu.org/other/past-anti-lgbt-religious-exemption-legislation-across-country

Andryszewski, T. (2008). *Same-sex marriage: Moral wrong or civil right?* Minneapolis, MN: Twenty-First Century Books.

Aoun, A. R. (2016). *The immigration challenges of same-sex binational couples and the impact on relationships, mental health, and well-being.* (Doctoral dissertation). Retrieved from ProQuest dissertations and theses. (AAI3663196)

Barnes, R. (June 26, 2013). *At Supreme Court, victories for gay marriage.* Retrieved from http://articles.washingtonpost.com/2013-06-26/politics/40195683_1_gaycouples-edith --windsor-doma

Blinder, A., & Perez-Pena, R. (2015, September 1). Kentucky clerk denies same-sex marriage licenses, defying court. *The New York Times.* Retrieved from https://www.nytimes.com/2015/09/02/us/same-sex-marriage-kentucky-kim-davis.html

Collins, K. M. T., Onwuegbuzie, A. J., & Jiao, Q. G. (2007). A mixed methods investigation of mixed methods sampling designs in social and health science research. *Journal of Mixed Methods Research, 1*(3), 267-294.

Creswell, J. W. (2013). *Qualitative inquiry & research design: Choosing among five approaches* (3rd ed.). Los Angeles, CA: Sage Publications.

Creswell, J. W., & Plano Clark, V. L. (2011). *Designing and conducting mixed methods research* (2nd ed.). Thousand Oaks, CA: Sage Publications.

Dominguez, D. G. (2015). *DOMA's demise: A victory for non-heterosexual bi-national families.* (Doctoral dissertation). Retrieved from ProQuest dissertations and theses. (AAI3581795)

Drescher, J. (2012). The removal of homosexuality from the DSM: Its impact on today's marriage equality debate. *Journal of Gay and Lesbian Mental Health, 16*(2), 124-135.

Freedom to Marry. (2013). *The defense of marriage act.* Retrieved from http://www.freedomtomarry.org/states/entry/c/doma

Gay and Lesbian Alliance Against Defamation (GLAAD). (July 2013). *Frequently asked questions: Defense of Marriage Act (DOMA).* Retrieved from http://www.glaad.org/marriage/doma

Goldberg, A. (2009). Lesbian, gay, and bisexual family psychology: A systemic, lifecycle perspective. In J. H. Bray & M. Stanton (Eds.), *The Wiley-Blackwell handbook of family psychology.* (576-587). Malden, MA: Blackwell Publishing.

Harris, E. A. (2017, June 20). Same-sex parents still face legal complications. *The New York Times.* Retrieved from https://www.nytimes.com/2017/06/20/us/gay-pride-lgbtq-same-sex-parents.html

Human Rights Campaign. (July 30, 2013). *Respect for marriage act.* Retrieved from http://www.hrc.org/laws-and-legislation/federal-legislation/respect-for-marriage-act?gclid=COXbopG2qLCFenm7AodRAMAzw

Killian, M. L. (2010). The political is personal: Relationship cognition policies in the United States and their impact on services for LGBT people. *Journal of Gay and Lesbian Social Services, 22*(1-2), 9-21.

Liptak, A. (2015). Supreme court ruling makes same-sex marriage a right nationwide. *The New York Times.* Retrieved from https://www.nytimes.com/2015/06/27/us/supreme-court-same-sex-marriage.html

Mathy, R. M., Kerr, S. K., & Lehmann, B.A. (2004). Mental health implications of same sex marriage: Influences of sexual orientation and relationship status in Canada and the United States. *Journal of Psychology and Human Sexuality, 15*(2-3), 117-141.

Mathy, R. M., & Lehmann, B. A. (2004). Public health consequences of the Defense of Marriage Act for lesbian and bisexual women: Suicidality, behavioral difficulties, and psychiatric treatment. *Feminism and Psychology, 14*(1), 187-194.

Morse, J. M. (1994). Designing funded qualitative research. In N. K. Denzin & Y. S. Lincoln (Eds.), *Handbook of qualitative research* (pp. 220-235). Thousand Oaks, CA: Sage Publications.

Moustakas, C. 1994. *Phenomenological research methods.* Thousand Oaks, CA: Sage Publications.

Pelts, M. D. (2014). A look back at the Defense of Marriage Act: Why same-sex marriage is still relevant for social work. *Journal of Women and Social Work, 29*(2), 237-247.

Pizer, J. C. (2016). *Lambda Legal condemns passage of anti-LGBT Mississippi bill HB 1523.* Retrieved from https://www.lambdalegal.org/blog/20160405_ms-hb-1523

Reilly, R., & Siddiqui, S. (June 26, 2013). *Supreme Court DOMA decision rules federal same-sex marriage ban unconstitutional.* Retrieved from http://www.huffingtonpost.com/2013/06/26/supreme-court-domadecision_n_3454811.html

Rimmerman, C. (2008). *The lesbian and gay movements: Assimilation or libera-*

*tion?* Boulder, CO: Westview Press.

Sterngass, J. (2012). *Same-sex marriage.* Tarrytown, NY: Marshall Cavendish Corporation.

Chapter 3

## How The Church Treats The LGBT Community

*Dudley Chancey*

*Oklahoma Christian University*

On June 26, 2015, the US Supreme Court ruled that the US Con-
stitution guarantees the right for same-sex couples to marry in all 50 US
states. "The Court, in this decision, holds same-sex couples may exercise
the fundamental right to marry in all States." (Obergefell et al. V. Hodges,
Director, Ohio Department of Health, et al., 2015).

### Introduction and Literature Review

Marriage is one of the great sacraments of the church. In 2001
North Americans opposed same-sex marriage 57% to 35%. A recent poll
reports a majority of North Americans (55%) support same-sex marriage,
with 37% opposing it (Pew Research Center, 2016). The Supreme Court
decision has fueled animosity toward the LGBT community. ("LGBT"
will be used throughout this paper to represent this marginalized community, understanding that "the struggle over the proper naming for the
complex of feelings and actions that are involved in same-sex relations —
gay men and lesbians, as opposed to homosexuals — is not trivial" (Gagnon, 1981, p. 560). Some examples of subgroups/minorities in this area
of study include Israeli Jews (Levin, 2013), Filipino Americans (Nadal &
Corpus, 2013), adolescents in India (Santoro, Benkhoukha, Ramanayake,
Suchday, & Kapur, 2015), Latino families (Koerner, Shirai, & Pedroza,
2013), secondary data analysis focusing on youth (Petts, 2014), African
American women (Lamis, Wilson, Lansford, Tarantino, & Kaslow, 2014),
Kuwaiti accident victims (Ashkanani, 2009), and adolescents (Goeke-Mo-
rey, Merrilees, Taylor, Shirlow, & Cummings, 2014)). The blame of a few,

for this animosity, gets laid at the feet of the church. Church people can be rude and violent, especially about this issue of same-sex marriage (Todd & Ong, 2012). Although the LGBT movement should not be compared to the Civil Rights movement, there are some similarities that are haunting when studying both. What some people did in the 1960's in the name of God, the church, and the Holy Bible was so wrong. Some of the same things happen today against minorities.

Original academic research on religiosity/spirituality (R/S) and health is voluminous. Koenig (2012) published a review of 1,200 quantitative studies between 1872 and 2000, and 2,100 quantitative studies between 2000 and 2010 covering these constructs. This review did not include qualitative studies on R/S that are numerous. There are multiple ways that R/S play out in the lives of many North Americans. There are wholesome effects on different areas of health including less depression and psychological distress (Ellison & Flannelly, 2009), greater satisfaction with life, happiness, and well-being (Ellison, Boardman, Williams, & Jackson, 2001; Krause, 2004) and higher levels of internal (perceived) control (Jackson & Bergeman, 2011; Fiori, Brown, Cortina, & Antonucci, 2006). R/S and church lie on a very wide continuum from extremely conservative (what some might call fundamentalist) to extremely liberal (what some call very progressive). Vincent, Parrott, and Peterson (2011) found that religious fundamentalism has many aspects, some of which increase risk for aggression toward gay men and lesbians whereas other aspects decrease this risk.

R/S have effects on different populations. Since the purpose of this investigation was to explore how the church treats the subgroup/minority LGBT community, it was important to find out if other groups had been studied connected with the R/S and health constructs, besides the seemingly default White, middle-class samples that are typically drawn for social science research as evidenced by the many studies published with LDS church members and R/S and health (Allen & Wang, 2014).

R/S are multi-faceted variables in the literature. For several years they were conceptualized synonymously (Nelson et al., 2009). Researchers lately have begun to define and operationalize them separately. Examples of *spirituality* would be a search for transcendent meaning expressed in a religious practice (Astrow, Pulchalski, & Sulmasy, 2001), a person's experience of a power not of their own (Mohr, 2006), and a set of principles that transcend all religions (Kaiser, 2000).

*Religion/religiosity* has been defined as a set of beliefs and practices generally based upon belief in a deity (Astrow, Pulchalski, & Sulmasy, 2001), religious beliefs shared by a group to connect to God (Davies, Brenner, Orloff, Sumner, & Worden, 2002), and a system for the expression of spirituality (Mohr, 2006).

It is within the context of church that many people experience religiosity and spirituality. The church today should be like the examples we have of the early church mentioned in Scripture. Many atrocities in the world are and have been caused by church people. What the Holy Bible defines as *the church* and how that is and has been lived out are mostly two different things. This paper is not defaming *the church* as it was originally meant to be in Scripture. The investigation and interviews contained herein provide the beginnings of an ethnographic study of some members of the LGBT community and their positive and negative experiences with church.

LGBT communities and R/S and church are not new topics in academic research. White (2008) provides a historical look at the roots of LGBT churches organizing in the United States beginning in Atlanta, Georgia in 1946. She makes a very important point in her research of this movement:

> By situating the gay church movement of the 1960s and 1970s in broader historical context, I chart the emerging spaces for discussing, performing, and proclaiming queer religious identities. Far from simply transplanting a political conception of gay identity into a religious arena, the religious movements I examine constructed and expressed a gay religious identity as an intrinsic — even divinely created — part of the self. Such a conception of identity countered opposing Christians' charge that homosexuality was a sinful behavior, and it provided the medium for reclaiming religious traditions that condemned homosexuality and gender variance. (p. 103)

The LGBT community discovered early on that established churches, especially conservative Protestant churches, were not friendly. Although conservative Christianity has not been the sole force behind producing and sustaining the historical antipathy toward the LGBT communities, it has exacerbated it because of its numerical majority and privilege in the United States (Russell & Bohan, 2014). Keep in mind that early in the 20th century homosexuality was changed from sin to sickness (mental illness) (Morin & Rothblum, 1991). It wasn't until 1973 that homosexuality was depathologized — 27 years after Helen Pappas and George Hyde founded the Eucharistic Catholic Church in Atlanta, Georgia. Point — we all have a part to play in social justice.

Having "all gay" churches does not address the root problem of how the church has and does treat the LGBT community. Ninety-eight percent of the participants interviewed for this paper grew up in a church — their church! To be kicked out or restricted from participating publically was traumatic for them and an injustice. Over and over the same is true in other fellowships. Johnson (2016) reports that gay LDS members have to decide whether they will go by the rules of the church or whether they will be excommunicated. Since many LDS children have their lives laid out for them from birth, a decision to go against this, to create a new life plan, is not a decision to take lightly.

So why does the LGBT community even bother with R/S and church? When R/S are separated from church experiences, positive and healthy attributes emerge for LGBT members such as increased self-esteem and identity affirmation, lower internalized homophobia, and fewer feelings of alienation (Lease, Horne, & Noffsinger-Frazier, 2005; Moleiro, Pinto, & Freire, 2013; Tan, 2005). It should be noted here that some in the LGBT community still suffer identity confusion and conflict even in churches that are highly gay-affirming (Smith & Horne, 2007). Members of the LGBT communities do not live in vacuums. Their lives intersect with the same variables (and others that are created against them) that all other humans face. Concerning identity with some in the LGBT communities, Wright and Stern (2015) found that spirituality was related to negative identity because of its association with a heightened sense of heteronormativity.

Specifically, in adolescence, Erikson's (1963) and Marcia's (1966) work point back to the important task of identity development at this age. Sexual identity and religious identity takes form during this foundational time. Yarhouse and Tan (2005) found a potential conflict with sexual identity and religious identity with adolescents as they developmentally attempt to answer, "Who am I?" Their traditional religious community tells them who they are, and the LGBT community tells them who they are. These two support groups for the emerging adolescent send opposing messages. This has been called the intersection of social identities by researchers (Jones & McEwen, 2000; Sherry, Adelman, Whilde & Quick, 2010; Sue & Sue, 1990). Ritter and Terndrup (2002) discuss LGB-centered religious communities that help young people reconcile traditional religious beliefs with minority sexual orientations.

Churches often create environments where the LGBT communities would find it difficult to integrate their spiritual and sexual identities (Sherry et al., 2010). This internalized conflict is associated with distress, internalized homophobia, depression, and suicidal ideation (Lease et al., 2005; Mahaffy, 1996; Schuck & Liddle, 2001). Such conflict certainly may contribute to the higher ratings in all of the above areas and others in the literature for gay men as compared to straight men (Hamilton & Mahalik,

2009; Lewis, 2009). It has been reported that the majority of gay men experience these conflicts when put in situations (i.e., group therapy, social settings) with straight men (Provence, Rochlen, Chester, & Smith, 2014).

For a moment, imagine being a Black man and gay. All of the above is magnified. Imagine being a Black man and gay and in a church. "You can't be gay and Black in a church. If you are gay you can't be a man. So why do you stay? We stay because church is our family. You don't abandon your whole family for one bad element." (from *Holler If You Hear Me: Black and Gay in the Church*, BET Documentary, directed by Clay Cane, 2015). Black LGBT members are more likely to continue participating in their churches than White LGBT members (Barnes & Meyer, 2012). Church and religious faith have been and are instrumental in positive mental health outcomes for African Americans (Walker & Longmire-Avital, 2013). The church is one of the great pillars of the Black community (Griffin, 2006; Miller, 2007). Tinson (2013) says:

> Historically the Black church has been a place for creating individual, systemic, and political change within the Black community. From its emergence in the late 18th century to its present day relevance, the Black church has and will always serve as a safe haven for African Americans, a place to worship God together, and a place where we are motivated to rebuild our communities. You can guarantee that on Sunday between the hours of 7 a.m. (early morning service) to 4 p.m. (afternoon service) there will be a large population of Blacks attending church. (para. 1)

In the Black church community religious faith still can contribute to higher levels of resiliency when there are struggles with internalized homonegativity (Walker & Longmire-Avital, 2013). Problems arise when the church is not tolerant, or even open to listening. The implications of this intolerance may be enduring according to Sowe, Brown, and Taylor (2014). They compared LGBT communities of religious, nonreligious, and formerly religious members, finding that despite having left the church, former Christians still reported high levels of homonegativity. There is also evidence in addition to the conflicts mentioned here of acts of microaggressions against people of color (POC) that contribute to negative effects for the Black LGBT communities (Balsam, Molina, Beadnell, Simoni, & Walters, 2011; Nadal et al., 2015). Black males who experienced these acts of microaggression reported more anxiety, distress, helplessness, hopelessness, and fear (Smith, Allen, & Danley, 2007). Intersect these microaggressions with being gay, and the abuse is multiplied.

Surely God did not make these people a minority — they must

be broken: Words from good intentioned families, pastors, and priests that haven't totally turned their back on their children and congregants, attempting to fix them. This fixing may be due to religious people's conservative views and a view of a just world (Lerner, 1980). This leads to victim blaming where people are unfairly held responsible for their misfortunes (Harber, Podolski, & Williams, 2015). Instead of blaming, research shows parents' attitudes and support moderate minority stress and depressive symptoms among those in the LGBT community (Feinstein, Wadsworth, Davila, & Goldfried, 2014; Pflum et al., 2015)

The church and some families exacerbate the confusion mentioned above by pressing those with same sex attraction (SSA) and even those fully out, to get "fixed," to become "ex-gay." The term "ex-gay" was introduced into the literature by Pattison and Pattison (1980). This fixing is discussed in the literature as conversion therapy, reparative therapy, or as sexual orientation change efforts (SOCE) (Dehlin, Galliher, Hyde, Bradshaw, & Crowell, 2015). The verdict is still out on the "curing power" of SOCE. Studies have shown the perceived benefits and the negative harmful takeaways from SOCE (Beckstead & Morrow, 2004; Haldeman, 1994; Nicolosi, Byrd, & Potts, 2000; Shidlo & Schroeder, 2002; Throckmorton, 2002). An APA (2009) SOCE task force concluded that no conclusive study to date proves that there are prevalent or frequent benefits or harms using SOCE. In 2010 the APA published its response to findings from another task force on SOCE, stating there were no adequate, rigorous studies to conclude whether or not SOCE works or does not work (Anton, 2010). There are several reviews in the literature that examine the different treatments used to fix homosexuals in the past (Drescher, 1998; Murphy, 1992; Stein, 1996). Conversion treatments are condemned by most agencies, counselors, and therapists. Several states are being pro-active against the use of conversion therapies and The Therapeutic Fraud Prevention Act of 2017 has been introduced into Congress. This bill, as a law, would prevent advertisements for conversion therapies that claim to change an individual's sexual orientation or gender identity, eliminate or reduce sexual or romantic attractions toward individuals of the same gender, or be harmless and without risk (Murray, 2017).

It seems that there is some progress being made in the struggle for equal rights for minority groups such as those in the LGBT communities. Will all churches ever affirm people that are same-sex attracted? Will all churches ever be tolerant of all peoples? Is it more important for some churches to keep their conservative identity and therefore possibly reject some people? Should same-sex attracted people forget the churches they grew up in and only attend all gay churches? Should all churches perform all of the sacraments for all people? Should other para-church and religiously-based organizations be tolerant toward LGBT communities? Should all family members be totally accepting of LGBT members that have come out? These are a few of the questions that drove the following investigation.

## Methodology

Clay Cane was asked (by a reporter after watching his documentary *Holler If You Hear Me: Black and Gay in the Church*) why he made his documentary. His answer was:

> I would say that. I'm not giving you some grand solution, but there's one takeaway that I hope people get: Spiritual violence and theological violence is just as damaging as emotional abuse. It is just as damaging as physical abuse. If you think you're doing things in the name of Christ, the name of "goodness," and you're damaging people, like Rev. Samuels says in the documentary, you're undermining all of your rightness. What happens to a young person's soul when they're taught you're an abomination? I have friends in their late 30's, in their 40's who are still trying to unlearn the lies they've been taught about themselves. I truly believe that if anything will make a shift, it won't be stats and numbers. It will be stories. (Cane, 2015)

Stories are powerful. This study set out to hear stories — not stats, not numbers — to listen.

A qualitative methodology fit this project well; specifically a grounded theory approach was used. Grounded theory is an approach for developing theory that is "grounded in data systematically gathered and analyzed" (Strauss & Corbin, 1994, p. 273). A common method used in grounded theory is the interview. Researchers using a grounded theory approach will learn about a culture or group by direct contact with them (Glaser & Strauss, 1967). Face-to-face interviews, Skype sessions, Facetime sessions, and phone calls were used to collect the stories in this research. With approval from our IRB, this data was collected under ongoing qualitative research at the Intergenerational Faith Center researching why persons stay and leave our fellowship. To date, two major projects are in process under this approval.

### The Sample

The participants in this study *(N=25)* were chosen from people the investigator knew personally, from participants bringing their friends, and from referrals. The participants self-identified as follows: Lesbian $N$=10, Gay $N$=13, Bi Sexual $N$=1, and Transgender $N$=1. Ages of participants ranged from 21 to 55. I did not interview teenagers to avoid having to gain parental permission and other human subjects issues with minors.

As the investigator, I began to realize how sensitive this topic was among the participants. Some participants would not meet in my home because they had been "ambushed" in homes of church leaders trying to fix them. Most asked to please not record the sessions, and above all, not use their names (some had to sign papers when leaving church or para-church positions saying they would not defame the institution or tell why they were "let go"). They were a little hesitant about meeting with me and me keeping my promise to not tell. One participant at my house leaned over to me one night as we sat around the table and said, "If you help us, they will fire you." Most of the participants old and young still asked, "Why would you help us?" There were no ulterior motives for doing this investigation, as in striking back at the church or other para-church organizations, monetary benefits, or even academic benefits. Although there is research describing social costs to being allies with the LGBT community (Cadieux & Chasteen, 2015), there is also current research being carried out on the benefits of being allies to the LGBT community (Rostosky, Black, Riggle, & Rosenkrantz, 2015). Perhaps I was attempting to "be the church" to these communities of people.

### The Context — In The Beginning

North America is full of religions/denominations/churches. They range from conservative exclusive to progressive inclusive, and all in between. No matter what theological stance most churches take, they are mostly filled with homogenous people. Dr. Martin Luther King, Jr. once said, "It is appalling that the most segregated hour of Christian America is eleven o'clock Sunday morning" (King, 1968; Barndt, 2011).

Bruner and Chancey (2013) describe the church of which 98% of the participants in this study grew up in:

> ...the Churches of Christ, one of three significant strands of the Stone-Campbell Restoration Moment: the Disciples of Christ (Christian Church), the Christian Churches/Churches of Christ, and the Churches of Christ, Non-instrumental. This movement grew rapidly in the United States in the early 19th century, rooted in the quest for church unity through the restoration of the principles and practices of the primitive first-century church. Initially rejecting the use of any but canonical materials to understand the primitive church, the careful reading of Scripture was of primary

importance among its members. The Churches of Christ are free churches, devoid of attachments to any over-arching government and eschewing clergy-laity distinctions, though, in practice, distinctions are sometimes implicit. One of the most distinctive features of this fellowship has been a capella congregational singing. Members typically have a high view of God and humanity. Churches in this faith group are more numerous in the south and southwest.

Of the 25 participants interviewed, only two are currently attending a church of Christ sporadically, and two participants attend on a full-time basis. This church fellowship is much like many others in North America. It is not without fault in how accepting it has been of "others." For example, there are "White" churches of Christ and there are "Black" churches of Christ. There are deep wounds in this fellowship that have not healed from the days of the civil rights movement. However, there does seem to be some agreement among Black and White church of Christ members—Gays Aren't Welcome! Stanford (2013) asks, "With same sex-marriage, are White evangelicals and Black Christian conservatives becoming one and the same?" Reverend Gregory Daniels told the *New York Times* (Clemetson, 2004): "If the KKK opposes gay marriage, I would ride with them." It has and continues to be a long road for White and Black people who grew up in our churches who have come out, to find acceptance among their church heritage. One of the participants in this investigation is male and Black. This participant has not come out even to family because of being so scared of what the Black and the White church would do.

I wondered if there ever was an all-gay church of Christ. I found a link to an archive of data, photos, and history of the LGBT communities of Houston, Texas. This link led to another link that led to a large file of history on a gay church of Christ in the Houston area (see *A Cappella Chorus and Houston's Montrose Church of Christ*). As of 7-27-16 I have not been able to track down anyone who knows anything about this church. It seems to have disappeared or perhaps changed its name and affiliation. I am confident that no mainline churches of Christ would have been in fellowship with this church during that era.

In my interviews, none of the 25 participants expressed a desire to go to an all-gay church (and none had ever heard of the church in Houston mentioned above). Many wished they could go to their home church. One participant shared that they were met in the foyer of the church of Christ that they grew up in, by an elder of that church and told, "we don't want your kind here." They actually have this conversation recorded on one of their phones. They still attend because the preaching minister is inclusive and their family still attends there. "The minister really speaks to my heart. I can put up with the occasional harassment of a few to hear good sermons and be with my family."

## Results — Some Initial Findings/Themes From This Investigation

This study began with a targeted select sampling procedure due to the sensitivity of the project. Great care has been taken to protect the identity of participants. No names are used. I have been careful in the use of pronouns such as him/her (used "their" or "them" which may be incorrect grammatically in some cases) to further protect the participants. Ryan and Bernard (2003) state the following about identifying themes in qualitative data: "At the heart of qualitative data analysis is the task of discovering themes. By themes, we mean abstract, often fuzzy, constructs which investigators identify before, during, and after data collection" (p. 85). The authors mention several techniques used by social scientists across a multiple of disciplines that assist in identification.

For this study, the literature review was helpful looking at what was reported in the early years versus what is being studied and reported currently. Much has been written (good and bad) since the passing of the Supreme Court ruling. Immediately after each interview session, I would sum up making notes of what had been talked about, looking for similar thoughts, concepts, key terms used, and quotes (on a couple of the long quotes here, I asked the participant if I could write them down during the interview). I asked all participants if it was okay to call them if I needed to clarify something from my notes. They all agreed that I could. I only called two for follow up.

Looking across the sample age-wise, an observation that rose to the top was:

**O1: *Fear of victimization does not disappear with age and experience.***
From a 21-year-old student being afraid of getting kicked out of university to the older couple afraid to meet in my home, the fear is real. One couple shared that they always have their power of attorney paperwork with them in case of emergencies, so that they can prove they are together. A gay couple even with the same last name is treated different, questioned, even harassed, unless they have a power of attorney.

With respect to age, I emailed seven big churches of Christ in the United States and asked them how LGBT friendly and accepting was their church. The responses were mostly apologetic for how they have treated the LGBT communities, and most said they pretty much are in

"Don't Ask, Don't Tell" mode. One minister referred me to their church's youth minister. He was even more apologetic, but also said the youth group was way more affirming and accepting of gay teens than the "big" church was. "We can do things down here that the adults just can't do or want do. If the senior minister was to push this, we would get 100 emails basically saying 'back off'." These comments lead to another theme that emerged:

### O2: How long before churches really start doing what the Bible says about loving people?

"It is like we are invisible as far as meeting any needs we might have that a loving church would normally provide to its members." "They use the Bible to beat us over the head with two verses while they fail to carry out so many verses that talk about responding to one another." These and other responses came from participants as they told their stories of trying to fit into their home churches. One participant is able to lead worship when they go back home and visit their home church. Another participant is also involved in the church's worship times and also involved in administration tasks in the church of which they are a member. Out of all of the current university students who I interviewed, only one still attends a church of Christ. The others mention that they miss some of the elements of the churches of Christ they grew up in, but that it is not worth the struggle and pain to try and be accepted. Some also pointed out, that there are also some theological elements that they have changed views on compared to the mostly conservative churches of Christ they grew up in. These differing views may assist them in choosing to go to a more open and accepting church. The fact is, they aren't going to churches of Christ (I am confident if I did these interviews with people who grew up in other conservative groups, the results would be very similar.)

Another observation seemed to fit under a theme of desperation:

### O3: Do the LGBT communities think about self-harm/suicide/death more than straight communities?

Yes! I was amazed at how many of the participants were on anti-depressants in the past and currently. Two had attempted suicide. Several of the younger participants discussed their suicidal thoughts after coming out. One participant came out to their spouse and then gathered their friends together to tell them. After coming out to their group of friends, the spouse divorced and the friends said they could not be friends anymore (these were church friends they had for almost four years at a "Christian" university). The participant said, "When I gathered my best friends together in our apartment and came out to them, they immediately rejected me and basically told me to get out of their lives. I had thoughts of harming myself because I felt so alone and betrayed. I didn't actually think about doing anything, but I remember thinking to myself, 'this is why people kill themselves.'"

These self-harm thoughts may be correlated with timing of coming out. Younger LGBT persons are twice as likely to self-harm than older members. My older participants who came out later in life reported that harming themselves was not a factor in their thoughts and decisions. Hickson, Davey, Reid, Weatherburn, and Bourne (2016) found that age was a factor in self-harm within the LGBT communities they studied.

One participant said, "I never thought about killing myself, but I would pray to God almost everyday to let me die—heart attack, car wreck, run over by a truck—didn't matter, just relieve the pain, loneliness, and rejection." Another participant shared the following: "Yes. When I was in college. I came to a breaking point. I was doing individual and group ex-gay focused therapy. I was involved with Exodus and after two years of digging up every 'root cause' of my sexuality I was ready to give up and wanted to die. I wanted to die. There were times I contemplated suicide—which made me feel even more guilty. So much of the journey is about shame, secrecy and deep feelings of inadequacy—failing at trying to overcome my 'struggle' just deepened all those feelings."

A fourth observation surfaced as some participants discussed sexuality:

## O4: Does celibacy work for some in the LGBT communities?

Two of the participants were adamant about being celibate for life. They felt for them that it honored God and they should be like any single heterosexual person should be who isn't married. Both of these individuals have no desire to marry. They both grew up in very strict church of Christ fellowships. Some in the LGBT communities believe "celibacy" is the new conversion therapy or "ex gay" therapy being thrown at them. Gay websites are full of stories and pros and cons of being celibate (e.g., https://www.gaychristian.net/greatdebate.php). There are also a few studies being done exploring this position (i.e., Creek, 2013). Several of the male participants expressed a desire to get married and have a family at some point in their lives. None of the participants, including the married ones, broached the subject of sex/sexuality during the interviews. One couple mentioned wearing shirts that said "We are gay and you can't watch."

A fifth theme that emerged concerned the spiritual side of the participants:

**O5: There are people in the LGBT communities who are very spiritual.**

Only one participant gave up on God and the church when they were in high school. "I had questions about God, the earth, sex, me – no one at the church even tried to help me find answers." One participant wanted to be a missionary. When school officials found out they were struggling with same-sex attraction, the participant was removed from a missionary program and told they couldn't participate until they got cured. Today, this participant does not engage in church and doesn't talk about God and Jesus in the sense that they were ready to give their life to in mission work. At best, the participant said they do believe in some of the principles that Jesus practiced, but choose to call them social justice issues and stay away from religion stuff.

The other participants range from very spiritual/religious in a church of Christ to occasionally attending highly liturgical churches such as Anglican or Episcopal on holidays. These have not lost their belief in God and Jesus. They do have varying opinions of the church, mainly because of how they have been treated by their former home churches. When I asked the participants why they stay involved in church and or why they keep going to church, they replied:

- All my friends are there.
- I want to make a difference with God's people so I need to be a part of it to do that.
- It is about our relationship with God (6X)
- It is the right thing to do.
- We want our adopted children to be brought up in the church.
- Taught that going to church is the thing to do when young and now owns it for myself.
- I love God. I want to be part of a church. I wish I could be part of the one I grew up in.
- My sense of faith community will never go away. Grew up living by a set of principles.
- At first I was angry at God, but not anymore. I go because I believe in God and I love God. I can see God more clearly now than when I was in high school.
- Loves God, loves Jesus, loves people.

My sixth observation is closely tied to observation number five:

**O6: Being spiritually involved in a church did not and does not come without a struggle.**

"The first fight is with yourself then you fight the church to keep your faith." I mentioned the couple feeling attacked in the church foyer by an elder. Another couple I interviewed was shy of visiting "friends" homes because of being surprised by church leaders trying to fix them when they would get to the home. Most of the participants had to find a new church to go to. Think about it. You grow up in a pretty conservative church atmosphere, and now you are in a totally different one if you choose to step outside of churches of Christ, as most of the participants have. Even if they stayed within the Restoration movement of churches described in the introduction, there are big differences to cope with. One participant described his new church as sort of a concert instead of a worship experience. "I miss the a cappella singing, no one does that better than us" (speaking of the a cappella churches of Christ). Another person told me they had found an Anglican church that was very inclusive, but they could not do much ministry there because they were not an ordained priest. "I used to lead worship, lead mission trips, and teach. I just go with my partner now and we sit, listen, and go home."

Ministries such as Glad Alliance (www.gladalliance.org) in the Restoration movement churches are welcoming, inclusive organizations dedicated to helping those in the LGBT communities become members of their churches (Disciples of Christ). Other church organizations are inclusive of LGBT communities world-wide (www.gaychurch.org). These organizations are very valuable in respect to persons looking for a church, for a place to get married, a youth group for their children, and last rites. One particular LGBT young woman says that she is so lonely on Sundays. No one understands where she is coming from at her big church. Shore (2013) confirms these feelings with a quote from one of the people he interviewed: "I hope that one day I can be out and proud before my fellow Christians at church. I know that there is nothing wrong with me."

Participants all had their different, stressful stories of coming out:

*O7: Coming out brings on multiple stressors because of the different contexts participants feel they need to come out to.*

*Family:* Participants in this study were conflicted when it came to coming out. We know from research that it is difficult for those in LGBT communities to come out in different contexts such as families, school, work, and church. Coming out to family is a big deal, perhaps the most difficult context (Savin-Williams, 2003). One participant could not even imagine meeting and telling his family face-to-face. The participant wrote letters to avoid the stress of being rejected in person. Coming out is seen as an important component in identity developmental theory (Willoughby, Malik, & Lindahl, 2006). Receiving favorable responses to coming out aids in a more positive development, whereas not receiving a positive response from others, especially parents, tends to increase adverse psychological outcomes (Rosario, Hunter, Maguen, Gwadz, & Smith, 2001). When some participants told their parents there were different types of reactions, from "get out the house and don't come back" to "we will help you get fixed." Some of the participants were outed by siblings, "friends," or supposedly confidential helpers. This made it even more difficult to have that first conversation. One participant recalled the following in their coming out experience with family:

> I was taught as a young person that singing with musical instruments in church was wrong—a sin. When I was older in college I was studying the Bible and biblical languages and came to the belief that using musical instruments in church was not wrong. I was home on break after that and told my parents that I now believed that it was not wrong to sing with instruments. That rocked my parents. My dad looked at me and said, 'It would only be worse if you were going out at night and murdering people, or if you were gay.' A few months later after graduation, I told my parents I was gay. I left home and have not been back.

Etengoff and Daiute (2014) found that some family members tend to use religious tools (e.g., God, Bible, other religious texts) to show the LGBT family member they are wrong, whereas others use the same tools and find ways to show support of the LGBT family member. Heatherington and Lavner (2008) have a good review and recommendations for family systems to come to terms with coming out.

*School*: Coming out at school whether middle school, high school, or college can be a dangerous choice for those in the LGBT communities. Evans and Chapman (2014) studied over 3,000 students with a model that included different types of bullying. Students who identified as LGBT received bullying from all the different types of bullying identified, especially *biased-based bullying* (Poteat, Mereish, DiGiovanni, & Scheer, 2013). Rivers (2004) studied adults who were out of school and university and found that many of those participating in the study reported that they still dealt with memories of being bullied by using drugs and alcohol. Seventeen percent of the sample exhibited PTSD symptoms. In addition to traditional bullying, there is a plethora of research out on microaggressions toward sexual minorities mentioned earlier, most unintentional (Sue, 2010), most hurtful by friends of the same orientation (Galupo, Henise, & Davis, 2014), and even coming from the helping communities (Kaufman, Baams, & Dubas, 2017), all contributing to minority stress.

Of the 25 people interviewed in this investigation, only five of them came out in high school. Being victims in school was not mentioned by them in any of our meetings together as a traumatic event. Ten of the participants came out in college, most by choice but a couple were outted by "friends" or confidants. The remaining participants in the sample came out as adults after college. Only one person in this sample has not come out to family. With this particular sample, there were not any war stories of getting beat up or persecuted in high school or university. This may speak well of the tolerance of millennial students in the 2000's and better diversity programs in schools (http://www.naspcenter.org/principals/nassp_glbqt.html). Better awareness on university campuses may contribute to better understanding, with over 200 universities in the United States that have a staffed LGBT center on campus (Marine & Nicolazzo, 2014). However, it is well documented that even if there is not outward physical and emotional abuse with LGBT students, many still have to deal with other stressors such as internalized homophobia (also called internalized sexual stigma) (Herek, Gillis, & Cogan, 2009).

*Work:* In an older review, Croteau (1996) reported that between 25% and 66% of LGBT employees reported experiencing sexual orientation discrimination at work. The fear of full disclosure in the workplace is common among LGBT communities and not easily resolved (Ragins, Singh, & Cornwell, 2007). Griffith and Hebl (2002) suggest having corporate policies in place and continual diversity training to ease the stress that LGBT employees and potential employees feel in the workplace. Not counting participants who were still students, all other participants were employed. One participant shared their story of being fired from a "Christian" organization when they found out from someone outside the organization that the participant was married to someone not of the opposite sex. Two participants had to retool for new careers because of not being allowed to be out and be ministers in churches of Christ. Many organizations are more LGBT friendly, whereas working for churches of Christ and most mainline Protestant churches is not an option for openly LGBT persons.

*Church:* Coming out in churches of Christ ensures that one will not be a member of that fellowship for long, as evidenced in this investigation (three of the participants parents were ministers). Twenty-two of the 25 participants grew up in churches of Christ, with only two of those currently attending a church of Christ. It must be noted here that more studies need to be done on individual fellowships (e.g., Church of Christ, Baptist, Church of God, Seventh Day Adventist) to determine if leaving these fellowships was caused by sexual orientation alone. Kinnaman (2011, reprint 2016) does a commendable job in his study of millennials as church dropouts. His research surfaced six major reasons why millennials are leaving mainline church fellowships (one reason being homophobia). Most of the participants who left by choice were not happy about leaving the church of Christ. One participant said, "I am not embittered, I am heartbroken. So many of us cannot be a part of our Tribe that we grew up in." Older participants shared mixed feelings about their church situation. One participant has come to see church as a "weapon" used against people. This participant shared the following about how church should be:

> I shared how gay bars made me know I wasn't alone and that if you got through the hatred getting to a bar it felt like a safe zone once inside. With that said, it would be so much better to have people feel they could go to a safe place/community that didn't involve the bad things that are associated with bar experiences like sex, drugs and alcohol. These things can often lead people down paths that impact them for a lifetime. Many community centers or other safe spaces are located in a "gay" neighborhood you would visit during the daytime. If someone wasn't out and got caught visiting such a place, it could have negative consequences. Wouldn't it be great if the church could serve that purpose? The church should bring ALL people together and not just select groups.

Although there are churches/church members working toward a better understanding of the LGBT communities (Rosik, Griffith, & Cruz, 2007), the Pew Research Center reports 37% of North Americans are still adamantly opposed to issues such as same-sex marriage, and homosexuality in general (Fingerhut, 2016). *Christianity Today* a popular evangelical magazine called for "A Better Conversation About Homosexuality" (Benson, 2012):

> Just at the point of exhaustion and irritability, when we think the debate on homosexuality in the church has reached its end—with every position articulated, every line drawn in the sand, every constituency ghettoized—other voices emerge to remind us that the conversation *must* proceed. Despite anxiety for ourselves and the church, the conversation must proceed because God has called us to this annoyance as he has called previous generations of Christians to other annoyances; the interpretation of Scripture requires us to think deeply and wait patiently upon God; the shalom of the church is at risk if we close down the search for agreement; and, lest we forget, some of God's precious children live upon the

rack (para. 1).

## Conclusion, Limitations, and Future Research

I asked participants "What do most churches need to know as to how to engage the LGBT communities?" Some of the respondents interviews were filled with "what the church should do" comments below:

*O8: What churches need to know.*

- Don't be hesitant to talk about the subject. Be open-minded. Most of all--LOVE
- Listen to us (5X)
- Don't mistreat my children
- Treat us like you would want to be treated
- Hear our stories (2X)
- Walk with us (2X)
- Churches should be a safe space
- Take a stand, do the right thing, even if not popular
- We are not bad people. Stumble along with us on this journey.
- Teach Love, Grace, Walk with us.
- Ignorance is a tool people use to not have to address the tough issues. There is a Void of Silence where the important, hard conversations are not happening. Don't make us Exiles. Stop using faith to keep bigotry and hate alive.
- Stop the rhetoric. Stem the hatred.
- Church is a great support group. We all need that.
- Hypocrites

The church of today must improve, to imitate its founder. This study is another reminder that we fall short of "Love God, Love Others," even with our own people, much less with the rest of humanity. The limitations of this investigation include a fairly homogeneous sample. Future samples should include more diversity in ethnicity, greater age range, and a greater variety of representation in what we try to define as LGBT. Another purposeful limitation was focusing on one denomination of church fellowships. Future comparisons should include others (i.e., Protestant, Catholic, Muslim). It would be interesting to interview people from "all-gay" churches to investigate any prejudices within those churches (i.e., L *vs.* G *vs.* B *vs.* T). Perhaps a mixed methods approach based off this study would help future studies to access more data for a better understanding of this population and their lives.

## References

*A Cappella Chorus and Houston's Montrose Church of Christ*. Retrieved from http://www.houstonlgbthistory.org/Houston80s/Misc/Churches/Church of Christ-A Cappella Chorus80-86.compressed.pdf

Allen, G. E. K., & Wang, K. T. (2014). Examining religious commitment, perfectionism, scrupulosity, and well-being among LDS individuals. *Psychology of Religion and Spirituality, 6*(3), 257-264.

American Psychological Association Task Force on Appropriate Therapeutic Responses to Sexual Orientation. (2009). *Report of the Task Force on Appropriate Therapeutic Responses to Sexual Orientation*. Washington, DC: American Psychological Association.

Anton, B. S. (2010). Proceedings of the American Psychological Association for the legislative year 2009: Minutes of the annual meeting of the Council of Representatives and minutes of the meetings of the Board of Directors. *American Psychologist, 65*, 385–475. doi:10.1037/a0019553

Astrow, A., Pulchalski, C., & Sulmasy, D. (2001). Religion, spirituality, and health care: Social, ethical, and practical considerations. *American Journal of Medicine. 110*, 283-287.

Balsam, K. F., Molina, Y., Beadnell, B., Simoni, J., & Walters, K. (2011). Measuring multiple minority stress: The LGBT people of color microaggressions scale. *Cultural Diversity and Ethnic Minority Psychology, 17*(2), 163-174.

Barndt, J. (2011). *Becoming the anti-racist church: Journeying toward wholeness*. Minneapolis, MN: Prisms of Fortress Press.

Barnes, D. M., & Meyer, I. H. (2012). Religious affiliations, internalized homophobia, and mental health in lesbians, *gay* men, and bisexuals. *American Journal of Orthopsychiatry, 82*(4), 505-515.

Beckstead, A., & Morrow, S. L. (2004). Mormon clients' experiences of conversion therapy: The need for a new treatment approach. *The Counseling Psychologist, 32*, 651-690.

Benson, C. (2012). A better conversation about homosexuality. *Christianity Today.* Retrieved from http://www.christianitytoday.com/ct/2012/julyweb-only/better-conversation-about-homosexuality.html

Breshears, D., & Beer, C. L. (2014). A qualitative analysis of adult children's advice for parents coming out to their children. *Professional Psychology: Research and Practice, 45*(4), 231-238.

Bruner, R., & Chancey, D. (2013). *Spiritual health and coping across three generations of faith.* Unpublished paper presented at the National Council on Family Relations, San Antonio, TX.

Cadieux, J., & Chasteen, A. L. (2015). You gay, bro? Social costs faced by male confronters of antigay prejudice. *Psychology of Sexual Orientation and Gender Diversity, 2*(4), 436-446.

Cane, C. (Director). (2015). *Holler if you hear me: Black and gay in the church* [Video Documentary]. United States: BET.

Clemetson, L. (2004). Both sides court Black churches in the battle over gay marriage. *New York Times.* Retrieved from http://www.nytimes.com/2004/03/01/us/both-sides-court-black-churches-in-the-battle-over-gay-marriage.html

Creek, S. J. (2013). Not getting any because of Jesus: The centrality of desire management to the identity work of gay, celibate Christians. *Symbolic Interaction, 36*(2), 119-136.

Croteau, J. M. (1996). Research on the work experiences of lesbian, gay and bisexual people: An integrative review of methodology and findings. *Journal of Vocational Behavior, 48,* 195–209.

Davies, B., Brenner, P., Orloff, S., Sumner, L., & Worden, W. (2002). Addressing spirituality in pediatric hospice and palliative care. *Journal of Palliative Care. 18,* 59-67.

Dehlin, J. P., Galliher, R. V., Hyde, D. C., Bradshaw, W. S., & Crowell, K. A. (2015). Sexual orientation change efforts among current or former LDS church members. *Journal of Counseling Psychology, 62*(2), 95-105.

Drescher, J. (1998). I'm your handyman: A history of reparative therapies. *Journal of Homosexuality, 36*, 19-42.

Erikson, E. H. (1963). *Childhood and society.* New York, NY: Norton.

Ellison, C. G., Boardman, J. D., Williams, D. R., & Jackson, J. S. (2001). Religious involvement, stress, and mental health: Findings from the 1995 Detroit Area Study. *Social Forces, 80*, 215–249.

Etengoff, C., & Daiute, C. (2014). Family members' uses of religion in post-coming-out conflicts with their gay relative. *Psychology of Religion and Spirituality, 6*(1), 33-43.

Evans, C. B. R., & Chapman, M. V. (2014). Bullied youth: The impact of bullying through lesbian, gay, and bisexual name calling. *American Journal of Orthopsychiatry, 84*(6), 644-652.

Feinstein, B. A., Wadsworth, L. P., Davila, J., & Goldfried, M. R. (2014). Do parental acceptance and family support moderate associations between dimensions of minority stress and depressive symptoms among lesbians and gay men? *Professional Psychology: Research and Practice, 45*(4), 239-246.

Fingerhut, H. (2016). *Support steady for same-sex marriage and acceptance of homosexuality.* Pew Research Center. Retrieved from http://pewrsr.ch/1rHRJ62.

Fiori, K. L., Brown, E. E., Cortina, K. S., & Antonucci, T. C. (2006). Locus of control as a mediator of the relationship between religiosity and life satisfaction: Age, race, and gender differences. *Mental Health, Religion, and Culture, 9*, 239–263.

Gagnon, J. H. (1981). Review of homosexuality. *American Journal of Orthopsychiatry, 51*(3), 560-568.

Galupo, M. P., Henise, S. B., & Davis, K. S. (2014). Transgender microaggressions in the context of friendship: Patterns of experience across friends' sexual orientation and gender identity. *Psychology of Sexual Orientation and Gender Diversity, 1*(4), 461-470.

Glaser, B., & Strauss, A. (1967). *The discovery of grounded theory: Strategies for qualitative research.* Chicago, IL: Aldine.

Griffin, H. L. (2006). *Their own receive them not: African American lesbians and gays in Black churches.* Cleveland, OH: Pilgrim Press.

Griffith, K. H., & Hebl, M. R. (2002). The disclosure dilemma for gay men and lesbians: Coming out at work. *Journal of Applied Psychology, 87*(6), 1191-1199.

Haldeman, D. C. (1994). The practice and ethics of sexual orientation conversion therapy. *Journal of Consulting and Clinical Psychology, 62*(2), 221-237.

Hamilton, C. J., & Mahalik, J. R. (2009). Minority stress, masculinity, and social norms predicting gay men's health risk behaviors. *Journal of Counseling Psychology, 56*, 132-141.

Harber, K. D., Podolski, P., & Williams, C. H. (2015). Emotional disclosure and victim blaming. *Emotion, 15*(5), 603-614.

Heatherington, L., & Lavner, J. A. (2008). Coming to terms with coming out: Review and recommendations for family systems-focused research. *Journal of Family Psychology, 22*(3), 329-343.

Herek, G. M., Gillis, J. R., & Cogan, J. C. (2009). Internalized stigma among sexual minority adults: Insights from a social psychological perspective. *Journal of Counseling Psychology, 56*, 32-43.

Jackson, B. R., & Bergeman, C. S. (2011). How does religiosity enhance well-being? The role of perceived control. *Psychology of Religion and Spirituality, 3*(2), 149-161.

Jones, S. R., & McEwen, M. K. (2000). A conceptual model of multiple dimensions of identity. *Journal of College Student Development, 41*, 405-414.

Jones, P. (2013). *Church zero: Raising 1st century churches out of the ashes of the 21st century church.* Colorado Springs, CO: David C. Cook Publishers.

Johnson, F. (2016). *Choosing love or the Mormon church.* The Atlantic. Retrieved from https://www.theatlantic.com/national/archive/2016/03/lgbt-mormons/475035/

Kaiser, L. R. (2000). Spirituality and the physician executive: Reconciling the inner self and the business of health care. *The Physician Executive. 26*(2). Retrieved from http://www.freepatentsonline.com/article/Physician-Executive/102342512.html

Kaufman, T. M. L., Baams, L., & Dubas, J. S. (2017). Microaggressions and depressive symptoms in sexual minority youth. *Psychology of Sexual Orientation and Gender Diversity, 4*(2), 184-192.

King, M. L. (1968). *Remaining awake through a great revolution. Sermon preached at National Cathedral in Washington, D.C., March 31, 1968.* Retrieved from http://kingencyclopedia.stanford.edu/encyclopedia/documentsentry/doc_remaining_awake_through_a_great_revolution.1.html

Kinnaman, D. (2011). *You lost me: Why young Christians are leaving church... and rethinking faith.* Grand Rapids, MI: Baker Books.

Koenig, H. G. (2012). Religion, spirituality, and health: The research and clinical implications. *ISRN Psychiatry, 2012,* 1-33.

Krause, N. (2004). Common facets of religion, unique facets of religion, and life satisfaction among older African Americans. *Journals of Gerontology, 59B,* S109–S117.

Lease, S. H., Horne, S. G., & Noffsinger-Frazier, N. (2005). Affirming faith experiences and psychological health for Caucasian lesbian, gay, and bisexual individuals. *Journal of Counseling Psychology, 52*(3), 378-388.

Lewis, N. M. (2009). Mental health in sexual minorities: Recent indicators, trends, and their relationships to place in North America and Europe. *Health & Place, 15,* 1029-1045.

Lerner, M. L. (1980). *The Belief in a Just World: A Fundamental Delusion.* New York, NY: Plenum Press.

Mahaffy, K. A. (1996). Cognitive dissonance and its resolution: A study of lesbian Christians. *Journal for the Scientific Study of Religion, 35,* 392-402.

Marcia, J. E. (1966). Development and validation of ego identity status. *Journal of Personality and Social Psychology, 3,* 551-558.

Masci, D., & Lipka, M. (2015). *Where Christian churches, other religions stand on gay marriage.* Washington, D.C: Pew Research Center.

Miller, R. L. (2007). Legacy denied: African American gay men, AIDS and the Black church. *Social Work, 52*(1), 51– 61.

Mohr, W. (2006). Spiritual issues in psychiatric care. *Perspectives in Psychiatric Care. 42*(3), 174-183.

Moleiro, C., Pinto, N., & Freire, J. (2013). Effects of age on spiritual well-being and homonegativity: Religious identity and practices among LGB persons in Portugal. *Journal of Religion, Spirituality & Aging, 25,* 93–111

Morin, S. F., & Rothblum, E. D. (1991). Removing the stigma: Fifteen years of progress. *American Psychologist, 46*(9), 947-949.

Murphy, T. (1992). Redirecting sexual orientation: Techniques and justifications. *Journal of Sex Research, 29,* 501-523.

Murray, P. (2017). *The therapeutic fraud prevention act of 2017.* Retrieved July 4, 2017, from https://www.congress.gov/bill/115th-congress/senate-bill/928

Nadal, K. L., & Corpus, M. J. H. (2013). Tomboys and baklas: Experiences of lesbian and gay Filipino Americans. *Asian American Journal of Psychology, 4*(3), 166-175.

Nadal, K. L., Davidoff, K. C., Davis, L. S., Wong, Y., Marshall, D., & McKenzie, V. (2015). A qualitative approach to intersectional microaggressions: Understanding influences of race, ethnicity, gender, sexuality, and religion. *Qualitative Psychology, 2*(2), 147-163.

Nicolosi, J., Byrd, A., & Potts, R. W. (2000). Retrospective self-reports of changes in homosexual orientation: A consumer survey of conversion therapy clients. *Psychological Reports, 86,* 1071-1088.

*Obergefell et al. V. Hodges, Director, Ohio Department of Health, et al.* (2015). Retrieved from http://www.cnn.com/2015/06/26/politics/scotus-opinion-document-obergefell-hodges

Pattison, E. M., & Pattison, M. L. (1980). Ex-gays: Religiously mediated change in homosexuals. *American Journal of Psychiatry, 137,* 1553-

1562.

Pew Research Center. (2016). *Changing attitudes on gay marriage*. Retreived from: http://www.pewforum.org/2016/05/12/changing-atti-tudes-on-gay-marriage/

Pflum, S. R., Testa, R. J., Balsam, K. F., Goldblum, P. B., & Bongar, B. (2015). Social support, trans community connectedness, and mental health, symptoms among transgender and gender nonconforming adults. *Psychology of Sexual Orientation and Gender Diversity, 2*(3), 281-286.

Poteat, V. P., Mereish, E. H., DiGiovanni, C. D., & Scheer, J. R. (2013). Homophobic bullying. In I. Rivers & N. Duncan (Eds.), *Bullying: Experiences and discourses of sexuality and gender* (pp. 75–90). New York, NY: Routledge.

Provence, M. M., Rochlen, A. B., Chester, M. R., & Smith, E. R. (2014). Just one of the guys: A qualitative study of gay men's experiences in mixed sexual orientation men's groups. *Psychology of Men & Masculinity, 15*(4), 427-436.

Ragins, B. R., Singh, R., & Cornwell, J. M. (2007). Making the invisible visible: Fear and disclosure of sexual orientation at work. *Journal of Applied Psychology, 92*(4), 1103-1118.

Ritter, K. Y., & Terndrup, A. I. (2002). *Handbook of affirmative psycho-therapy with gay men and lesbians*. New York, NY: Guilford Press.

Rivers, I. (2004). Recollections of **bullying** at **school** and their long-term implications for lesbians, **gay** men, and bisexuals. *Crisis: The Journal of Crisis Intervention and Suicide Prevention, 25*(4), 169-175.

Rosario, M., Hunter, J., Maguen, S., Gwadz, M., & Smith, R. (2001). The coming out process and its adaptational and health-related associations among gay, lesbian, and bisexual youths: Stipulation and exploration of a model. *American Journal of Community Psychology, 29*, 133–160.

Rosik, C. H., Griffith, L. K., & Cruz, Z. (2007). Homophobia and conservative religion: Toward a more nuanced understanding. *American Journal of Orthopsychiatry, 77*(1), 10-19.

Rostosky, S. S., Black, W. W., Riggle, E. D. B., & Rosenkrantz, D. (2015). Positive aspects of being a heterosexual ally to lesbian, gay, bisexual and transgender (LGBT) people. *American Journal of Orthopsychi-*

*atry, 85*(4), 331-338.

Rostosky, S. S., Riggle, E. D. B., Horne, S. G., Denton, F. N., & Huellemeier, J. D. (2010). Lesbian, gay, and bisexual individuals' psychological reactions to amendments denying access to civil marriage. *American Journal of Orthopsychiatry, 80*(3), 302-310.

Russell, G. M., & Bohan, J. S. (2014). Toward a contextual understanding of psychology trainees' religious conflicts. *Psychology of Sexual Orientation and Gender Diversity, 1*(4), 293-301.

Ryan, G. W., & Bernard, R. (2003). Techniques to identify themes. *Field Methods, 15*(1), 85-109.

Savin-Williams, R. C. (2003). Lesbian, gay and bisexual youths' relationships with their parents. In L. D. Garnets & D. C. Kimmel (Eds.), *Psychological perspectives on lesbian, gay, and bisexual experiences* (2nd ed., pp. 299–326). New York: Columbia University Press.

Schuck, K. D., & Liddle, B. J. (2001). Religious conflicts experienced by lesbian, gay, and bisexual individuals. *Journal of Gay and Lesbian Psychotherapy, 5,* 63-82.

Smith, B., & Horne, S. (2007). Gay, lesbian, bisexual and transgendered (GLBT) experiences with Earth-spirited faith. *Journal of Homosexuality, 52,* 235-248.

Sherry, A., Adelman, A., Whilde, M. R., & Quick, D. (2010). Competing selves: Negotiating the intersection of spiritual and sexual identities. *Professional Psychology: Research and Practice, 41*(2), 112-119.

Shildo, A., & Schroeder, M. (2002). Changing sexual orientation: A consumers' report. *Professional Psychology: Research and Practice, 33,* 249-259.

Shore, J. (2013). *Unfair: Christians and the LGBT question.* Charleston, SC: Createspace Independent Publishing Platform.

Smith, W. A., Allen, W. R., & Danley, L. L. (2007). Assume the position . . . you fit the description: Psychosocial experiences and racial battle fatigue among African American male college students. *American Behavioral Scientist, 51,* 551-578.

Sowe, B. J., Brown, J., & Taylor, A. J. (2014). Sex and the sinner: Comparing religious and nonreligious same-sex attracted adults on internalized homonegativity and distress. American Journal of Orthopsychiatry, 84(5), 530-544.

Stein, T. (1996). A critique of approaches to changing sexual orientation. In R. Cabaj & T. Stein (Eds.), *Textbook of homosexuality and mental health* (pp. 525-537). Washington, DC: American Psychiatric Press.

Strauss, A., & Corbin, J. (1994). Grounded Theory Methodology. In N. K. Denzin & Y. S. Lincoln (Eds.) *Handbook of Qualitative Research* (pp. 273-285). Thousand Oaks, CA: Sage Publications.

Sue, D. W., & Sue, D. (1990). *Counseling the culturally different: Theory and practice* (2nd Ed). Oxford, England: John Wiley & Sons.

Sue, D. W. (2010). *Race, gender, and sexual orientation.* Hoboken, NJ: Wiley.

Tan, P. P. (2005). The importance of spirituality among gay and lesbian individuals. *Journal of Homosexuality, 49,* 135–144.

Throckmorton, W. (2002). Initial empirical and clinical findings concerning the change process of ex-gays. *Professional Psychology: Research and Practice, 33*(3), 242-248.

Tinson, N. (2013). *The role of the Black church in creating change.* Congressional Black Caucus Foundation, Inc. Retrieved from http://www.cbcfinc.org/thevillage/2013/10/08/the-role-of-the-black-church-in-creating-change/

Todd, N. R., & Ong, K. S. (2012). Political and theological orientation as moderators for the association between religious attendance and attitudes toward gay marriage for Black Christians. *Psychology of Religion and Spirituality, 4*(1), 56-70.

Vincent, W., Parrott, D. J., & Peterson, J. L. (2011). Effects of traditional gender role norms and religious fundamentalism on self-identified heterosexual men's attitudes, anger, and aggression toward gay men and lesbians. *Psychology of Men & Masculinity, 12*(4), 383-400.

Walker, J. J., & Longmire-Avital, B. (2013). The impact of religious faith and internalized homonegativity on resiliency for Black lesbian, gay, and bisexual emerging adults. *Developmental Psychology, 49*(9), 1723-1731.

White, H. R. (2008). The historical roots of LGBT religious organizing, 1946-1976. *Nova Religio: The Journal of Alternative and Emergent Religions, 11*(4), 102-119.

Willoughby, B. L. B., Malik, N. M., & Lindahl, K. M. (2006). Parental reactions to their sons' sexual orientation disclosures: The roles of family cohesion, adaptability, and parenting style. *Psychology of Men and Masculinity, 7*(1), 14-26.

Wright, A. J., & Stern, S. (2016). The role of spirituality in sexual minority identity. *Psychology of Sexual* Orientation and Gender Diversity, 3, 71-79.

Yarhouse, M. A., & Tan, E. S. N. (2005). Addressing religious conflicts in adolescents who experience sexual identity confusion. *Professional Psychology: Research and Practice, 36*(5), 530-536.

## Appendix A

**Interview Questions**
1. How were you introduced to church?
    a. born into the church from birth
    b. converted to church as a teen
    c. converted to church as an adult.
2. Tell me about your church experience.
3. If experience was bad, what are you doing for church now?
4. If experience was/is good, what makes it that way? Why do you stay?
5. Are you allowed to teach or be in any type of leadership position? Explain.
6. If the answer to 5 is "no", once again, why do you stay?
7. Would you talk about how you "came out" to your family and what the results of that was like.
8. In your opinion, what do most churches need to know about how to engage with the LGBT community?
9. Any closing thoughts, pet peeves, soapboxes?

*Chapter 4*

## Increased Recognition–For Better or For Worse?

## Transgender Individuals, Couples, and Families

## in the 21st Century

*Alicia Bosley*

*Hofstra University*

*Atticus Ranck*

*Bradbury-Sullivan LGBT Community Center*

### Introduction

"It is revolutionary for any trans person to choose to be seen and visible in a world that tells us we should not exist."
- Laverne Cox, actress and transgender activist (in Jones, 2014)

In recent years, transgender individuals have become increasingly visible in American society. From television shows such as I am Jazz and Transparent, to the growing recognition of "out" transgender people including Laverne Cox and Caitlyn Jenner, more people are becoming aware of the lives and struggles of the transgender community (Hope et al., 2016; Jones, 2016; World Professional Association for Transgender Health (WPATH), 2011). Legal and political movements affecting transgender Americans have also rapidly advanced, providing more rights and recognition for the community (National Center for Transgender Equality, 2017). These advancements have resulted in heated public debates and countermovements by groups such as the American Family Association and Focus on the Family (Hains, 2015; Isidore, 2016). It is in this sociopolitical climate that trans-identified people and their families are learning to navigate their lives. In this article, we will balance the existing literature with our experience as direct service providers to the transgender community, in the effort to better equip professionals and scholars working with transgender individuals and their partners and families.

## Recent Changes

Important legal progress for transgender rights has been made in recent years. The 2013 and 2015 Supreme Court rulings legalizing same-sex marriage, despite not being specifically intended to do so, have positively affected marital rights for many transgender individuals in same-sex relationships (Bosley, 2014; Human Rights Campaign, 2017b). These rulings provided access to over 1,000 federal benefits and protections to same-sex couples for the first time, positively affecting sociopolitical standing and emotional well-being (Bosley, 2014; Human Rights Campaign, 2017b). Further, in May 2013, the federal government mandated that public schools must allow transgender students to use bathrooms that correspond with their gender identity (Mason, 2016). This ruling, colloquially deemed the "Bathroom Bill", soon spread into policy in over a dozen states; 125 cities; and many colleges, agencies, and companies (Mason, 2016). Finally, in 2015, former military service members who had previously been denied military benefits due to their transgender identity were formally included in the extension of these benefits, and on June 30, 2016, the Pentagon lifted transgender military service ban, allowing transgender individuals to openly serve in the military (National Center for Transgender Equality, 2017). Similar to the repeal of the "Don't Ask, Don't Tell" policy on gay, lesbian, and bisexual (GLB) military service, these rulings marked a significant shift in national understandings of the legitimacy and nonpathology of transgender and gender-nonconforming identities.

However, awareness does not necessarily preclude equal rights and respect, and many transgender individuals are still marginalized, victimized, and threatened daily (Grant et al., 2011). As with many of the advances in the rights of GLB community, with most victories made for transgender rights or recognition, there has been pushback from opposing groups. For example, Target's bathroom policy, which allows customers to use bathrooms which correspond with their gender identity, as well as its decision to eliminate gendered marketing for its toys and children's bedding, resulted in public opposition and boycotts from some individuals and conservative organizations such as the American Family Association and the Billy Graham Evangelistic Association (Hains, 2015; Isidore, 2016). Following the introduction of bathroom bills in schools and businesses, multiple state legislators made movements to introduce laws restricting access to restrooms and other sex-segregated facilities such as locker rooms on the basis of gender assigned at birth, regardless of current legal, psychological, or physical gender (Kralik, 2017).

Additionally, President Donald Trump hinted at potential changes to transgender-inclusive military policies in July 2017 when he tweeted that transgender people would not be allowed to serve "in any capacity" in the United States Military effective immediately (Hirschfield Davis & Cooper, 2017). It is important to consider that tweets are not considered policy change and there has not been any official change to this ban as of this writing. In fact, the Commander of the Coast Guard said he would not break faith with transgender service members and vowed to support them (Cohen, 2017). Although the nation and military are uncertain as of summer, 2017 on the stance of transgender people in the military, it is clear that conversation around transgender people has made national headlines and therefore has potential for far-reaching effects on transgender communities.

It is difficult to ascertain whether legal changes occurred prior to, due to, or alongside shifts in social opinion; however, they assisted in bringing the existence and needs of transgender individuals, couples, and families to light. Sociopolitical debates and efforts can have very real effects on transgender individuals, as well as their significant others: Over half of respondents to a joint study between the National Center for Transgender Equality (NCTE) and the National Gay and Lesbian Task Force (NGLTF) reported experiencing verbal harassment or disrespect in public accommodations such as hotels, restaurants, and retail stores (Grant et al., 2011). Outcomes such as these often result in psychological or behavioral responses including social anxiety, agoraphobia, or behavioral modifications such as avoiding public places during peak hours (Israel, 2004; Kenaghy, 2005; Kenaghy & Bostwick, 2005). These effects were not unique to trans-identified individuals themselves; intimate partners, spouses, and family members have also reported stress related to harassment or unequal treatment of their loved ones (Grant et al., 2011). In fact, several significant others have experienced harassment or discrimination directly: fourteen percent of respondents to the NCTE/NGLTF survey reported that their spouse or partner had experienced job discrimination due to their gender identity, and eleven percent reported their child had experienced discrimination (Grant et al., 2011). Therefore, the current sociopolitical climate related to transgender visibility and rights has significant effects for trans-identified individuals and their significant others.

## Murder rates

With increased recognition and visibility of the transgender community, there has been a pushback in the form of murder rates. In 2016, 26 transgender-identified individuals were murdered in the United States. In the first 7 months of 2017, 16 trans people were murdered, presumably simply because they existed. We can compare these numbers to previous years: in 2015, 19 transgender people were murdered; in 2014, 11 trans people were killed; 11 in 2013; and 14 in 2012 (List of Unlawfully Killed Transgender People, 2017). Transgender people have always existed, so why is the murder rate increasing?

Although it is possible that transgender individuals are being murdered at higher rates than ever before, it is also possible that the media and law enforcement are better at recognizing when it is a trans person who has been murdered and therefore the record keeping is better. For example, if a biological male was found murdered while wearing a dress, even as late as the 1990s, their death may not have been recorded as a transgender murder (Human Rights Campaign, 2016). Now authorities generally know better, or at least know enough to investigate the death to determine if a gender-based hate crime is the cause of the murder (Human Rights Campaign, 2016).

It is not possible to determine the cause in the rise of transgender murders, but professionals and experts can speculate. One potential reason is because the visibility of transgender individuals has increased. Now that society knows transgender people exist, some have realized they do not agree with people "switching" genders and so they fight back with violence (Grant et al., 2011; Human Rights Campaign, 2016). Another speculation is that transgender people have been murdered at relatively the same rate for years but that the visibility of the trans community has made its way into law enforcement and the media; thus, society may be better equipped to recognize a gender-based hate crime against a trans person than they have in years past (Human Rights Campaign, 2016).

## Laws

Since transgender people have come into the national spotlight, there has been an increase in the legal ramifications for trans and gender nonconforming people, mostly bills and laws trying to regulate and/or norm trans bodies (ACLU, 2017). The bills in this section are broken down into two affirmative nondiscrimation bills and harmful-anti-LGBT bills (see Tables 1 and 2).

Affirmative nondiscrimination bills can be further divided into two categories: comprehensive protection and incomplete protection. Comprehensive protection bills prevent discrimination based on sexual orientation and gender identity and do so in a range of contexts, including employment, housing, and public accommodations (ACLU, 2017). Incomplete protection bills leave out gender identity, do not prevent discrimination in all key contexts, and contain broad religious exemptions or carve-outs for sex-segregated facilities (ACLU, 2017).

| Status | Affirmative Nondiscrimination | Harmful Anti-LGBT Bills |
|---|---|---|
| Dead | 46 | 113 |
| Withdrawn prior to introduction | 0 | 1 |
| Introduced | 7 | 4 |
| Active | 8 | 9 |
| Vetoed | 0 | 4 |
| Became law | 1 | 6 |

*Table 1. 2016 U.S. Legislative Sessions*

| Status | Affirmative Nondiscrimination | Harmful Anti-LGBT Bills |
|---|---|---|
| Dead | 55 | 76 |
| Withdrawn prior to introduction | 0 | 0 |
| Introduced | 4 | 10 |
| Active | 0 | 2 |
| Vetoed | 0 | 2 |
| Became Law | 0 | 3 |

*Table 2. 2017 U.S. Legislative Sessions*

Harmful anti-LGBT bills are divided into four categories: religious exemption bills, Bills pre-empting local protections, anti-transgender bills, and other anti-LGBT bills (ACLU, 2017). Bills pre-empting local protections prevent cities and other government entities from passing nondiscrimination protections greater than the protections offered at the state level (ACLU, 2017). Anti-transgender bills target trans people for discrimination, such as barring access to or criminalizing the use of appropriate facilities, including restrooms, or restricting trans students' ability to fully participate in school (ACLU, 2017).

Religion exemption bills, which fall under the category of harmful anti-LGBT bills, can also be divided further into six categories: religious freedom restoration acts, adoption and foster care, college and university student groups, access to health services, other exemption bills, and marriage-related religious exemption laws (ACLU, 2017). In addition, the marriage-related religious exemption laws has four subcategories, which are first amendment defense acts, government employees, commercial wedding services, and other marriage exemption bills (ACLU, 2017). For further discussion of these bills, we direct readers to the full ACLU report.

To illustrate the results of the increased visibility of the trans community, we have created a table highlighting the affirmative nondiscrimination bills and the harmful anti-LGBT bills during the United States 2016 legislative session (see Table 1) as well as the U.S. 2017 legislative session from January 1 through July 31, 2017 (see Table 2). Legislative sessions are times during which state legislatures convene in each state for the purpose of lawmaking (ACLU, 2017). States do not all meet at the same time or for the same length of time, and state legislature sessions are state specific. The tables provide a comprehensive summary of laws in all 50 states. As noted from the tables, despite some positive legal moves for the trans community, between 2016 and the first 7 months of 2017, there have also been nine laws passed which are harmful to LGBT people and only one law to protect the LGBT community (ACLU, 2017).

Nevertheless, there is some good news for transgender rights and protections. Although the 2017 legislative sessions are not all complete yet, if the year is on course for the next 5 months as it is for the first 7 months, 2017 is turning out to be less harmful than 2016 in terms of the percentage of protective to harmful LGBT bills, based on ACLU data (2017). In the 2016 legislative sessions, there were 219 affirmative and harmful LGBT related bills, 62 of which were affirmative to the LGBT community. This means 28.3% of LGBT-related bills in the 2016 U.S. legislative sessions are affirmative nondiscrimination bills. In the first 7 months of the 2017 U.S. legislative sessions, there have been 153 bills related to the LGBT community, 60 of which are affirmative nondiscrimination bills. This means 39.2% of LGBT-related bills in the 2017 U.S. legislative sessions are affirmative to the LGBT community. That is a positive difference for the LGBT community of 10.9% in just one year of (incomplete) legislative sessions (ACLU, 2017). Although there have been 9 harmful anti-LGBT laws passed and only 1 affirmative nondiscrimination law passed in 2016 and the first 7 months of the 2017 U.S. legislative sessions, there has still been forward progress for the LGBT community.

## Community Needs and Challenges

### Employment

As both authors are direct service providers working with the transgender and gender-nonconforming community, and one author (Atticus Ranck) is a self-identified trans person, we are aware of many of the needs and challenges those in the trans community face. One of the most significant community needs is in regards to job security. Even when the law and company policy is on their side, trans people continue to face employment discrimination. According to Grant et al. (2011), transgender people experience unemployment at twice the rate of the general population with rates for trans people of color up to four times the national unemployment rate. When trans people are able to secure employment, almost 90% of trans people report having been harassed or mistreated at work (Grant et al., 2011). As a former Director of Transgender Services, Atticus attests that he could have spent his entire working career on simply seeking employment and equity on the job site for trans people.

**Housing**

Another ongoing challenge in the trans community is housing and access to homeless shelters. Although housing is a basic human right, those in the trans community are discriminated against when it comes to access to housing and housing shelters. Nineteen percent of transgender people have been denied a home or apartment because they are trans and 11% claim to have been evicted because they are trans (Grant et al., 2011). At the extreme end of housing discrimination, 19% of transgender people report they have been homeless because they are trans or gender non-conforming (Grant et al., 2011). In addition, homelessness leads to a slew of other issues, such as incarceration, engaging in sex work for income, higher likelihood of contracting HIV, and being more likely to attempt suicide.

When a transgender person is able to find a shelter with an open bed (quite a challenge in itself in South Florida, where both authors have worked with the transgender and gender nonconforming community), 29% of trans people reported being turned away and 42% were housed with the wrong gender (Grant et al., 2011). Even if a trans person is accepted into a shelter, 55% reported being harassed, 25% were physically assaulted, and 22% were sexually assaulted (Grant et al., 2011).

One of the tasks Atticus had as Director of Transgender Services was to find homeless shelters that were willing to accept transgender individuals. According to the Fair Housing Act and HUD rules for federally-funded housing, it is illegal to discriminate against gender identity, sexual orientation, and marital status in all federally-funded housing programs. In addition, the county in which we worked also has legal protection in place to prohibit discrimination against trans persons when it comes to access to housing and homeless shelters (National Center for Transgender Equality, 2017b). Nevertheless, this was one of the most challenging aspects of Atticus's position, for a few reasons. First, finding shelter in Broward County, Florida is difficult whether a client is cisgender or transgender. There are consistently many homeless people in need of assistance and once a bed opens at a shelter, it is almost immediately claimed by someone who may have been on a waiting list for months or years. Second, there are relatively few homeless shelters capable of taking decent care of a transgender person under their charge. Many of our transgender clients reported back to us that they felt harassed, isolated, placed with the wrong gender, deadnamed (referred to by the name assigned to them at birth, rather than their affirming name), or staff refused to use their affirming pronouns. Although our experiences are only relevant to the locations in which we have worked, existing literature supports that these problems may be applicable in many areas of the United States (Grant et al.; Israel, 2004; Kenaghy, 2005; Kenaghy & Bostwick, 2005).

As a side note, we do not generally out our clients as transgender; however, it is necessary in some cases. In the case of housing it is often necessary to out a trans person with their permission if their legal name and gender marker are at odds with their current name and gender identity. Someone who identifies as female but is legally male needs to be housed with female clients, and a legal female who identifies as male should similarly be housed with males (Grant et al., 2011; National Center for Transgender Equality, 2017).

**Legal Name and Gender Marker Change**

Another important aspect of direct service to the transgender community involves assistance with legal name and gender marker changes. In our experience, some trans people want to legally change both their name and gender, and some only want one or the other. In both cases, the process is complex, intrusive, and often prohibitively expensive (National Center for Transgender Equality, 2017d). Multiple visits to medical and mental health providers are generally required for these legal changes to be made. This is often easier said than done as many transgender people are wary of physicians and/or mental health therapists and, for example, turn to the black market to self-administer their hormone replacement therapy (HRT) (WPATH.org, 2011; National Center for Transgender Equality, 2017d). Additionally, many medical and mental health professionals are ill-equipped or uncomfortable working with transgender clients (Grant et al., 2011).

To add to the complexity of these processes, although the gender marker change procedure is the same regardless of state, name change differs on a state-by-state, and even county-by-county, basis. These can again be very complex: In Miami-Dade county, where many of our clients reside, a trans person needs to pick up the name change packet from the court in the county in which the client legally resides. This can be a hindrance because the packet itself has a cost; for example, $32 in Miami-Dade County, and filing a name change petition in Broward County, Florida costs $401. This is prohibitive to many people, especially transgender people, who are often underemployed and living well below the poverty line (Grant et al., 2011). In addition, the trans person needs to have lived in that county for six consecutive months, which can be a burden for some trans people who move often due to job insecurity, underground employment, and/or family and housing issues. Depending on the county, the person may be required to appear before a judge to finalize their new name. Again, this can be intimidating to many trans people, who often do not trust law enforcement and related agencies, often rightfully so, and thus many want support from a friend, family member, or trusted community member.

## Emerging Issues in Families

### Coming Out and Discrimination

As many marriage and family-oriented professionals know, issues which affect an individual also affect the significant others in their lives. Respondents to the NCTE/NGLTF study indicated that their significant others, particularly romantic partners and children, had experienced discrimination based on their association to their transgender family member (Grant et al., 2011). Often, witnessing acts of discrimination against their transgender loved one results in distress for significant others, including feelings of helplessness, anger, or shame (colage.org, 2017). Additionally, many romantic partners and family members struggle with simultaneously supporting their trans-identified loved one, while navigating their own coming-out process and experiences of discrimination. Often, partners or family members must navigate these new relational statuses alone, as most do not know anyone else with a transgender significant other (collage.org, 2017; Human Rights Campaign, 2017a). Specific to romantic partners is the need to navigate new relationship dynamics and labels: a man who has identified as gay his whole life is suddenly in a heterosexual relationship; a woman who is used to her partner's socially sanctioned masculine emotional stability must learn to navigate the partner's estrogen-fueled mood changes. These issues are sensitive and powerful factors within relationships and deserve careful consideration in therapy and other social service work.

### Developmental Considerations

A significant factor in the lives of couples and families is the age of the transgender individual. When the transgender-identified person is a young child, often the most support is needed for parents and family members, to assist in supporting and protecting the child (Human Rights Campaign, 2017a; WPATH, 2011). Hormone replacement therapy, which is used to increase testosterone levels in transgender men and estrogen levels in transgender women, is generally contraindicated at this age; rather, hormone blockers, which are reversible and prevent the onset of puberty, are more useful (WPATH, 2011).

As children grow into adolescence, support is often helpful for both the teen and family members, both individually and in a family format. Peer support becomes more important, and groups such as gay-straight alliances may be helpful in connecting adolescents to supportive friendships. Additionally, teens are more likely than their older counterparts to identify outside of the traditional male-female binary (Macpherson, 2015; Marsh, 2016); many adolescents and young adults prefer identities such as gender-fluid or genderqueer. Hormone blockers may continue to be appropriate through adolescence while HRT may become appropriate in the late teens (WPATH, 2011). Other medical interventions may become appropriate in late adolescence and early adulthood, including top surgery (augmentation or removal of breasts) (WPATH, 2011). Legal changes, such as names or gender on birth certificates or government-issued forms of identification, may be undertaken at this phase of life as well.

In adulthood, additional considerations become important. Although family support continues to be helpful, transgender adults often have more responsibilities for significant others, rather than primarily receiving primary support (colage.org, 2017; Grant et al., 2011; McShane, 2015). Thus, a more systemic assessment of needs and multiple forms of support may be indicated. Due to the significant prevalence of workplace discrimination, occupational support is often crucial for transgender adults (Grant et al., 2011). Additionally, as adulthood is often when medical transitions are undertaken, medical and health factors, as well as related financial effects, can be significant stressors (Grant et al. 2011; WPATH, 2011).

As adults age, social support becomes increasingly important due to the frequency of social isolation in older adults. Isolation is often compounded by the regularity of at least some family rejection following the coming out of a transgender person (Grant et al., 2011; McShane, 2015). The rates for transgender adults who have no contact with their children ranges from thirty percent (Grant et al., 2011) to nearly half (McShane, 2015). Couple relationships suffer as well; nearly half of the respondents to the NCTE/NGLTF study reported that their relationships ended after they came out to their partner (Grant et al., 2011). Thus, family, couple, and larger social support may be of higher importance for older adults. Medically, older adults face more risks related to surgery and medical interventions, and age-related health concerns may delay the process (McShane, 2015). Further, assisted living facilities are often ill-equipped to house transgender adults, and discrimination is a concern (Grant et al., 2011).

**Discussion: How Professionals (and Nonprofessionals) Can Help**

Although increased visibility and rights have made life easier for many transgender and gender-nonconforming individuals and their significant others, many barriers to true equality remain, or have increased (Bosley, 2014; Grant et al., 2011; Hope et al., 2016; Human Rights Campaign, 2017b). It is therefore important for professionals to be familiar with issues facing the community, and to make efforts to help, including direct support and advocacy work.

In order to orient readers to the myriad possibilities for supporting the transgender and gender-nonconforming community, we will include brief personal summaries here. Both authors have provided education and training on how to be a trans ally to various social service organizations, college and high school students, addiction recovery centers, and hospitals. Atticus also provided direct services to the trans community by assisting clients through the legal name and gender marker change process, and consulted clients on resumes and job applications. Additionally, Atticus has worked on multiple transgender health efforts, including tobacco cessation and prevention, diabetes screening, free HIV and STD testing and counseling, and inclusive Pap testing guidelines and campaign for the transgender community. Alicia has provided direct therapy for transgender individuals, couples, and families. She worked with individual clients on their personal gender exploration and identification, the coming out process, managing stress and emotional difficulties related to transphobia and discrimination, internalized transphobia, and substance abuse and other behavioral issues, many of which were perceived by clients as directly stemming from their experiences of rejection, discrimination, and victimization related to their gender status. She has written many WPATH letters for assistance with hormone replacement therapy (HRT) as well as gender confirmation surgery, also known as sex reassignment surgery (SRS). Alicia has also worked with spouses, parents, children, and significant others of transgender clients to assist them in their own processes related to their loved ones' coming out and transitioning. Both authors have facilitated support groups for self-identified transgender adults, transgender youth, and families, friends, and significant others of transgender individuals. Perhaps most rewarding has been our personal work as vocal and active allies for transgender and LGBTQ rights, participating in marches, rallies, and community support meetings.

One does not have to be a professional directly within the LGBT nonprofit community or in higher education in order to help. In one's own personal life, there are many options to support the transgender community. We have compiled a list, based on our own experience, to assist readers in developing their own ideas and plans to support transgender and gender-nonconforming individuals and their families. This list is certainly not exhaustive, some suggestions include:

- Have your organization and colleagues trained in LGBTQ competency and inclusivity
- Purchase a health insurance plan that covers hormone replacement therapy, gender-identity therapy, and gender confirmation surgeries
- Advocate for transgender clients (gently) in couple or family sessions
- Know how to write WPATH letters - and do it! Instructions at http://www.wpath.org/
- Use of proper pronouns and affirming names

Despite this list, it is not always appropriate or possible to advocate for transgender people through one's place of work. There is plenty that can be done as a private citizen, too:

- Support your local PFLAG, or LGBTQ nonprofit organization(s)
- Get involved in community events
- Be open about being an LGBTQ ally
- Challenge anti-transgender jokes or remarks in public spaces
- Support all-gender public restrooms and/or the right of trans people to use self-identified restrooms
- Listen to transgender people, remain open, and believe them

## Conclusion

Transgender and gender nonconforming individuals have always existed, but usually at the margins of society, unnoticed and often ignored by the mainstream. With the public notoriety of trans people such as Chaz Bono, Laverne Cox, Jazz Jennings, and Caitlyn Jenner, trans individuals and issues have come front and center in the media. This increased recognition has pushed transgender issues into the spotlight, which has been a double-edged sword for the community. On one hand, there is a lot of good to be had for being recognized. We cannot work on solving transgender issues if we do not know what the issues are. With the trans revolution, the larger society is becoming aware of some of the more pressing issues facing the trans community, such as prejudice and inequality, job insecurity, and housing discrimination. However, the negative side of any mainstream advocacy for the trans community may be related to the increase in transgender-targeted violence and murder, as well as harmful anti-LGBT bills and laws being introduced and passed. Although many are hopeful good will prevail for the transgender community in line with the progress of the gay and lesbian community, the backlash has been challenging and demeaning for many, particularly recent political losses under the Trump administration (Hirschfield Davis & Cooper, 2017; Shear & Savage, 2017).

We will further note here that many of our sources come from news articles and transgender-related websites, rather than from scholarly sources. This is primarily due to the fact that many issues relating to transgender people and their families were occurring as we were writing this article, therefore not providing time for more scholarly literature to be published on the subject. Additionally, there is a paucity of existing scholarly literature in family and development journals, as well as in other professional journals, related to transgender civil rights and societal treatment of the community. We therefore hope that others will continue to explore this topic, conduct research, and add to our voices in supporting the process toward greater rights and recognition of the transgender community. It seems that our work, as allies and professionals of the transgender community, their partners and families, has only just begun.

## References

American Civil Liberties Union. (2017). *Past LGBT Nondiscrimination and Anti-LGBT Bills Across the Country.* Retrieved from https://www.aclu.org/other/past-lgbt-nondiscrimination-and-anti-lgbt-bills-across-country

Bosley, A. (2014). *Same-sex couples' lived experiences of the repeal of the Defense of Marriage Act's (DOMA) Section Three.* (Doctoral dissertation). Retrieved from ProQuest Open Access Dissertations and Theses. (10107072).

Cohen, Z. (2017, August 1). *Coast guard chief vows to support transgender personnel after Trump tweets ban.* Retrieved from http://www.cnn.com/2017/08/01/politics/coast-guard-chief-transgender-ban/index.html

Colage.org. (2017). *People with trans parents.* Retrieved from http://www.colage.org/resources/people-with-trans-parents/

Goldman, R. (2014). *Here's a list of 58 gender options for Facebook users.* Retrieved from http://abcnews.go.com/blogs/headlines/2014/02/

heres-a-list-of-58-gender-options-for-facebook-users/

Grant, J. M., Mottet, L. A., Tanis, J., Harrison, J., Herman, J., & Keisling, M. (2011). *Injustice at every turn: A report of the national transgender discrimination survey.* Washington, D.C.: National Center for Transgender Equality and the National Gay and Lesbian Task Force.

Hains, R. (2015). Target will stop labeling toys for boys or girls. Good. *The Washington Post.* Retrieved from https://www.washingtonpost.com/posteverything/wp/2015/08/13/target-will-stop-selling-toys-for-boys-or-for-girls-good/?utm_term=.146fc2f53bdd

Hirschfield Davis, J., & Cooper, H. (2017, July 26). Trump says transgender people will not be allowed in the military. *The New York Times.* Retreived from https://www.nytimes.com/2017/07/26/us/politics/trump-transgender-military.html

Hope, D. A., Mocarski, R., Bautista, C. L., & Holt, N. L. (2016). Culturally competent evidence-based behavioral health services for the transgender community: Progress and challenges. *American Journal of Orthopsychiatry, 86*(4), 361-365.

Human Rights Campaign. (2016). *Addressing anti-transgender violence: Exploring realities, challenges, and solutions for policymakers and community advocates.* Retrieved from http://hrc-assets.s3-website-us-east-1.amazonaws.com//files/assets/resources/HRC-AntiTransgender-Violence-0519.pdf

Human Rights Campaign. (2017a). *Talking to grandparents and other adult family members.* Retrieved from http://www.hrc.org/resources/transgender-children-and-youth-talking-to-grandparents-and-other-adult-fami

Human Rights Campaign. (2017b). *Transgender people and marriage: The importance of legal planning.* Retrieved from http://www.hrc.org/resources/transgender-people-and-marriage-the-importance-of-legal-planning

Isidore, C. (2016). Target's $20 million answer to transgender bathroom boycott. *CNN Money.* Retrieved from http://money.cnn.com/2016/08/17/news/companies/target-bathroom-transgender/

Israel, G. (2004). Supporting transgender and sex reassignment issues: Couple and family dynamics. In J. J. Bigner and J. L. Wetchler (Eds.). *Relationship therapy with same-sex couples,* (53-63). Philadelphia, PA:

Haworth Press.

Johnston, J. (2015). *Understanding "transgenderism"*. Retrieved from http://www.focusonthefamily.com/socialissues/sexuality/transgenderism/understanding-transgenderism

Jones, J. (2016). *TransTV: Transgender visibility and representation in serialized television*. (Electronic Thesis or Dissertation). Retrieved from Ohiolink Electronic Theses and Dissertations Center. (miami1469625819).

Jones, S. (2014). *Laverne Cox is the woman we've been waiting for. Buzfeed LGBT*. Retrieved From https://www.buzzfeed.com/saeedjones/laverne-cox-is-the-woman-weve-been-waiting-for?utm_term=.jya2pB5Ro#.ec8gbGkZP

Kenagy, G. (2005). The health and social service needs of transgender people in Philadelphia. *International Journal of Transgenderism, 8*(2/3), 49-56.

Kenagy, G., & Bostwick, W. (2005). Health and social service needs of transgender people in Chicago. *International Journal of Transgenderism, 8*(2/3), 57-66.

Kralik, J. (2017). *"Bathroom Bill" Legislative Tracking. National Conference of State Legislature*. Retrieved from http://www.ncsl.org/research/education/-bathroom-bill-legislative-tracking635951130.aspx

*List of Unlawfully Killed Transgender People*. (2017). Retrieved on August 2, 2017 from Wikipedia: https://en.wikipedia.org/wiki/List_of_unlawfully_killed_transgender_people

Macpherson, A. (2015). Gender fluidity went pop in 2015 – and it's not just a phase. *The Guardian*. Retrieved from https://www.theguardian.com/music/musicblog/2015/dec/28/gender-fluidity-went-pop-in-2015-miley-cyrus-angel-haze-young-thug

Marsh, S. (2016). The gender-fluid generation: Young people on being male, female, or non-binary. *The Guardian*. Retrieved from https://www.theguardian.com/commentisfree/2016/mar/23/gender-fluid-generation-young-people-male-female-trans

Mason, J. (June 2, 2016). *Obama says transgender bathroom directive based on law*. Retrieved from http://www.nbcnews.com/feature/nbc/obama-says-transgender-bathroom-directive-based-law-n584691

McShane, C. (2015). The challenges of being transgender and over 60. *BBC News*. Retrieved from http://www.bbc.com/news/magazine-34454576

National Center for Transgender Equality. (2017). *Issues.* Retrieved from http://www.transequality.org/issues

National Center for Transgender Equality. (2017b). *Know your rights: Housing and homeless shelters.* Retrieved from http://www.transequality.org/know-your-rights/housing-and-homeless-shelters

National Center for Transgender Equality. (2017c). *Issues: Housing and homelessness.* Retrieved from http://www.transequality.org/issues/housing-homelessness

National Center for Transgender Equality. (2017d). *Issues: Identity documents and privacy.* Retrieved from http://www.transequality.org/issues/identity-documents-privacy

Shear, M. D., & Savage, C. (2017, July 27). In one day, Trump administration lands 3 punches against gay rights. *The New York Times.* Retrieved from https://www.nytimes.com/2017/07/27/us/politics/whitehouse-lgbt-rights-military-civil-rights-act.html

World Professional Association for Transgender Health. (2011). *Standards of care for the health of transsexual, transgender, and gender nonconforming people, Version 7.* Retrieved from https://s3.amazonaws.com/amo_hub_content/Association140/files/Standards%20of%20Care%20V7%20-%202011%20WPATH%20(2)(1).pdf

*Chapter 5*

# Consideration of the Benefits and Drawbacks of Alternate Relationship Paradigms for Sexual and Gender Minority Clients

*Jeni Wahlig*

*Suzanne Mueller Sherman*

*Resonant Relationships*

Acknowledgements: I (Jeni) would like to acknowledge my wife, Stephanie, for walking down this poly path with me, and for being so committed and supportive when relationships get hard and messy.

## Introduction

Sexual and gender identities intersect to inform the way people perform relationships, particularly partnered or intimate relationships. In the dominant sexuality and gender paradigms (read heterosexual, male-female sex/gender binary) the performance of partnered relationships is well-scripted. For example, it is easy to imagine, solely based on knowing that someone identifies as a heterosexual man, how he might act on a date, engage sexually (and with whom), and create a family. For sexual and gender minorities, however, such assumptions are not so easily made. Dominant discourses rarely offer clear scripts for the performance of sexual or gender identities that exist outside of the heteronormative cisgender boxes, to say nothing of how these identities might intersect to influence how one engages in relationships.

In the dominant paradigm, sex and gender (which are presumed to be the same thing) organize sexuality (van Anders, 2015). If you are a man attracted to a woman, you are heterosexual. If you are man or woman attracted to someone of the same sex/gender, you are a homosexual. However, the reality is that gender and sex are neither synonymous nor dichotomous. Being born male, for example, does not guarantee how one will come to identify with or express one's gender. In fact, the ways in which people today are identifying and expressing gender are constantly expanding, as terms such as genderqueer, trans* or transgender, gender fluid, genderful, agender, bigender, androgynous, and two-spirit illustrate. In the dominant paradigm, where the sex/gender of each partner dictates sexual orientation, one can no longer draw easy conclusions about the sexual orientation of, say, a genderfluid male who partners with an agender trans* man. Nor can clinicians draw easy conclusions about how such a couple might engage in relationship with one another.

Sexual identities are also far more complex than the dominant discourses typically allow. For example, the idea of *sexual orientation*, which tends to group people into categories based on the sex/gender binary (gay, lesbian, bisexual, and heterosexual), makes no space for the diversity of experiences of attraction within the intersection of sexuality and gender (van Anders, 2015). As van Anders (2015) illustrates, "It fails to account for heterosexual men interested in feminine women versus those aroused by breasts, vulvas, or vaginas, regardless of gender" (p. 1180). Similarly, the term lesbian assumes a woman who is attracted to women, but it does not differentiate between women who are attracted to butch women versus those attracted to femme women. Additionally, sexuality and attraction are not limited to one's sex characteristics or even gender identity or expression. By assuming that a person's sexual attraction is based solely on the sex characteristics or gender identity of a partner, one denies many other aspects of a person's sexuality. Sexual attraction can, and often does, involve things like intelligence, physical characteristics, personality traits (Horncastle, 2008), spiritual connection, or romantic affection. Like gender identities, ways that people understand and describe their sexual identities continue to expand and might include labels such as lesbian, gay, bisexual, queer, pansexual, asexual, aromantic, demisexual, skoliosexual, gynesexual, androsexual, and kinky (see Killerman, 2017, for an easy online reference to many of these and other terms). Finally, van Anders (2015) argues that preferred and actual number of sexual partners is also an important part of exploring and understanding one's sexuality. Indeed, for many people, a *polyamorous identity*—identifying as someone who can and does love and engage in relationships with more than one person—is an important sexual identity location.

As people affirm and express identity locations that are more complex, fluid, and multi-faceted, the dominant discourses directing the performance of relationships, and even of self within relationships, no longer apply. Sexual and gender minorities are left to explore and navigate uncharted territory. The intersection of a person's queer sexual and/or gender identities with how they engage in relationships can become complicated and unclear. It is likely that many will attempt, perhaps unconsciously, to perform relationships based on the expectations set forth by dominant discourses. For some, this will work, but for others, doing so may result in a denial of parts of their identity

Clinicians have recently been called to apply an intersectional lens to their work with clients (Addison & Coolhart, 2015; Harris & Bartlow, 2015). "The power of an intersectional lens is the way it frames individuals' experiences of identity and power as complex, dynamic, subjective, and specific, rather than as single-axis, static, autonomous, and generalized" (Addison & Coolhart, 2015, p. 440). In applying such a lens, sexual and gender identities are often considered. However, relationship orientation or paradigm is rarely, to our knowledge, called out as an identity location for consideration in intersectionality. Although the intersection of sexual identity, gender identity, and relationship orientation is a part of all of clients' experiences, it may be especially important to attend to when working with sexual and gender minorities, particularly if there is a conflict, tension, anxiety, or mismatch between the authentic expression of a person's identity locations and their internal or relational systems.

In considering how to support clients through these challenges, helping professionals have begun to turn their attention to the value of critically questioning, expanding, deconstructing, and queering one's understanding of sexual and gender identities. Although we believe that this attention to sexual and gender identity locations is necessary, it may not be enough for all clients. Living authentically as a sexual or gender minority may require not only a deconstruction and reconstruction of the dominant discourses surrounding how a person performs their sexual or gender identity, but also how they perform relationships.

Monogamy is the dominant paradigm for how to perform partnered relationships, and it is so deeply ingrained and normalized that it is rarely questioned, nor are alternate relationship paradigms considered — a phenomenon which feminists have termed *compulsory monogamy* (Willey, 2015). Both clients and therapists alike are subject to this internalized monogamy paradigm, or *mononormativity* (Cohen, 2016; Finn, Tunariu, & Lee, 2012). Furthermore, dominant discourse tends to stigmatize alternate relationship paradigms, as pathological, problematic, and even immoral (Conley, Moors et al., 2013). Even reportedly poly-friendly therapists are not immune to perpetuating the internalized discourses that suggest monogamy is the preferred and healthier relationship paradigm and that engaging in alternate relationship paradigms is indicative of some underlying issue (Finn et al., 2012, Weitzman, 2006). When alternate relationship paradigms are neither considered nor explored, options for how to perform self, relationships, and even family become limited to what is acceptable within the monogamy paradigm. Thus, the beauty, complexity, and sophistication one might otherwise identify in a myriad of sexual and gender identities and relationship paradigms are instead viewed as "other", abnormal, and undesirable (Horncastle, 2008). For sexual and gender minorities in particular, this may mean that parts of one's identity have to be denied — personally, relationally, socially, and politically.

We believe that helping professionals have a responsibility to support their clients in understanding and considering as many options as possible for how to live most authentically in all of their identity locations. To do that, however, helping professionals need to have awareness that other options are available and of the benefits and drawbacks of those options. This includes a consideration of alternate relationship paradigms. Because of their queer identity location(s), we believe that a consideration of alternate relationship paradigms is especially important in their work with sexual and gender minorities. In writing this, we do not intend to take the position that alternate relationship paradigms are at all superior for sexual and gender minorities. Indeed, they may not work for a majority of queer clients! Rather, we are attempting to bring a critical lens to assumptions about monogamy and to highlight both the potential benefits and drawbacks of alternate relationship paradigms to sexual and gender minorities. Although we do not explore or explain all of the different kinds of non-monogamous paradigms that may be available, we challenge clinicians to consider their role in bringing these considerations into the therapeutic dialogue and supporting clients who may be interested or are already engaging in alternate relationship paradigms. It is also essential that clinicians bring critical consciousness to their own biases and beliefs regarding relationship paradigms, and we offer suggested questions for this reflective practice.

## A Note About Language

In this article, we will often use the term *poly* to denote alternate relationship paradigms. To say "alternate relationship paradigm" is to point to the reality that people have choices in the ways in which they perform relationships; aside from monogamy, there are a number of other, or alternate, paradigms from which one might choose, to say nothing of the unlimited unique ways in which a person can negotiate and co-create relationships within or outside of any paradigm. The drawback of solely using the language of "alternate relationship paradigm", or of using other common terms, like consensual non-monogamy, is that we risk further privileging the expected normativity of monogamy by naming what a relationship *is not* (Horncastle, 2008). Non-monogamous paradigms become *othered*; they are the "other" or "alternate" choices. The term *polyamory* is often used as an umbrella term that captures the more defined alternate relationship paradigms, such as open relationships, group marriage, and swinging (Munson & Steboum, 1999). However, it could be validly argued that polyamory is its own relationship paradigm (and identity location), and one that is importantly distinct from other types of consensual non-monogamy (Sheff & Tesene, 2015).

For these reasons, we chose to use the term poly as an overarching umbrella term that captures the myriad of choices available to people in the performance of partner relationships. This term is a reference to what Anapol (1997) named *new paradigm poly*. Halpern (1999) summarized the idea of new paradigm poly well:

> New paradigm poly appears to assume a basic respect for all forms of expression of sexual-loving feelings in ways that facilitate individual growth, with the assumption that there can be no a priori limitation placed upon the number or nature of intimate relationships among consenting individuals. (p. 161)

As an affirming term for what alternate relationships are, we thought Anapol's (1997) concept of new paradigm poly, or poly as we will refer to it, was a fitting choice.

Similarly, we will often use the word *queer* to refer to sexual and gender minority identities so that we may point toward and affirm what these identities *are* – lesbian, gay, bisexual, transgender, queer, questioning intersex, asexual, pansexual (LGBTQQIAP) and so on – rather than what they are *not* – heterosexual and cisgender (the majority).

## Monogamy – The Traditional Relationship Paradigm

Monogamy, it seems, is a difficult term to find defined in literature, perhaps because it is assumed to be inherently understood. Monogamy might be defined as a relationship paradigm wherein a person is expected to partner with (mate), and remain mutually sexually and romantically exclusive for life. Dominant discourse suggests that monogamy is the preferred, best, pervasive, and most natural way of being in relationship (Conley, Ziegler et al. 2013). However, when more closely examined, these beliefs come into question. Globally and historically monogamy is not as normative as one might think. Research estimates that 4% to 5% of American people are in poly relationships (Conley, Ziegler et al., 2013). Lifelong monogamy – staying with only one sexual partner for life – is actually quite rare. Instead, many people engage in what is sometimes referred to as serial monogamy, or engaging in sexual exclusivity with one partner at a time, but still changing partners throughout one's life. Furthermore, even within reportedly monogamous relationships, sexual exclusivity is not often the case. An estimated 25% of married men and 15% of married women have at least one affair during their lifetime (Blow & Harnett, 2005). Given the stigma around infidelity, and potential differences in how cheating is defined, it is likely that these numbers are underreported (Sheff & Tesene, 2015).

With divorce rates climbing higher and increased reports of marital affairs (Taormino, 2008, p. xvi), trusting a partner to be faithful can be anxiety provoking, and then emotionally devastating, when not upheld. Anapol (2010) writes that

> …most observers agree that traditional marriage is floundering… rising divorce rates, declining marriage rates, and the skyrocketing incidence of infidelity on the one hand and sexless marriage on the other hand have many people concerned about their prospects for marital bliss. (p. 2)

The increase in cohabiting unmarried couples further suggests that people may no longer feel as comfortable settling into a commitment to one life-long partnership (Anapol, 2010).

Despite these realities, monogamy is so entrenched that most people rarely question it (Perel, 2006). Perel (2006) describes monogamy as a "ship sinking faster than anyone can bail it out" (p. 178) and notes that most people "would rather kill a relationship than question its structure" (p. 177). The idea that a monogamy paradigm might not be as sound and beneficial is somehow terrifying. The beliefs that monogamy is inherently superior, more beneficial, and is more likely to work are widely held (Conley, Moors et al., 2013). According to Conley, Ziegler et al. (2013) the perceived benefits of monogamy include an improved sex life, decreased risk for sexually transmitted infections (STIs), improved relationship quality, greater commitment and less jealousy, benefits to the family, and the social acceptability of this form of relationship. Although it is likely that many couples experience these benefits from a monogamous relationship paradigm, a more critical examination of monogamy suggests that this paradigm may not be as indisputably beneficial as most would assume (see Conley, Ziegler et al., 2013 for a review).

## Alternate Relationship Paradigms

Although we choose to use the term poly to refer to alternate relationship paradigms, other frequently used terms include "open" relationships, consensual non-monogamy, and polyamory (Benson, 2017). On the surface, poly may be understood as in opposition to monogamy; where monogamy is commitment to one person, poly is an openness to more than one (Anapol, 2010). Although true, this simple contrast does not capture the complexity and diversity for engaging in relationships that poly paradigms offer.  Poly relationships include ways of connecting to multiple partners that "may encompass many elements, including love, friendship, closeness, emotional intimacy, recurring contact, commitment, affection, flirting, romance, desire, erotic contact, sex and a spiritual connection" (Taormino, 2008, p. 71). Anapol (2010) asserts that engaging in poly can also include "freely chosen monogamy" (p. 230), or monogamy that is desired and wanted. In a poly paradigm, this means that those who choose to have a monogamous relationship would do so because it fits and that the relationship agreement does not necessitate a strict agreement of only engaging in a monogamous relationship for the entirety of the relationship.

The underlying essence of alternate relationship paradigms is to allow for conscious, consensual, ethical, and authentic choices, rather than cultural, religious, or discursive prescriptions, to dictate the form and flow of a relationship over time. It is critical to recognize that poly relationships do not imply permission to have affairs (Taormino, 2008).  Rather, the form and boundaries of each relationship are openly discussed, developed, and agreed upon by those involved. Each partnered configuration may come up with their own rules and ideals for expectations, but they are clearly defined, not assumed, and they can be renegotiated as people, lives, and relationships change.

Within the overarching construct of a new poly paradigm (Anapol, 1997), it is important to recognize that there are many different relationship configurations from which a person might choose. Some of these include: monogamish, polyfidelity, solo polyamory, open, swinging, and primary/secondary polyamory (see Veaux, 2017a for definitions of these and other poly terms). These relationship paradigms may be an important resource for clients looking to better understand the options available to them, as they offer a framework for what a relationship within that paradigm might look like. Although a discussion of each of these types of poly relationships is beyond the scope of this article, clinicians should educate and familiarize themselves with these, and other, ways of engaging in relationships. (Helpful starting resources might include: Sheff & Tesene, 2016; Taormino, 2008; Veaux, 2017b, or Weitzman, 2006) At the same time, it behooves clinicians to remember that there is no one way to do poly relationships, even within a particular paradigm. The gift, and challenge, of poly relationships is that they allow for a space for people to ethically perform relationships in ways that feel authentic and affirming of one's multi-faceted self.

## Considerations for Sexual and Gender Minorities

Alternate relationship paradigms are not for everyone, but they may offer important benefits and solutions to queer clients. In order for clinicians to be most effective in supporting queer clients in exploring alternate relationship options, clinicians need to be aware of both the benefits and the drawbacks that they may experience.

### Benefits

Poly relationships offer numerous benefits to anyone who chooses to engage in them. For sexual and gender minorities, however, some of these benefits may be particularly relevant, and others may be unique to queer identities. Benefits of poly relationships to sexual and gender minorities include self-actualization, healthy and fulfilling relationships, sex and sexual satisfaction, and expanded family.

**Self-actualization.** Engaging in a poly relationship paradigm can facilitate an acceleration of personal and spiritual growth (Anapol, 2010; Taormino, 2008). Because of its very nature, a successful poly relationship demands the development of many beneficial personal qualities and relationship skills, including communication skills, self-awareness, radical honesty, the ability to set and respect boundaries, trust, fidelity, and commitment (Taormino, 2008). New relationships also bring new experiences and can facilitate a sense of personal freedom (Cohen, 2016; Taormino, 2008). Additionally, poly relationship can bring forth the best in a person, illuminate areas of personal growth, and facilitate self-discovery (Richards, 2010; Weitzman, 2006). Poly paradigms may allow for expressions of different facets of self, sexuality, and gender, which may facilitate further revelations of one's authentic self (Richards, 2010). The more relationships in which one engages, the more parts of one's self that a person gets to identify, experience, explore, and grow. This benefit may be especially relevant to the queer community, as the constraints and stigmas within the dominant discourses can stunt one's ability to identify, articulate, discuss, and represent the wide array of authentic sexual, gender, and relationship experiences (Horncastle, 2008).

For example, consider the potential benefits of poly relationships for trans* individuals, whose gender and sexualities may change throughout their identity actualization and potential gender transition. "Polyamory opens up extra spaces within a trans person's intimate relationships for the comfortable foregrounding of various genders at various times, which in turn opens up opportunities for further growth and exploration of gender and intimacy" (Richards, 2010, p. 132). Furthermore, trans* bodies do not fit the dominant sex/gender paradigm, but poly relationships can provide a space to identify and create a self where dominant heteronormative and binary gender discourses do not necessarily exist. There is a tendency to experience greater acceptance of differences in body types and sexual expressions within poly paradigms (Weitzman, 2006). These multiple opportunities to perform gender in different relationships can allow for a richer exploration of one's own self and thus result in greater opportunities for self-actualization (Richards, 2010).

Similarly, for sexual minorities whose identities include an attraction to more than one expression of sex/gender, such as bisexual and pansexual, poly relationships allow for the full expression and experience of sexual attraction and desire. Weitzman (2006) asserts that poly paradigms offer these folks the benefits of not needing to eliminate partners based on gender, greater freedom to speak about one's attractions and fantasies, the ability to form relationship configurations of any gender combination, being able to enjoy the differences in genders, the transcendence of gender, and greater visibility of one's sexual identity.

Although poly may be a way for many sexual and gender minority clients to affirm other parts of their identities, it is important to recognize that people choose poly for a number of reasons. For example, a bisexual person may not choose poly just to be able to date both men and women. Instead, they may choose it because a poly paradigm offers other valuable factors or because being poly simply fits their authentic self and the way they understand and perform love and relationships (Halpern, 1999; Weitzman, 2006). For people whose *identity* includes being poly, engaging in poly relationship paradigms may feel necessary to their full self-actualization.

**Healthy and fulfilling relationships.** Alternate relationship paradigms allow for many relationship characteristics that hold the potential for healthy, satisfying, high quality relationships. Indeed, one study found that people in alternate relationships identified feeling fulfilled and closer to their partner as some of the benefits of their relationship paradigm (Cohen, 2016). Conley, Ziegler et al. (2013) report evidence from research that suggests that folks in poly relationships "report high degrees of honesty, closeness, happiness, communication, and relationship satisfaction" (p. 133). A study of gay male couples suggests that agreed upon poly contracts helped to facilitate deepened trust, emotional bonds, and boundaries in the relationship (Hoff & Beougher, 2010).

Poly paradigms allow for greater flexibility, enrichment, and fulfillment in relationships. They allow for an openness to loving (Benson, 2017) and the ability to experience connections as deeply and authentically as it feels right to (Blasband & Peplau, 1985). As mentioned previously, successful poly relationships require the development of important relationship skills, such as the ability to communicate around relationship needs and boundaries (Weitzman, 2006). The communication, boundaries, and support may lead to increased trust and security. Poly relationships encourage mutual support of one another's authentic experiences and commitment to work through jealousy and other difficult feelings (Weitzman, 2006). Poly relationships benefit those involved by offering a sense of unity, the ability to forgive, an increase in consciousness, and altruism (Anapol, 2010). It requires a conscious commitment to intentional unselfish love within relationships. As Anapol (2010) writes, "Polyamory breaks down cultural patterns of control as well as ownership and property rights between persons and… [replaces] them with a family milieu of unconditional love, trust, and respect…" (p. 239). Poly relationships, therefore, can be a "training ground for unconditional love" (Anapol, 2010, p. 237).

Although dominant cultural discourse suggests that love and relationships should feel like a Hollywood romance—exciting, passionate, connection with a soul-mate who provides one everything a person could ever want in a life-partner—this narrative is far from reality. Perhaps more than ever before in history, people are relying on their spouses to fulfill all kinds of roles — lover, friend, confidant, fellow-adventurer, co-parent, income-earner, household maintainer, fulfiller of dreams, and so-on. It is rare, however, that any single person could successfully fulfill all of these roles. Poly paradigms take the pressure off of one person having to meet all of another person's needs (Bettinger, 2005; Weitzman, 2006). It allows for each person to enrich and fulfill the lives of one another, without the demand that they be everything.

Although it is still possible to experience infidelity within an alternate relationship paradigm, the openness and consensual permission for romantic or sexual engagement with other partners likely minimizes this risk. Jealousy often arises in response to fears around what is not allowed, such as having sex with another person (Conley, Ziegler et al., 2013). Thus, it is unsurprising that jealousy, if present at all, tends to be less of an issue and better managed in poly relationships than in monogamous ones (Conley, Moors et al., 2013). Furthermore, engaging in poly relationships allows for the experience of *compersion*, which can be understood as the opposite of jealousy (Taormino, 2010). Compersion is essentially experiencing one's own personal joy in response to a partner's pleasure or happiness with others (Taormino, 2010), and it can be a beautiful and connecting experience between partners.

There may also be additional benefits of alternate relationship paradigms to relationship quality for sexual and gender minorities. Poly relationships may be particularly beneficial to people who identify as asexual, for example, because they invite new, not necessarily sexual, ways of performing relationships, understanding intimacy and connection, and meeting needs (Scherrer, 2010). Munson and Steboum (1999) suggest that poly relationships may also be particularly relevant to lesbians, because they could offer solutions to some of the stereotypical relationship challenges that lesbian couples might encounter, such as moving in with one another too quickly, merging identities, and experiencing a decrease in sexual involvement. She argues that these challenges arise, in part, because of internalized messages to women about what it means to have good sex, be in a good relationship, and be a good partner. Although it could be validly argued that these stereotypical "challenges" are unnecessarily pathologized (e.g., Iasenza, 2002), it is nevertheless possible that, for lesbian-identified women who are reporting such challenges in their relationships, a poly relationship could open doors to greater relationship satisfaction and well-being.

At the very least, an exploration of the potential for poly relationships is likely to open discursive doors that critically examine the internalized messages about how one should be, act, and feel in the performance of relationships. This process may be especially important for sexual and gender minority clients, whose identities already position them in ambiguous territory when it comes to the intersection of these identities within relationships. The discursive exploration of the performance of self within relationships and the availability of more choices for authentic living allows for increased opportunities to co-create mutually healthy and satisfying relationships.

**Sex and sexual satisfaction.** Some people may choose an alternate relationship paradigm for the benefit of experiencing greater sexual satisfaction, (Cohen, 2016; Sheff, 2005; Taormino, 2008), agency (Sheff, 2005), and fantasy fulfillment (Taormino, 2008). To be sure, many poly relationship paradigms allow for the opportunity to engage in sexual relationships with more than one person. For members of the queer community, this opportunity may be especially important.

Some sexual and gender minorities do not recognize that they are queer until they are already partnered in a relationship with someone whose sexual or gender identity is not the right fit for them. In a monogamy paradigm, this often means that the relationship ends, or that neither partners engage in sexual activity (Wolkokmir, 2009). The most obvious example of this situation is a presumed heterosexual relationship in which one partner later comes out as gay or lesbian (Wolkokmir, 2009). However, this may also occur in any partnering configuration when one partner discovers that their sexual or gender identity is somehow different from what they originally believed, such as when one recognizes that they are trans*, asexual, or kinky. Engaging in an alternate relationship paradigm, then, offers a solution for such couples to be able to continue their relationship while also meeting each person's sexual needs.

Furthermore, people's sexual behaviors, desires, and fantasies change over time (Devor & Dominic, 2015). In such cases, limiting one's self to one partner would then require that aspects of one's sexuality may never be explored or expressed, unless, both changed together or the relationship ended. For trans* people, particularly those who undergo transition, this may be especially so, both because of the effects of hormone treatments and because of the psychological effects of living and being perceived as their authentic gender (Devor & Dominic, 2015). It is not uncommon for trans* people to find that their sexual attractions change as their gender identities change. When this occurs within an established monogamous relationship, it is likely to cause problems and may necessitate that the sexual relationship between partners shifts, becomes nonsexual, or ends. The benefit of a poly paradigm is that there is room for these changes to occur and for the all partners to be able to explore and fulfill their sexual desires, with less likelihood for relationship distress or dissolution (Devor & Dominic, 2015; Wolkokmir, 2009).

Literature suggests that many gay men may prefer being in open relationships (e.g., Adam, 2010; Bettinger, 2005; Martell & Prince, 2005), perhaps especially for couples who have been together longer and have already established security and confidence in their relationship (Adam, 2010). This highlights the importance of recognizing and being open to talk about alternate relationship paradigms with gay couples in therapy; assuming a mononormative experience may deny, albeit unintentionally, an important aspect of a gay couples' relationship. Although engaging in casual sexual relationships with multiple partners is often presumed to be an expectation of gay lifestyle (Adam, 2010), gay couples negotiate poly relationships in many ways. In one study, gay men who struggled with the limitations of monogamy dealt with it by having sex together with a third man; others developed open relationships with a primary partner which distinguished between sex-as-play and sex-as-love (Adam, 2010).

Bauer (2010) argues that queer folks who identify as kinky or whose sexual proclivities include BDSM practices may also benefit greatly from poly relationships, as these sexual desires are often diverse and specific, and one person is not likely to be able to meet all of those needs. In fact, there are many skills needed to be successful in the kink/BDSM community, such as communication, negotiation, considering ethics, exploring new ways of relating, and greater comfort with behaving in socially frowned upon ways, that make for greater success in both the kink/BDSM world and poly relationships (Bauer, 2010).

**Expanded family.** Relationship paradigms are about more than sex and sexuality, of course; they are about how one understands and performs interactions with other people (Scherrer, 2010). Munson and Steboum (1999) note that "a sexual connection is not necessary for passionate love to exist" (p. 4). Indeed, poly relationships can include nonsexual partnerships. Poly households may experience several benefits, including greater financial (Bettinger, 2005; Weitzman, 2006), physical, and emotional resources (Weitzman, 2006). Even when partners in a poly relationship do not live together, they experience the benefit of an expanded kinship network, which can help provide support with things like chores, child care, and pet sitting (Weitzman, 2006). Because of their sexual and gender identity locations, many queer people experience rejection from their families of origin and an overall lack of social support. In response to this, many queer individuals create a family of choice (Green & Mitchell, 2008). These relationships, although rarely framed as such, could already be considered part of an alternative relationship paradigm (Bettinger, 2005).

Poly relationships bring the added benefit, for many queer individuals, of being able to become a parent or caregiver to children. Because of their sexual or gender identity locations, it is difficult for many queer people to bring children into their lives. For example, same-sex couples cannot procreate together, and trans* folk who transition using hormone replacement therapy will likely lose their ability to reproduce. Options for bringing children into the family for such folks in a monogamous paradigm are limited and often challenging and expensive (Goldberg, 2010). Certain poly relationships, however, can open new avenues of being or becoming a parent or caregiver.

Furthermore, there is no evidence that poly relationships are detrimental to children (Conley, Ziegler et al., 2013; Sheff, 2010), and in fact may be beneficial (Sheff, 2010). One study found that poly relationship may provide important benefits, including more emotionally intimate relationships between children and caregivers and more access to resources (Sheff, 2010). Children may benefit from individualized time with adults, less time in day care, exposure to diverse skills and hobbies, learning to be sex positive, and seeing their parents as people (Sheff, 2010). Furthermore, the additional healthy attachments to adults whose availability to offer support, supervision, and play is likely to benefit children's intellectual and emotional growth (Halpern, 1999).

## Drawbacks

Although they offer many benefits, alternate relationship paradigms also come with their own set of challenges, particularly for sexual and gender minorities. Drawbacks include increased stigma, a lot of work, and ambiguity.

**Increased stigma.** Research shows that alternate relationship paradigms are highly stigmatized (Conley, Moors et al., 2013). Common misperceptions and stigma associated with poly relationships include beliefs that poly individuals are experiencing psychological problems, have difficulty with or fear of intimacy or commitment, are confused, are promiscuous, are prone to cheating (Taormino, 2008), or that poly relationships are only about having permission to have sex with other people. Thus, social disapproval, discrimination, and lack of support and acceptance from family, friends, and social institutions are very real drawbacks of engaging in an alternate relationship paradigm (Anapol, 2010; Benson, 2017; Cohen; 2016).

For sexual and gender minorities, whose identity locations are already highly stigmatized, and for whom social support may already be limited, the added stress of engaging in another socially stigmatized location may not be worthwhile. Bisexuality, for example, is often discriminated against not only by heterosexuals but also by other queer folks and by monogamists (Horncastle, 2008; Weitzman, 2006). In our current cultural climate, trans* or nonbinary gender identities are under a cultural and political spotlight and have fewer protections under the law (Addison & Coolhart, 2015). These individuals may therefore be even more susceptible to the internal, social, legal, and safety consequences of participating in another stigmatized identity location, particularly if they are out about it. Being "monogamous and stable" (Horncastle, 2008, p. 45), therefore, may seem like a socially safer option.

For those who do engage in poly relationships, coming out about their poly relationships may be challenging, should they choose to come out at all. A queer person who comes out as poly may invite further judgment and discrimination (Conley, Moors et al., 2013; Rambukkana, 2004). Furthermore, Rambukkana (2004) suggests that "To come out of the closet as poly is to risk alienating oneself from the straight (-edged) world, but perhaps also from the sex-radical community" (p. 149), perhaps because becoming visible as a poly person makes alternate relationship paradigms seem too mainstream. Additionally, one person's coming out as poly risks outing other members of the poly relationship. This is not only problematic because it discloses a person's engagement in an alternate relationship paradigm, but also because it may out a person's sexual identity. For sexual and gender minorities, whose minority identity locations may not yet be disclosed nor affirmed in some of their personal circles, being outted as polyamorous could be detrimental (Halpern, 1999).

Creating a poly family risks having to experience stigma, discrimination, and exclusion, even from close family and friends, for everyone involved (Halpern, 1999). This is one of the major drawbacks of poly relationships that involve children (Sheff, 2010). For kids whose parents or caregivers are also sexual and gender minorities, the misunderstandings, discrimination, and lack of family representation may be even more challenging.

**A lot of work.** Alternate relationship paradigms can be a lot of work; there is "a lot of emotional work, time, and energy being expended on more than one partner" (Benson, 2017, p. 36). Successful poly relationships require informed consent, a lot of communication (Benson, 2017; Sheff & Tesene, 2015), and relationship skills (Bettinger, 2005). There is often constant negotiation around identity, behaviors, relationship dynamics (Benson, 2017), emotions (Sheff & Tesene, 2015), and the practicalities of being in relationship with multiple people (Anapol, 2010). Such practicalities include negotiating how the limited resources of time, energy, and attention are managed, and coordinating schedules and a variety of individual needs, preferences, and dreams (Anapol, 2010). Some of the relationship skills that one needs to employ in successful poly relationships include respect, time management, boundaries, communication and assertiveness, relationships with other members of the system, honesty, honoring of commitments, a sense of one's own needs, and a nonjudgmental attitude (Bettinger, 2005). Many of these skills require learning, expending emotional energy, engaging in personal growth, being vulnerable, practicing, and repairing, all of which can be challenging and feel like too much work for many people.

Poly relationships can also bring up fears, insecurities, jealousy, and possessiveness, which take emotional energy, communication, and relationship skills to successfully navigate (Bettinger, 2005). A person may come up against internalized beliefs that there is something inherently wrong with them for not being able to fit the monogamy paradigm (Halpern, 1999). As a society, people are conditioned to believe that the monogamous marriage, and its success, is a sign of personal success or failure (Block, 2008). Furthermore, monogamy is often deemed to be morally right, especially within most contemporary religions, thus risking a moral dilemma should one want to engage in a poly relationship (Conley, Ziegler et al., 2013).

Queer people often struggle with similar internal struggles as it relates to their queer identity locations, thus risking a compounding of self-doubt, criticism, loathing, or even shame. For example, for some sexual minorities, dating an opposite-sex partner can isolate a person from queer discourses and spaces (Rambukkana, 2004). Halpern (1999) asserts that in poly relationships where one or more member identifies as bisexual, additional fears may come up as they relate to myths about what it means to be bisexual. Some of these myths include: that bisexuality is not real, bisexuals just cannot decide, bisexuals just want to have it both ways, bisexuals do not want to give up heterosexual privilege, and bisexual women are "not feminists because they sleep with the enemy" (Halpern, 1999, p. 162). For women in particular, when a female bisexual partner engages in a relationship with a man, this may bring up fears around one's worth and feelings around the privileging of heterosexuality. Being involved with a man may feel threatening to a relationship that previously only included women.

People who are in an initial monogamous relationship but who want to shift into an alternate relationship paradigm may also encounter fears that the addition of a new partner will break or take away from the initial pair bond (Halpern, 1999). For many people, fear of loss and abandonment can be the biggest obstacle to the acceptance of poly relationship paradigms (Halpren, 1999). This loss may feel especially threatening for queer individuals, whose pool of and access to potential partners may be limited. Although jealousy and trust issues may be generally less or more manageable in poly relationships, they still occur (Cohen, 2016), especially initially, and are challenging experiences to walk through. As a whole, poly relationships bring a lot of emotional complexity; thus, much of the communication needs in poly relationships centers around emotional experiences (Sheff & Tesene, 2015). However, communication (Cohen, 2016) and emotional awareness, expression, and regulation are skills that many may find challenging.

Because poly relationships tend to be a lot of work, they can also increase stress (Anapol, 2010) and may be especially difficult to manage when other life stressors are also occurring. It takes a certain amount of privilege to be successful in alternate relationship paradigms; members need access to time, opportunities to learn, resources, and support to manage stigma and stress (Sheff & Tesene, 2015). Thus, the more layers of marginalization one adds — sexuality, gender, race, class, education, spiritual background, ability, community environment — the more difficult polyamory may be (Noël, 2006).

**Greater ambiguity.** Although not necessarily always beneficial, dominant discourse around sexuality, gender, and relationships offer people a set of expectations for who and how to be. Few such expectations can be found when engaging in an alternate relationship paradigm. Poly relationships do not necessarily have a clear or standard trajectory, or even sometimes a clear beginning or end (Conley, Ziegler et al., 2013). For children, the dissolution (Sheff, 2010) and presumably also the ambiguity around the creation and meaning of multiple relationships may be challenging, although these challenges may also be present in serial monogamy paradigms (Sheff, 2010). There are many ways of engaging in poly relationships, and each partner's expectations and desires for what the relationship will look like may differ (Benson, 2017). Additionally, poly relationships often change over time and are not always consistent across partners (Benson, 2017). Those who choose a poly relationship also face a profound lack of role models for their relationship (Anapol, 2010).

Benson (2017) warns that "It is very easy for polyamorous people to posit polyamorous relationships as a kind of queer ideal and utopian option" (p. 36), but that this is not the case. Poly relationships are full of ambiguity (Conley, Ziegler et al., 2013) and require that one must let go of the safety and familiarity of their previous scripts and relationship conditioning (Anapol, 2010). This may be difficult for many people, particularly those who prefer clarity or see the world in more black and white terms (Conley, Ziegler et al., 2013). Furthermore, queer people already lack clear scripts and strong role models for their sexual and gender identity locations. For queer people, then, the intersection of sexuality, gender, and poly relationships may become a very murky and gray location in which to exist.

## Clinical Considerations

Clinicians need to prepare themselves for the potential of working with queer clients who may benefit from, who are interested in, and who are already engaging in alternative relationships paradigms. Because of the stigma that surrounds poly relationships, and the pervasiveness of mononormativity, it is possible that many queer clients are already engaging in alternate relationship paradigms, but their clinicians simply do not know about it (Barker, 2005; Hegarty, 2013). Hegarty (2013) states "LGB [lesbian, gay, and bisexual] people could be described as leading in the deconstructing of the 'halo effect' surrounding monogamy in the United States society" (p. 32).

We believe clinicians have a responsibility to ask about engagement in alternate relationship paradigms. For those monogamous clients who are struggling with aspects of their sexual or gender identities, especially as they intersect with relationships, we believe clinicians have a responsibility to present the subject for exploration. Therapists can wonder, consider, suggest, provide psychoeducation, and support clients in exploring the potential of alternate relationship paradigms to benefit their lives. Some individuals will be most comfortable with monogamy, and others will need support on their quest towards engaging in healthy and positive poly relationships. As clinicians, however, it is important to be aware that some clients may not even recognize that poly is an option for them.

If clinicians themselves are not aware of the possibilities offered by alternate relationship paradigms, however, they cannot hope to be successful in offering them to their clients. Although this paper presents a consideration of benefits and drawbacks of poly relationships to sexual and gender minorities, clinicians must go beyond this information to further educate themselves about the types, experiences, and needs of poly relationships. Clinicians must also become aware of the dominant discourses that saturate their own and their clients' assumptions about identity and relationships so that we might examine, deconstruct, and reconstruct them in a more life-affirming way. Finally, in order to be truly effective in supporting their queer clients in the exploration, negotiation, and navigation of poly relationships, it is critical that clinicians examine their own ideas, biases, and prejudices.

**Supporting poly clients.** There are several important ways that clinicians can support their queer poly clients. One of the most important is to know what poly is and to treat it as a choice as equally viable as monogamy (Finn et al., 2012; Herbert & Zika, 2014). Often, problems that arise within a poly relationship are assumed to be caused by the poly relationship (Anapol, 2010; Finn et al., 2012). Instead of suggesting a return to monogamy as a solution to their challenges, clinicians can support clients in exploring options for engaging more successfully in their chosen poly relationship paradigm. Herbert and Zika (2014) recommend that therapists go a step beyond this by recognizing and affirming the courage that it takes to search for and live a type of relationship outside of the social norms. For sexual and gender minorities, whose lives and identities already exist outside of social norms, this courage is magnified, and certainly deserves recognition and affirmation.

For clients who are just beginning to consider or explore alternate relationship paradigms, clinicians can play an important role in helping them to identify what kind of poly relationship might work best (Weitzman, 2006). Clinicians can then help clients to negotiate initial expectations, rules, boundaries, choosing partners, sex, privacy, balancing of multiple needs, and management of time around this (Weitzman, 2006). When clients begin their journey into alternate relationship paradigms from an established monogamous couple relationship, clinicians should also bring attention to supporting the initial couple system or primary partners to rekindle the spark, keep perspective, and stay healthy in their relationship (Weitzman, 2006). It is important to recognize that partners in an initial couple system may be in very different places in terms of their orientation toward poly relationships. Sometimes, one partner may be interested in changing the status of their relationship paradigm, but the other partner is not. Poly/mono relationships, as they are often called, add additional challenges to the relationship (Veaux, 2017), and clinicians can play a critical role in helping these partners to explore their options, negotiate compromises, and manage difficult feelings so that the relationship can work.

Clinicians should also be mindful of other intersecting identity differences within client systems (Addison & Coolhart, 2015), as these can and do affect partners' experiences of poly relationships (Noël, 2006). Racial, cultural, class, age, (dis)ability, sexual identity development, gender identity development and other differential developmental differences between partners in poly systems are likely to affect experiences of power, safety, comfort, stigma, and needs within relationships. For example, differences in coming out, generational stages, and relational stages have been identified as challenges for same-sex couples (Connolly, 2004). By adding additional partners to the picture, these differences, and their effect on relationship dynamics, are likely to multiply. Applying a broad intersectional lens can help to bridge connections and facilitate bonding between partners over their shared experiences without disregarding any differences, advantages, or disadvantages that partners may experience (Addison & Coolhart, 2015). Clinicians should therefore address identity location and developmental differences openly in therapy, so that they may support clients in understanding and navigating challenges and identifying strengths that these differences present within their poly relationships.

Other ways one can support clients in alternate relationship paradigms include assisting them with things like coming out (Herbert & Zika, 2014; Weitzman, 2006); choices around how to involve multiple partners in different aspects of life; coping with stigma, judgment, discrimination, and exclusion, as well as internalized judgments and fears; and navigating the ongoing process of negotiation, communication, and decision-making with partners (Herbert & Zika, 2014). Finally, clinicians can help clients remember to slow down and proceed with caution (Weitzman, 2006). "The reality of polyamory is more complicated than the theory… [and] should be embarked on as a very slow process" (Weitzman, 2006, p. 155).

Sometimes, clients may need support for poly relationships ending. These relationships can end for all of the same reasons as monogamous ones, and they are likely to need the same kind of support. What may be different, however, is the possible experience of shame around not being able to make the relationship work or fear that others will judge the dissolution as evidence of poly's inferiority to monogamy (Weitzman, 2006) or as indicative of the wrongness of one's sexual or gender identity. Furthermore, clinicians should be aware that a shift in relationship status for poly folks may not look like the same kind of break up as in monogamous relationships (Weitzman, 2006). In poly relationships, staying together or breaking up are not the only options. This may be especially so for some sexual and gender minorities, as they may be more inclined to maintain friendships with their ex's.

Identifying, examining, and deconstructing dominant discourses are important ways that clinicians can support queer poly clients. Many of the struggles, fears, biases, and challenges that queer poly clients experience are likely a result of internalized and externally reinforced discourses about who and how a person should perform sexuality, gender, and relationships (Finn et al., 2012; Halpern, 1999; Hegarty, 2013). Hegarty (2013) asserts "An analysis of the stigma of CNM [consensual non-monogamy] will be strengthened by keeping the deep-rooted historical reasons for that stigma in view, and their relationship to long-standing heteronormative constructions of gender differences" (p. 33). Similarly, Finn et al., (2012) suggest that clinicians can more effectively support clients by better understanding the contextually situated nature of their identities, exploring different aspects of themselves and their identities through alternate relationship paradigms, and "actively affirming ambiguity over the ostensible stability and coherency of a politically conducive mononormativity" (Finn et al., 2012, p. 213). The contextually situated location of a sexual and/or gender minority engaging in alternate relationship paradigms is one that is loaded with powerful and often oppressive discourses. Identifying and exploring these can open up much-needed space for affirming authentic expressions of self and relationships.

**Self-examination.** Without critical examination of one's own internalized beliefs, one is at risk of unintentionally upholding mononormative performances of identity, sexuality, and relationships (Finn et al., 2012). It is therefore vitally important for clinicians to consider their own biases, fears, assumptions, and attitudes about poly relationships.

Herbert and Zika (2004) offer many helpful questions for such self-reflection, which we have modified and added to here as a starting point for clinicians:

- What are my beliefs and assumptions about monogamous relationships?
- How much do I really know about alternate relationship paradigms, such as polyamory, swinging, open relationships, group marriage, solo polyamory, don't-ask-don't-tell, or nonsexual marriages?
- What are my beliefs, assumptions, or preferences about alternate relationship paradigms as a whole and specific forms of poly relationships in particular?
- What are the dominant discourses that inform my beliefs? Where do such beliefs come from, and how might they be informing the work that I do with clients, and sexual and gender minority clients in particular?
- How might my thoughts, feelings, and beliefs about different forms of relationships interfere with my therapeutic work, especially if I am working with someone who is or wants to engage in an alternate relationship paradigm?
- Which of my personal beliefs about the performance of relationship do I want to let go of? Of those that I choose to hang on to, how might these affect my potential as a clinician?
- How might my current forms, practices, theories, and interventions be perpetuating limiting mononormative discourses, and how might I shift these?

## Conclusion

Just as clinicians do for sexual and gender minority locations, they also have a responsibility to be informed, respectful, and culturally sensitive to alternate relationship paradigms, regardless of one's own feelings about them. For clients who struggle with issues such as infidelity, commitment issues, or experiencing romantic or sexual feelings toward multiple people, and perhaps especially for queer clients whose identity locations may be, in part, denied within the monogamous paradigm, knowledge of the benefits and drawbacks of alternate relationship paradigms, and a critical examination of one's role and one's biases, can help clinicians to support their clients in finding unique solutions.

## References

Adam, B. D. (2010). Relationship innovation in male couples. In M. Barker & D. Langridge (Eds.), *Understanding non-monogamies* (pp. 55-69). New York, NY: Routledge.

Addison, S. M., & Coolhart, D. (2015). Expanding the therapy paradigm with queer couples: A relational intersectional lens. *Family Process, 54*(3), 435–453.

Anapol, D. (2010). *Polyamory in the 21st century*. Lanham, MD: Rowman & Littlefield Publishers, Inc.

Anapol, D. M. (1997). *Polyamory: The new love without limits: Secrets of sustainable intimate relationships* (Revised Edition). San Rafael, CA.: Intinet Resource Center.

Barker, M. (2005). This is my partner, and this is my...partner's partner: Constructing a polyamorous identity in a monogamous world. *Journal of Constructivist Psychology, 18*(1), 75–88.

Bauer, R. (2010). Non-monogamy in queer BDSM communities: Putting sex back into alternative relationship practices and discourse. In M. Barker & D. Langridge (Eds.), *Understanding non-monogamies* (pp. 142-153). New York, NY: Routledge.

Benson, K. L. (2017). Tensions of subjectivity: The instability of queer polyamorous identity and community. *Sexualities, 20*(1–2), 24–40.

Bettinger, M. (2005). Polyamory and gay men: A family systems approach.

*Journal of GLBT Family Studies, 1*(1), 97.

Blasband, D., & Peplau, L. A. (1985). Sexual exclusivity versus openness in gay male couples. *Archives of Sexual Behavior, 14*(5), 395–412.

Block, J. (2008). *Open: Love, sex, and life in an open marriage.* Berkeley, CA: Seal Press.

Blow, A. J., & Hartnett, K. (2005). Infidelity in committed relationships I: A methodological review. *Journal of Marital and Family Therapy, 31*(2), 183–216.

Cohen, M. (2016). An exploratory study of individuals in non-traditional, alternative relationships: How "open" are we? *Sexuality & Culture, 20*(2), 295–315.

Conley, T. D., Moors, A. C., Matsick, J. L., & Ziegler, A. (2013). The fewer the merrier?: Assessing stigma surrounding consensually non-monogamous romantic relationships. *Analyses of Social Issues & Public Policy, 13*(1), 1–30.

Conley, T. D., Matsick, J. L., Moors, A. C., Ziegler, A., & Rubin, J. D. (2015). Re-examining the effectiveness of monogamy as an STI-preventive strategy. *Preventive Medicine, 78,* 23–28.

Conley, T. D., Ziegler, A., Moors, A. C., Matsick, J. L., & Valentine, B. (2013). A critical examination of popular assumptions about the benefits and outcomes of monogamous relationships. *Personality and Social Psychology Review, 17*(2), 124–141.

Connolly, C. (2004). Clinical issues with same-sex couples: A review of the literature. *Journal of Couple & Relationship Therapy, 3*(2/3), 3–12.

Devor, A. H., & Dominic, K. (2015). Trans* sexualities. In J. DeLamater & R. F. Plante (Eds.), *Handbook of the sociology of sexualities* (pp. 181–199). Cham, Switzerland: Springer International Publishing.

Goldberg, A. E. (2010). *Lesbian and gay parents and their children: Research on the family life cycle.* Washington, DC: American Psychological Association.

Green, R.-J., & Mitchell, V. (2008). Gay and lesbian couples in therapy: Minority stress, relational ambiguity, and families of choice. In A. S. Gurman (Ed.), *Clinical handbook of couple therapy* (4th ed.) (pp. 662–680). New York, NY: Guilford Press.

Halpern, E. L. (1999). If love is so wonderful, what's so scary about MORE? *Journal of Lesbian Studies, 3*(1–2), 157–164.

Harris, A., & Bartlow, S. (2015). Intersectionality: Race, gender, sexuality, and class. In J. DeLamater & R. F. Plante (Eds.), *Handbook of the sociology of sexualities* (pp. 261–271). Cham, Switzerland: Springer International Publishing.

Hegarty, P. (2013). Deconstructing the ideal of fidelity: A view from LGB psychology. *Analyses of Social Issues & Public Policy, 13*(1), 31–33.

Herbert, M., & Zika, E. (2014). Why (not) simply loving? Polyamorous reflections. *International Journal of Narrative Therapy & Community Work,* (3), 17–20.

Hoff, C., & Beougher, S. (2010). Sexual agreements among gay male couples. *Archives of Sexual Behavior, 39*(3), 774–787.

Horncastle, J. (2008). Queer bisexuality: Perceptions of bisexual existence, distinctions, and challenges. *Journal of Bisexuality, 8*(1/2), 25–49.

Johnson, S. M. (2004). *The practice of emotionally focused couple therapy: Creating connection* (2nd ed.). New York, NY: Routledge.

Killermann, S. (2017). Comprehensive* list of LGBTQ+ vocabulary definitions. Retrieved from: http://itspronouncedmetrosexual.com/2013/01/a-comprehensive-list-of-lgbtq-term-definitions/#sthash.pr0qJ70u.dpbs

Martell, C. R., & Prince, S. E. (2005). Treating infidelity in same-sex couples. *Journal of Clinical Psychology, 61*(11), 1429–1438. https://doi.org/10.1002/jclp.20192

Munson, M., & Steboum, J. P. (1999). Introduction: The lesbian polyamory reader: Open relationships, non-monogamy, and casual sex. *Journal of Lesbian Studies, 3*(1/2), 1.

Noël, M. J. (2006). Progressive polyamory: Considering issues of diversity.

*Sexualities, 9*(5), 602–620.

Perel, E. (2006). *Mating in captivity*. New York, NY: Harper.

Rambukkana, N. P. (2004). Uncomfortable bridges: The bisexual politics of outing polyamory. *Journal of Bisexuality, 4*(3/4), 141–154.

Richards, C. (2010). Trans and non-monogamies. In M. Barker & D. Langridge (Eds.), *Understanding non-monogamies* (pp. 121-133). New York, NY: Routledge.

Sheff, E. (2005). Polyamorous women, sexual subjectivity and power. *Journal of Contemporary Ethnography, 34*(3), 251–283.

Sheff, E. (2010). Strategies in polyamorous parenting. In M. Barker & D. Langridge (Eds.), *Understanding non-monogamies* (pp. 169-181). New York, NY: Routledge.

Sheff, E., & Tesene, M. M. (2015). Consensual non-monogamies in industrialized nations. In J. DeLamater & R. F. Plante (Eds.), *Handbook of the sociology of sexualities* (pp. 223–241). Cham, Switzerland: Springer International Publishing.

Scherrer, K.S. (2010). Asexual relationships: What does asexuality have to do with polyamory? In M. Barker & D. Langridge (Eds.), *Understanding non-monogamies* (pp. 154-159). New York, NY: Routledge.

Taormino, T. (2008). *Opening up: A guide to creating and sustaining open relationships*. San Francisco, CA: Cleis Press.

van Anders, S. (2015). Beyond sexual orientation: Integrating gender/sex and diverse sexualities via sexual configurations theory. *Archives of Sexual Behavior, 44*(5), 1177–1213.

Veaux, F. (2017a). Glossary of poly terms: Learning the lingo. Retrieved from https://www.morethantwo.com/polyglossary.html

Veaux, F. (2017b). More than two: Franklin Veaux's polyamory site. https://www.morethantwo.com

Weitzman, G. (2006). Therapy with clients who are bisexual and polyamorous. *Journal of Bisexuality, 6*(1/2), 137–164.

Willey, A. (2015). Constituting compulsory monogamy: Normative femininity at the limits of imagination. *Journal of Gender Studies, 24*(6), 621–633.

Wolkomir, M. (2009). Making heteronormative reconciliations: The story of romantic love, sexuality, and gender in mixed-orientation marriages. *Gender & Society, 23*(4), 494–519.

*Chapter 6*

**The Sexual Trajectory Map: A Model for Examining**

**Sexual Identity Development**

*Sharon M. Ballard*

*Rebecca Senn*

*East Carolina University*

An important developmental task during adolescence and emerging adulthood (Arnett, 2000) is the exploration of one's identity, including gender identity and sexual identity. Regardless of their sexual behavior status, many young people struggle with questions about their development as sexual beings. These questions are more complicated than simply choosing with whom, where, and when to have sex; rather they engage in a process of making meaning related to their own sexuality. In their attempts to construct such meanings, youth often look to their social contexts for clues about what constitutes acceptable sexual behavior or what is sometimes referred to as a sexual script (Berntson, Hoffman, & Luff, 2014).

This paper is based on a qualitative study that examined sexual socialization from an ecological approach (Bronfenbrenner, 1992). The purpose of the study was to examine the influence of social context during adolescence on sexual identity development and sexual decision making using a sample of emerging adults (Arnett, 2000). Emerging adulthood includes ages 18-26 and is a unique time in which individuals are maturing and are able to reflect on their adolescence (Arnett, 2000). Adolescent experiences may provide an important foundation from which emerging adults construct their sexual identity and make decisions regarding their sexual behavior (Allen, Husser, Stone, & Jordal, 2008). As such, in this study, emerging adults were asked to reflect on sexual socialization and sexual decision making during their adolescence and relate it to their current sexual decision making. This paper reviews literature relevant to sexual socialization during adolescence followed by a brief description of the methods used in the study. The purpose of this paper is to present the sexual trajectory map, a model of sexual socialization and decision making that emerged from the data.

## Literature Review

Shtarkshall, Santelli, and Hirsch (2007) distinguished between sex education and sexual socialization, indicating that whereas education is more structured and intentional, socialization is ongoing and informal. Sexual socialization may occur both in and outside the home, including influences of community, media, culture, and religion: It is within this broader context that identity and subsequent sexual behavior evolves. Although there are risks to early sexual involvement, sexuality should be framed as a positive aspect of life that does not always result in negative consequences. The goal is to help all young people make good decisions that are right for them, to develop a healthy sexual identity, and to become sexually-healthy adults encompassing all dimensions of health including physical, emotional, mental, and social well-being (World Health Organization, 2006).

In support of the goal of sexual health, there are an increasing number of researchers who are advocating for a paradigm shift in adolescent sexuality from one that views adolescent sexual activity as a deviant behavior to one that views adolescent sexual activity as a normative developmental task (Diamond & Savin-Williams, 2009; Gross, 2009; Halpern, 2010; Harden, 2014). Overall, condom and birth control use, absence of substance use, and having sex within a monogamous relationship all constitute more positive or competent sexual decision making (Gross, 2009). Competent sexual decision making among adolescents can result in positive outcomes such as positive well-being (Harden, 2014; Vrangalova & Savin-Williams, 2011), higher self-esteem (Goodson, Buhi, & Dunsmore, 2006), lower stress reactivity (Brody, 2002), positive-affect (Connolly & McIsaac, 2011), decreased likelihood of substance use (Manlove, Ryan & Franzetta, 2003), improved academics (Manlove, Ryan & Franzetta, 2003, and improved adult sexual functioning (Tolman & McClelland, 2011). Romantic relationships among adolescents can provide a learning experience that influences the development of future romantic relationships. Harden (2014) hypothesized that those who do not experience hugging, kissing, or romantic relationships during adolescence may fall behind in development and thus feel the need to catch up during emerging adulthood. This developmental progression described by Harden (2014) supports the idea of examining sexual decision making as a developmental process that is an integral part of sexual identity development.

## Sexual Decision-Making

There is a myriad of studies that have explored factors that affect adolescent sexual decision making (e.g., Fantasia, 2008; Hensel, Hummer, Acrurio, James, & Fortenberr, 2015) and this sexual decision making often is framed as the decision to have sex for the first time as well as aspects of competent or safe decision making. For example, age has been identified as an important factor in sexual risk, yet, early first intercourse does not necessarily equate with incompetent decision making (McKee et al., 2010; Symons, Vermeersch, & Van Houtte, 2014). Relationship status at the time of first intercourse greatly influences emotional readiness and satisfaction with the first experience (Symons et al., 2014). Other relationship factors such as high commitment and satisfaction within the relationship (Harden, 2014; Manlove et al., 2003; Meier, 2007), minimum age difference between partners (Mercer et al., 2006; Symons et al., 2014), and having an element of control in making the decision to have sex (Allen, Husser, Stone, & Jordal, 2008; Symons et al., 2014) result in having a more positive sexual experience, less risk-taking, and more satisfaction with the decision to have sex. Receiving positive recognition regarding academic or extra-curricular activities positively influences sexual decision making (Lohman & Billings, 2008) and high academic achievement can be a protective factor in delaying sexual initiation (Lafflin, Wang, & Barry, 2008).

In regard to gender, males are more likely to engage in risky sexual behavior in early adolescence, while females are more likely to engage in risky sexual behavior in late adolescence (Cavazos-Rehg, et al., 2009; Fergus, et al., 2007). Males are more likely to have strongly desired their first sexual initiation, whereas, females are more likely to have mixed feelings around sexual initiation (Anonymous, 2006). Yet, despite these differences one of the most important similarities between men and women is in their contraception use — male and female adolescents use contraception at similar rates (Anonymous, 2006; Cavazos-Rehg, et al., 2009).

Although many of these studies adopt a more positive approach and identify influences on positive sexual experiences, they often lack an ecological perspective that encompasses a variety of environmental influences including community. Much research has been found to support the influence that community has in adolescent sexual decision making (Jones, Jensen, & Selzer-King, 2014; Kraft, Kulkarni, Hsia, Jamieson, & Warner, 2012; Volpe, Morales-Aleman, & Teitelman, 2014). Using Arnett's broad and narrow socialization theory (1995), communities that adopt a broad sexual socialization provide sexual health information and create an atmosphere where sexuality is an open topic, thereby allowing adolescents to ask questions and feel more prepared in their sexual decisions (Akers, Muhammad, & Corbie-Smith, 2011; Arnett, 1995; Williams et al., 2014). A community that socializes sexuality in a narrow way is one that promotes abstinence and does not encourage discussions on sex or sexual exploration. Broad and narrow communities can be either urban or rural and have varying degrees of religiosity. It is how the community approaches sexuality that defines it as either broad or narrow rather than being labeled by the characteristics that make it up (i.e., geographical location, religiosity, and state requirements). Additionally, a community's socialization practices may vary based on gender with the socialization practices of girls often narrower than the socialization practices of boys (Arnett, 1995).

An ecological perspective also can frame different types of sexual decisions and how they might link together to create a sexual trajectory. Through an ecological lens, Bronfenbrenner's (1979) concept of the chronosystem captures an individual's history and accounts for the time frame in which environments are experienced. The chronosystem allows for an individual's development to be mapped and viewed as a process; rather than viewing events separately. Emerging adults have the developmental capacity to reflect on their past experiences. Therefore, this developmental timeline reflected by the chronosystem allows for mapping sexual identity development while integrating contextual influences. Examination over time allows us to see that sexual decision making is a process and not a one-time event. Each time an individual engages in sexual intercourse, he or she is making multiple decisions such as giving consent to have sex, whether to do so while under the influence of a substance, or whether or not to use a form of birth control. Each sexual decision made is a part of the individual's sexual map, which will then influence future sexual encounters and decisions. Additionally, the individual meaning that develops through these reciprocal influences provides an additional lens through which to gain understanding.

From a symbolic interaction perspective, meaning is created from interaction with others, including parents, peers, educators, culture, and media (LaRossa & Reitzes, 1993; White, Klein, & Martin, 2015). The process of developing a sexual identity entails the interpretation and synthesis of multiple perspectives into a personal meaning in which one's role as a sexual being emerges. This meaning then guides role enactment or sexual behavior. A person is more likely to be satisfied in his or her role of sexual being when the expectations of that role are clear; however, role strain is more likely when there is lack of consensus on the norms relative to that role (White et al., 2015). This meaning making is driven systemically through reciprocal interaction within multiple contexts. Gender is one such context and one that may exacerbate role ambiguity in relation to sexual identity, particularly for women. Women still report a sexual double standard in sexual decision making in which the sexual activity of men and of women is evaluated differently based solely on gender (Allen et al., 2008). Women's sexual behavior is still likely to be viewed more negatively than men's sexual behavior (Zaikman & Marks, 2014) and women have more trouble than men do in seeing themselves as agents in their own sexuality (Allen et al., 2008).

## The Study

Shoveller, Johnson, Langille, and Mitchell's (2003) study centered upon the assumption that the experiences and perceptions of youth are integral to understanding young people's current sexual experiences. Following on this perspective, this research from which the sexual trajectory map emerged was conducted by the first author. Theoretical sampling was used to maximize variation resulting in a sample of 10 males and 10 females, ages 18-24, enrolled in a Southeastern university. The mean age was 20 years old. Sixty percent of the participants were Caucasian ($n$ = 12), 20% were African American ($n$ = 4), 15% were Hispanic/Latino ($n$ = 3), and 3% were multiracial ($n$ = 1). The majority of participants (60%, $n$ = 12) grew up in suburbs and 90% of participants self-identified as being from average to well-off families. Almost all participants were exclusively heterosexual (90%, $n$ = 18) and half of all participants reported that they were currently single and not involved in a sexual relationship, whereas the other half were either casually or exclusively dating or cohabitating.

A male interviewer conducted interviews with male participants and a female interviewer conducted female interviews. At the beginning of each interview, study participants completed a brief survey to capture socio-demographic characteristics, sexual histories during teenage years, and current sexual behavior patterns. Interview questions focused on the following areas of sexual socialization during adolescence: community level norms (e.g., community's approach to sexual health issues among teenagers), religion, education, personal decision making, familial influences, peer influences, and media influences. Examples of interview questions were: "How would you describe the general attitude in your community toward sexual activity among teenagers?", "How did you decide what was best for you when you were making decisions about sex as a teenager?", and "As you were growing up, what did your parents think about teenagers having sex?" Interviews lasted an average of 45 minutes, were audio-recorded, and subsequently transcribed. Each participant received an honorarium in the form of a gift card that was worth $20. Approval to conduct this study was granted from the Institutional Research Board at the first author's institution.

Data from this study depicted emerging adults' perceptions of contextual influences on their sexual socialization and sexual behavior. The specific aim of this paper is to share "The Sexual Trajectory Map" which emerged from the data as a model of sexual identity development and sexual decision making.

## The Sexual Trajectory Map

Grounded theory methodology (LaRossa, 2005) was used to analyze the data and help move the data toward theory development. A three-step process of coding was used for both the male and female data: open coding, axial coding, and selective coding. Early in the open coding process, the category of "sexual decision-making trajectory" emerged which captured the ideas of sexual decision making as a process rather than a one-time event and that the factors influencing sexual decision making, and the meanings associated with sex, may change over time. This initial category evolved into the concept of a sexual trajectory map (See Figure 1). In this model, the word "trajectory" is used to describe the path that one takes as part of sexual identity development. The sexual trajectory map captures socialization and sexual identity development as an ongoing process that includes sexual messages received, factors influencing sexual decisions (push/pull factors), attitudes toward sex, sexual decisions made, and consequences from sexual decisions (see Figure 1). Each sexual decision made is a part of the individual's sexual map, which will then influence future sexual decisions.

A map was created from each participant's interview data and use of the map as a framework for each participant facilitated constant comparison and development of key concepts. Specifically, the initial interviews were compared to the information included in the map to determine if the map fully represented the participant's sexual trajectory, to view the data through a symbolic interaction lens, and to identify patterns across participants. During the selective coding process, specific quotes were selected that illustrated the concepts identified in the sexual trajectory map during the open and axial coding stages. Contextual factors such as gender, race, and urban or rural background provide a context for the map (See Figure 1). Sexual messages were identified and examined for consistency. Many of these messages fed into the trajectory with several acting as push/pull factors influencing various sexual decisions. The decision to have sex for the first time is the central decision on the map but other decisions may be depicted before and after this central decision of sexual initiation along with consequences of sexual decisions. Changing attitudes toward sex were captured at the bottom of the map and may have a reciprocal influence with the decisions being made. Each component of the map is discussed below with participant quotes to illustrate each concept.

## Sexual Messages as Push/Pull Factors

Messages received about sexuality fell into five overarching domains of influence: family, peers, religion, school, and media. Some of these messages served as pull factors (pulling one away from engaging in sexual activity) and others as push factors (pushing one toward sexual activity). Each source of sexual messages (e.g., friends, religion, parents) could be either a pull or a push factor depending on context and perspective.

Overall, participants indicated a lack of discussion ("it wasn't talked about in my house"), implied messages ("we just knew…") or surface-level messages that focused on birth control, condoms, or reproduction ("It's very limited. We had maybe one or two classes about it"). This lack of information, coupled with the pervasive idea that everyone was having sex, acted as a push factor for some participants. One female participant whose only message from parents and church was to wait until marriage said:

> I don't know. I guess since everybody was doing it, I wanted to try it. Then it was kinda like, I don't know. I guess like peer pressure from everybody, including my boyfriend at the time, to do it, so. It's probably why I did it.

Media was a strong socializing agent described by the participants and some of them described the media as a push factor or a factor that pushed them toward having sex. One male participant described it this way:

> They [media] definitely made it seem like you know you needed to have sex to be cool, to fit in. You know growing up I kind of felt like, you know if I don't have sex then you're not going to be the cool guy, you're going to be the nerd on every sitcom.

Peers are another important socializing factor in terms of sexual identity, and peers emerged as both a push and a pull factor for participants. One male participant talked about how his peers acted as a pull factor for him and helped him refrain from engaging in sex: "I guess that it would help a lot when all of your peers and everything are on the same level as you are, thinking the same way you are." Others did not get consistent messages from peers: "Several of us were engaging in it [sex] and then several of us were completely against it" which allowed some to hear different perspectives. For example, an 18-year-old female participant who had not yet engaged in sexual intercourse said: "I guess lots of my friends were sexually active, so they were talking about having sex, pros and cons."

In family discussions, dads were less strict with sons than with daughters. Moms also appeared less strict, but still were the ones telling their sons to wait to have sex and "not get a girl pregnant." Rather than acting as an initial pull factor, family communication often facilitated a more positive trajectory for participants by providing more information and tools to make healthy decisions, even if that decision was to be sexually active. One 19-year-old male participant whose parents discussed sex and potential consequences of sex with him described a healthy decision making process that emerged as a teenager:

> As a teenager, I discussed with the person who I had sex with, like we just talked about how that's what we really want to do and we are ready for that and it wasn't anything rushed, it didn't like just happen or anything. We definitely talked about it before. That's what influenced me to do it because we both felt comfortable with it.

Other parents revised their messages as their children got older. One male participant described it this way:

> At a younger age, it was 'don't have sex'. But as I started to get older, my mom realized that she couldn't stop me from having sex, so she was going to prepare me 'okay if you do have sex, here be safe.' As I started to get older and develop more, she started to give me more information and tell me what it is.

Other male participants described a similar dynamic with their mothers in that mothers did not necessarily say no but did put some parameters around sexual activity. For example, one male participant said, "So mom was like you're going to respect my house and not have sex in here until you're of appropriate age or whatever." Another male participant described how his mom helped him to see potential consequences of having sex with an underage girl and therefore served as a pull factor.

> I had discussions with my mom about sex because this year I was

dating a girl who was still in high school and she was worried she was too young or something like that. She told me to not do it, like she said if I wanted to I could but not with her because I could go to jail or something.

Participants who had parents who attempted conversation about sexuality (even if they were not successful) and were perceived as approachable often made safer sexual decisions. They acknowledged that their parents were available to discuss sex even if they did not take advantage of it: "I always knew that I could go to her to ask her anything" or "there was always like an open-door policy, like if we wanted to talk about anything with my parents, we could."

Siblings can also be a source of messages for both males and females. One male participant's brother served as a pull factor:

My older brother, he would be like you don't want babies. We do not want to raise no babies or whatever. You may not be financially stable to raise a baby so you may need to take that into perspective I guess.

Some participants recognized that earlier experiences influence their sexual decision making in emerging adulthood. When talking about a sexuality teacher in high school, a female participant stated, "she definitely laid a foundation for me and my knowledge and so I could build on it..." Many did not immediately recognize the lasting value of previous education, but were still able to reflect on a few salient points.

Finally, several female participants cited pull factors such as their own maturity level or aspirations for the future: "I mean, I just, I feel like in high school, especially like, you are so young, you don't need to be having sex, or whatever." Another said: "I want to finish up school, stuff like that. That's my main priority right now. So basically, it's school, my family, and... that's it."

### Consistency of Messages

Framing the data for each participant using the sexual trajectory map allowed us to discern the intersecting influence of various socialization agents and how various combinations of messages influenced decisions as well as the meaning associated with these decisions. Some of these intersecting influences resulted in consistent messages. For example, many participants discussed the intersection of religion and peers in influencing their sexual decision making. One female participant described the fact that she chose friends with whom she shared similar attitudes and values and how this acted as a pull factor for her.

> Well, most of my friends were Christians. And now that I moved here, most of my friends are Christians. And they think the same way. I'm not gonna say all of them follow, but we believe, and if they don't, I mean, that's their decision. But I'll stick to my decision. I will not actually be sexually active, because they do it. I will remain pure because I want to and it's my decision.

One participant described how media messages conflicted with her parents and affected her decision making in this way.

> I would firstly think media definitely says have sex, have sex, it's ok. So, I guess it makes decisions harder. You know, do I follow what mom and dad say? Or do I do what everyone else is doing what, you know, TV shows. So, it just made it harder to make my decision.

Another described the discrepancy between media messages and church messages regarding sexuality: "they [church members] say abstain, abstain, abstain, but it's so hard when sex is being thrown at you constantly from you know watching TV."

Rather than consistency of messages, the data pointed to the importance of receiving a balance of positive and negative messages. A consistent message of abstinence was not always as effective as a balance of messages in producing a positive sexual trajectory. An example of balanced messages was from a female participant who was reflecting on her changing attitudes toward sex:

> I guess just seeing that sex isn't always a bad thing. You know, I see people who have sex and have a great relationship. I guess friends kind of made me see that sex isn't a bad thing. And at the same time, church kind of keeps me from it, from just running around.

## Decisions

Although the decision to have sex for the first time was used as a focal point on the sexual trajectory map, other sexual decisions were captured as well in order to examine the way in which decisions were cumulative. For example, participants shared decisions such as who to have sex with, decisions about condom use or other birth control, or decisions to use drugs and how that in turn influenced decisions about having sex.

Aside from the decision to have sex for the first time, one of the most important decisions discussed by male participants was the decision to use a condom and this decision was consistent over time. This was perceived to be the most important piece of information learned in sexuality education programs in schools and the message that they were most likely to remember. One 23-year-old male participant admitted that most of the information that he got in school sexuality education classes was not useful but he did learn one important lesson: "…cause the only useful bit of information that I got was you know wear a condom. And I mean that it affects my sexual activity today whereas you know I wear a condom." Boys, in particular, received a variety of creative messages about the importance of condoms, often from their mothers. One described advice his mother gave him about condoms:

> …just because I give you this, don't mean you can run around doing every girl you see. Everything that glitters is not gold. Be careful. What did she say?… before you go in a storm make sure you have a rain coat. That's what she said. That's her saying.

Whereas boys focused on condoms and didn't mention other types of contraception, girls talked about both birth control pills and condoms and were more likely to be aware of services such as Planned Parenthood or other places to get contraception. One female participant recognized the importance of both the birth control pill and condoms: "You can take the pill and use condoms to prevent pregnancy, also condoms to prevent spreading the STDs."

Other participants realized that some of the other decisions that they made led to the decision have sex. A female participant stated, "I decide before I start drinking, I'm not going to have sex and make sure that it doesn't happen." Another female participant stated that her decision to use drugs was her decision to have sex knowing that drug use generally leads to sex.

> And then once I started having sex, the decision-making process was due to drugs and alcohol…my first time was also the first night I did cocaine and I really didn't make the decision. It just sort of happened. And I didn't even know the guy. So, there were a few years of just recklessness and people I didn't know. Then I kinda straightened up, met my boyfriend, and since then, it's been monogamous.

Socialization agents work together in different ways and often, if a teen experienced more positive socialization factors, they were more likely to experience competent decision making. One female participant illustrates this positive intersection of socialization influences by discussing peers, school activities, family, and school sex education and then describing her decision-making process. First, she described her peers:

> None of my friends were sexually active in high school. Maybe some were senior year. I guess we talked about it. I wasn't, they were like tell me about stuff and I mean we always talked about being safe and they were with their boyfriends so it wasn't like they were sleeping around.

School activities acted as another pull factor: "I was really really busy in high school and I never had a boyfriend." This participant also had open family communication:

> I guess my mom does a lot of it [talking about sex] just telling us different things and stuff, I mean we all participate. I mean around my dad it's a little awkward, we didn't talk about it with my dad, but with my brother and my mom and I, it gets kind of funny. But we know it's serious.

Finally, she talked about what she learned in school sexuality education: "I guess you always have to think about what we've learned, the STD's and pregnancy...now I guess I've learned to develop safe sex." This intersection of positive socialization sources resulted in healthy decision making for this participant:

> I was in like a yearlong relationship until now and I haven't had sex with anyone else since that relationship. I guess with that person, we had a love relationship. It was more intimate, and that kind of thing. So having, I guess having sex wasn't as big of a deal.

## Consequences of Sexual Decisions

Some participants established conditions for having sex (e.g., only within marriage), and the level of adherence to these established conditions when making decisions about sexual behavior often influenced the outcome or perceptions of the event. For some, this might have been a negative influence (e.g., guilt or regret) and for others it was viewed as more of a learning experience or fulfillment of different goals during that developmental period. Two female participants established the condition of waiting until marriage before having sex and neither met this condition. However, one experienced gut-wrenching guilt and regret; whereas, the other expressed some regret but was able to move forward and learn from her "mistake."

> I know for me, it [religion] played a large role, because I have always seen myself waiting because of my religion. That does not end up happening, but I dated my first boyfriend, who I actually ended up losing my virginity to. He was the same way I was, you know, don't have sex until marriage. And that actually was what ended up breaking us up. It was just we both kind of gave into it. I think we were just really disappointed in ourselves and maybe almost resented each other a little bit for it. It was a pressure, a lot of pressure.

The gut-wrenching guilt experienced by this participant was evident throughout the interview. However, another female participant was able to look back at some of her earlier sexual activity and put it in place in her trajectory. Even though her behavior can be considered risky, she described her period of drug use and sleeping around as awesome. But, now she only has sex with her boyfriend. "Well, I went through a period where I sort of slept around. And I would talk to my other girlfriends who enjoyed that too. You know, like real serious descriptive. We discovered sex and it was awesome."

### Attitudes about Sex

Participants discussed attitudes and feelings related to sexual decisions and reflected on how they have progressed or matured in their ability to make decisions over time. Additionally, the meaning associated with sex changed since adolescence and many of the comments reflected this process of making meaning out of being a sexual being and the development of their sexual identity. For example, many female participants described a change in attitudes toward sex from more negative to more positive. One female participant stated,

> I guess just being that you know, kind of sex is a bad thing. If you have sex, you are gonna get pregnant, you are gonna get STD. But there's ways to prevent that. So sex isn't necessarily a bad thing.

Another female participant talked about her changing attitudes this way:

> I used to think sex was so scary in high school. I couldn't imagine.

Then I guess I came to college and I realized more people were having sex and it was not as big a deal as I thought it was. But to me, it was still a big deal and I guess now, it still scares me to be honest. But now, it may be not as huge of a deal because I've done it and I know what it is. But it's still a big deal to me. I don't take it as something light.

One female talked about how peer pressure had influenced her when she was in high school. When asked about how she made decisions currently, she said "I'm not as easily influenced by other people. I'm a lot more independent than what I was then. Other people don't influence my decisions; I do what's best for me or whatever I think is best at the time."

Many participant comments reflected shifting goals within their relationships. In particular, male participants were getting more serious in their developmental task of finding a mate so their decisions were made more carefully. One male participant described it this way: "it's more relationships, just getting to know the person, I guess. It might sound cheesy, but that's how I view it now." Another male participant said, "But I think now with my friends, getting older, like we started thinking about like dang, alright, I need to stop messing around and actually try to find somebody to settle down with."

## Discussion

Reframing sexual decision making to move beyond a focus on sexual initiation provided insight into the factors that can determine the level of sexual health one might experience as an adult. Socialization is an ongoing process that involves many different sexual messages from a variety of sources, push and pull factors, and attitudes about sex. Sexual decision making encompasses many different types of decisions and these decisions link together to influence future sexual decision making and future outcomes. The sexual trajectory map provided a longitudinal perspective of decision making that supports the paradigm shift of viewing sexual activity as a normative developmental task (Diamond & Savin-Williams, 2009; Gross, 2009; Halpern, 2010; Harden, 2014).

One example of competent decision making was in protection against unwanted pregnancy and sexually transmitted infections. Both male and female participants mentioned the regular use of the birth control pill and/or condoms, which is consistent with previous literature that found that men and women were similar in their contraception use (Anonymous, 2006; Cavazos-Rehg et al., 2009). However, data revealed that female participants were more likely than males to mention the birth control pill, whereas, male participants mainly talked about condoms.

Consistent with the findings of previous literature (Allen et al., 2008; Symons et al., 2014), the sense of being in control of sexual decisions seemed to result in a more positive experience and therefore, more positive trajectory; whereas, participants who expressed feelings of losing self-control tended to express feelings of guilt associated with their decisions. From a symbolic interaction perspective, one's perception of events, in this case sense of control, was important and the meaning made from the decisions was important in consequences. As Allen et al. (2008) found, participants did not necessarily characterize their behavior as making mistakes but rather learning life lessons, which is turn contributes to one's developmental progression and identity development (Harden, 2014).

However, it is important to keep in mind the variety of decisions that comprise one's trajectory and to think about what control looks like for each of these types of decisions. For example, the female participant who chose to use drugs and subsequently had sex might initially appear as having a lack of self-control. But her comments suggested that she was very much in control of her decision to use drugs and that she was fully aware that this also meant that she would end up having sex. Although her behavior could certainly be considered risky, she expressed satisfaction with her experiences. In contrast, the female participant who, along with her boyfriend, was planning to wait until marriage to have sex but "gave in to it," experienced intense dissatisfaction with this decision to have sex. Although she ultimately appeared to have made a clear decision (wait until marriage), she lost control and had sex, which resulted in the negative consequences of a break-up with her boyfriend and intense guilt. These two examples illustrate the importance of looking at the context for multiple decisions rather than just the dichotomous decision to have sex or not. Future research might examine variables such as perceived control over sexual decision making and satisfaction with various decisions made.

Influences interact to create a new influence. It is not necessarily consistent messages that lead to positive and healthy decisions but a balance of messages that helped them to see multiple aspects of sexual decisions. Having more information about sexuality and an exposure to a broad array of sexual perspectives may provide an element of control in sexual decision making. Those who consistently had narrow socialization (Arnett, 1995) had more difficulty negotiating their sexual decisions. In other words, those who had consistency among their socialization sources but the messages left little room for deviation (e.g., wait until marriage, little comprehensive information) seemed to have more negative consequences of their decisions, such as feelings of guilt and regret. This supports research that suggests that adolescents are more likely to experience regret after sexual decisions if they are going against religious values (Osorio et al., 2011). Additionally, female participants were more likely than male participants to express regret regarding their sexual decisions, which supports the idea that socialization experiences of girls often are narrower than the socialization experiences of boys (Arnett, 1995).

In looking at sexual identity development and the sexual decision-making process from symbolic interaction and ecological perspectives, understanding is gleaned from more than the actual decisions but from the perception and meaning made from a decision and from the interpretation of consequences. The sexual trajectory map illustrates these theoretical perspectives in that the participant's current sexual identity was not dependent on the actual decisions made (e.g., had sex or not) but on the context for the decision making (which was captured by the model).

Limitations of this study include the small sample size and the fact that the sample was predominantly heterosexual and seemingly cis-gender. Further research with a larger and more varied sample is needed to support and to further expand the sexual trajectory map. However, this model can be used to further understand the complexity of sexual identity development and those factors that can influence whether or not one achieves a state of sexual health. Overall, the sexual trajectory map provides a model for examining how sexual socialization factors work together to influence sexual decision making and identify development over time.

## References

Allen, K. R., Husser, E. K., Stone, D. J., & Jordal, C. E. (2008). Agency and error in young adults' stories of sexual decision making. *Family Relations, 57*, 517-529. doi: 10.1111/j.1741-3729.2008.00519

Anonymous. (2006). Sexual initiation. *American Sexual Behavior*, 3-31.

Arnett, J. J. (1995). Broad and narrow socialization: The family in the context of a cultural theory. *Journal of Marriage and Family, 57*, 617-628. doi:10.2307/353917

Arnett, J. J. (2000). Emerging adulthood: A theory of development from the late teens through the twenties. *American Psychologist, 55*, 469-480. doi: 10.1037/0003-066X.55.5.469

Aronowitz, T., Rennells, R. E., & Todd, E. (2006). Ecological influences of sexuality on early adolescent African American females. *Journal of Community Health and Nursing, 23*, 113-122. doi: 10.1207/ s15327655jchn2302_4

Barnett, R. V., Jackson, T. L., Smith, S., & Gibson, H. J. (2010). The effects of religiosity and sibling relationships on the timing of sexual debut. *Family Science Review, 15*, 66-83.

Berntson, M. A., Hoffman, K. L., & Luff, T. L. (2014). College as context: Influences on interpersonal sexual scripts. *Sexuality & Culture 18*, 149–165. doi 10.1007/s12119-013-9180-7

Blackburn, T. (2009). The influence of sex education on adolescent health: Abstinence-only vs. comprehensive programs. *The Journal of Undergraduate Nursing Writing, 3*, 3-10.

Brody, S. (2002). Age at first intercourse is inversely related to female cortisol stress reactivity. *Psychoneuroendocrinology, 27*, 933-943. doi: 10.1016/S0306-4530(02)00007-0

Bronfenbrenner, U. (1986). Ecology of the family as a context for human development: Research perspectives. *Developmental Psychology, 22*, 723-742. doi: 10.1037/0012-1649.22.6.723

Bronfenbrenner, U. (1992). Ecological systems theory. In R. Vasta (Ed.), *Six theories of child development: Revised formulations and current issues.* London, England: Jessica Kingsley Publishers Inc.

Cavazos-Rehg, P. A., Krauss, M. J., Spitznagel, E. L., Schootman, M., Bucholtz, K. K., Peipert, J. F., … & Bierut, L. J. (2009). Age of sexual debut among US adolescent. *Contraception, 80*, 158-162. doi: 10.1016/j. contraception.2009.02.014

Connolly, J., & McIsaac, C. (2011). Romantic relationships in adolescence. In M. K. Underwood & L. H. Rosen (Eds.), *Social development: Relationships in infancy, childhood, and adolescence.* New York, NY: Guilford Press.

Davis, S., & Tucker-Brown, A. (2013). Effects of black sexual stereotypes on sexual decision making among African American women. *The*

*Journal of Pan African Studies, 5,* 111-128.

Diamond, L. M., & Savin-Williams, R. C. (2006). The intimate relationships of sexual-minority youths. In G. R. Adams & M. D. Berzonsky (Eds.), *Blackwell handbook of adolescence.* Oxford, UK: Blackwell Publishing Ltd.

Fantasia, H. C. (2008). Concept analysis: Sexual decision-making in adolescence. *Nursing Forum, 43,* 80-90. doi: 10.1111/j.1744-6198.2008.00099

Fergus, S., Zimmerman, M. A., & Caldwell, C. H. (2007). Growth trajectories of sexual risk behavior in adolescence and young adulthood. *American Journal of Public Health, 97,* 1096-1101. doi: 10.2105/AJPH.2005.074609

Goodson, P., Buhi, E. R., & Dunsmore, S. C. (2006). Self-esteem and adolescent sexual behaviors, attitudes, and intentions: A systematic review. *Journal of Adolescent Health, 38,* 310-319. doi: 10.1016/j.jadohealth.2005.05.026

Gross, K. (2009). Adolescent sexual competence: A paradigm shift. *Family Science Review, 14,* 33-47.

Harden, K. P. (2014). A sex-positive framework for research on adolescent sexuality. *Perspectives on Psychological Science, 9,* 455-469. doi: 10.1177/1745691614535934

Hensel, D. J., Hummer, T. A., Acrurio, L. R., James, T. W., & Fortenberry, J. D. (2015). Feasibility of functional neuroimaging to understand adolescent women's sexual decision making. *Journal of Adolescent Health, 56,* 389-395. doi: 10.1016/j.jadohealth.2014.11.004

Jones, C. L., Jensen, R. E., & Selzer King, A. (2014). Future sex educator perceptions of rural versus urban instruction: A case for community-centered sexual health education. *American Journal of Sexuality Education, 9,* 464-484. doi: 10.1080/15546128.2014.976299

Kraft, J. M., Kulkarni, A., Hsia, J., Jamieson, D. J., & Warner, L. (2012). Sex education and adolescent sexual behavior: Do community characteristics matter? *Contraception, 86,* 276-280. doi: 10.1016/j.contraception.2012.01.004

Laflin, M. T., Wang, J., & Barry, M. (2008). A longitudinal study of adolescent transition from virgin to nonvirgin status. *Journal of Adolescent Health, 42,* 228-236. doi: 10.1016/j.jadohealth.2007.08.014

Larossa, R. (2005). Grounded theory methods and qualitative family research. *Journal of Marriage and Family, 67,* 837-857. doi: 10.1111/j.1741-3737.2005.00179

LaRossa, R., & Reitzes, D. C. (1993). Symbolic interactionism and family studies. In, P. G. Boss, W. J. Doherty, R. LaRossa, W. R. Schumm, and S. K. Steinmetz (Eds.), *Sourcebook of family theories and methods: A contextual approach.* New York, NY: Plenum.

Lohman, B. J., & Billings, A. (2008). Protective and risk factors associated with adolescent boys early sexual debut and risky sexual behaviors. *Journal of Youth and Adolescence, 37,* 723-735. doi: 10.1007/s10964-008-9283

Manlove, J., Ryan, S., & Franzetta, K. (2003). Patterns of contraceptive use within teenagers' first sexual relationships. *Perspectives on Sexual and Reproductive Health, 35,* 246-255. doi: 10.1363/psrh.35.246.03

McKee, A., Albury, K., Dunne, M., Grieshaber, S., Hartley, J., Lumby, C., & Mathews, B. (2010). Healthy sexual development: A multidisciplinary framework for research. *International Journal of Sexual Health, 22,* 14-19. doi: 10.1080/19317610903393043

Meier, A. M. (2007). Adolescent first sex and subsequent mental health. *American Journal of Sociology, 112,* 1811-1847. doi: 10.1086/512708

Mitchell, K., & Wellings, K. (1998). First sexual intercourse: Anticipation and communication. Interviews with young people in England. *Journal of Adolescence, 21,* 717-726. doi: 10.1006/jado.1998.0191

Mueller, T. E., Gavin, L. E., & Kullkarni, A. (2008). The association between sex education and youth's engagement in sexual intercourse, age at first intercourse, and birth control use at first sex. *Journal of Adolescent Health, 42.* 89-96. doi:10.1016/j.jadohealth.2007.08.002

Murray, K. M., Ciarrocchi, J. W., & Murray-Swank, N. A. (2007). Spirituality, religiosity, shame and guilt as predictors of sexual attitudes and experiences. *Journal of Psychology and Theology, 35,* 222-234.

Osorio, A., Lopez-del Burgo, C., Carlos, S., Ruiz-Canela, M., Delgado, M., & de Irala, J. (2012). First sexual intercourse and subsequent regret in three developing countries. *Journal of Adolescent Health, 50,* 271-278. doi: 10.1016/j.jadohealth.2011.07.012

Pearson, J., Muller, C., & Frisco, M. L. (2006). Parental involvement, family structure, and adolescent sexual decision making. *Sociological Perspectives, 49,* 67–90, doi: 10.1525/sop. 2006.49.1.67

Shoveller, J. A., Johnson, J. L., Langille, D. B., & Mitchell, T. (2004). Socio-cultural influences on young people's sexual development. *Social Science and Medicine, 59,* 473-487. doi: 10.1016/j.socscimed.2003.11.017

Shtarkshall, R. A., Santelli, J. S., & Hirsch, J. S. (2007). Sex education and sexual socialization: Roles for educators and parents. *Perspectives on Sexual and Reproductive Health, 39,* 116-119. doi: 10.1363/3911607

Smith, V. C., & Shaffer, M. J. (2013). Gone but not forgotten: Virginity loss and current sexual satisfaction. *Journal of Sex & Marital Therapy, 39.* 96-111. doi: 10.1080/0092623X.2012.675023

Symons, K., Vermeersch, H., & Van Houtte, M. (2014). The emotional experiences of early first intercourse: A multi-method study. *Journal of Adolescent Research, 29,* 533-560. doi: 10.1177/0743558414528976

Tolman, D. (2002). *Dilemmas of desires: Teenage girls talk about sexuality.* Cambridge, MA: Harvard University Press.

Tolman, D. L., & McClelland, S. I. (2011). Normative sexuality development in adolescence: A decade in review, 2000-2009. *Journal of Research on Adolescence, 21,* 242-255. doi: 10.1111/j.1532-7795.2010.00726

Vivancos, R., Abubakar, I., Phillips-Howard, P., & Hunter, P. R. (2013). School-based sex education is associated with reduced risky sexual behaviour and sexually transmitted infections in young adults. *Public health, 127,* 53-57. doi: 10.1016/j.puhe.2012.09.016

Volpe, E. M., Morales-Aleman, N. M., & Teitelman, A. M. (2014). Urban adolescent girls' perspectives on romantic relationships: Initiation, involvement, negotiation, and conflict. *Issues in Mental Health Nursing, 35,* 776-790. doi: 10.3109/01612840.2014.910582

Vrangalova, Z., & Savin-Williams, R. C. (2011). Adolescent sexuality and positive well-being: A group-norms approach. *Journal of Youth and Adolescence, 40,* 931-944. doi: 10.1007/s10964-011-9629-7

White, J., Klein, D., & Martin, T. (2015). *Family theories: An introduction* (4th ed.). Thousand Oaks, CA: Sage Publications.

World Health Organization (2006). *Sexual and reproductive health.* Retrieved from    http://www.who.int/reproductivehealth/topics/sexual_health/sh_definitions/en/

*Chapter 7*

**Predicting First Sex among African American Adolescents:**

**The Role of Gender, Family, and Extra Familial Factors**

*Helyne Frederick*

*University of North Carolina-Chapel Hill*

*Judith L. Fischer*

*Texas Tech University*

*Jacquelyn D. Wiersma-Mosley*

*University of Arkansas-Fayetteville*

This research uses data from Add Health, a program project directed by Kathleen Mullan Harris and designed by J. Richard Udry, Peter S. Bearman, and Kathleen Mullan Harris at the University of North Carolina at Chapel Hill, and funded by grant P01-HD31921 from the Eunice Kennedy Shriver National Institute of Child Health and Human Development, with cooperative funding from 23 other federal agencies and foundations. Special acknowledgment is due Ronald R. Rindfuss and Barbara Entwisle for assistance in the original design. Information on how to obtain the Add Health data files is available on the Add Health website (http://www.cpc.unc.edu/addhealth). No direct support was received from grant P01-HD31921 for this analysis.

Risky sexual behavior can take many forms, including early intercourse, multiple partners, and inconsistent use of protection. Early age of first sex (initiation before age 16) is an important indicator of exposure to the risk of pregnancy and risk of sexually transmitted infections during adolescence (Jordahl & Lohman, 2009). Of particular concern are the reports from the Centers for Disease control (CDC) that identify African American adolescents as initiating sexual intercourse at an earlier age than do other ethnicities (CDC, 2014). Current understanding about risk factors for early sexual debut among African Americans is limited due to use of small, nonrepresentative samples, and cross-sectional analyses (Luster & Small, 1994). There is a critical need for greater understanding of predictors of sexual risk taking for African Americans that can guide policies for prevention of STDs and delay of sexual initiation within this group.

The socio-ecological framework (adapted from Bronfenbrenner's ecological perspective) proposed by DiClemente, Salazar, Crosby, and Rosenthal (2005) suggests that various factors within the individual (including psychological characteristics), the family, and other social contexts may be associated with adolescents' behaviors, particularly sexual risk behaviors. Researchers have identified parenting and familial factors such as communication about sex, family structure, and monitoring, as key correlates of sexual initiation and sexual risk behaviors (e.g., Hutchinson, 2002; Luster & Small, 1994; Majumdar, 2005). A second aspect involves adolescents' relationships outside of the immediate family in the neighborhood and school as predictors of sexual debut (e.g., Browning, Leventhal, & Brooks-Gunn, 2004). Thirdly, religiosity and academic performance are examples of individual level factors associated with initiation of first sex (e.g., Frisco, 2008; Meier, 2003).

Informed by DiClemente et al.'s (2005) socio-ecological theoretical framework, the purpose of this study is to examine how, studied together, individual, family, and community factors predict the initiation to first sex among African American adolescents. The research is a secondary analysis of a large national longitudinal data set.

## Socio-ecological Model

According to DiClemente et al.'s (2005) socioecological model, individuals' behaviors should be examined from multiple contexts, including psychological factors, family, relational, and community/societal contexts. In the current study, factors at the individual level (religiosity, academic aspirations, self-esteem, depression), family (social relationships, communication, and family support), and community/societal (neighborhood connectedness and school connectedness) are considered. Adolescents are exposed to each of these interdependent levels on a daily basis. In support of the socio-ecological theoretical framework, Ritchwood, Traylor, Howell, Church, and Bolland (2014) examined self-worth, social relationships (parents and peer), and neighborhood factors and their associations with sexual behaviors of adolescents among African American male and female adolescents in the Deep South. They found that individual, parental, and neighborhood factors were predictive of sexual behaviors (Ritchwood et al., 2014). Such findings emphasize the importance of understanding prior individual and social factors that are directly associated with and interact with gender to also predict later sexual behaviors. As well, such research should be expanded to embrace youth represented in a national data set.

## Individual Factors and Sexual Initiation

Adolescents play a role in their own sexual behavior and sexual decision-making processes (Buhi & Goodson, 2007). Often referred to as intrapersonal factors, attributes such as religiosity, academic aspirations, self-esteem and depression, are correlates of adolescent sexual behaviors and initiation to first sex.

### Adolescent Religiosity

Religiosity has been defined in multiple ways. For this study, adolescent religiosity is conceptualized as beliefs and participation in religious activities, including church attendance (Meier, 2003; Thornton & Camburn, 1989). According to Thornton and Camburn (1989), religious groups tend to discourage premarital sex and adolescents may hear frequent messages about the dangers of premarital sex. Meier (2003) and Rostosky, Regenerus, and Wright (2003) found that high religiosity reduced the probability of having sex for adolescents of various ethnic backgrounds. A definitive conclusion about whether or not these beliefs deter African American adolescents from initiating intercourse is yet to be established.

Similarly, Manlove, Terry-Humen, Erum, Ikramullah, and Moore (2006) examined the relationships between parent and family religiosity and timing of sexual initiation and contraceptive use, using a sample of sexually inexperienced youth between 12 to 14 years old at base line. Follow-up was conducted five years later. The results from this longitudinal study indicated that more frequent parent religious attendance and activities were related to later age of sexual initiation. African American parents were about twice as likely to attend religious services more than once per week compared to Hispanic and White parents (Manlove et al., 2006). However, family religiosity was independent of sexual initiation among African American adolescents. Their study did not address adolescents' own religiosity.

There is consistency in the literature regarding the protective nature of religiosity for adolescents. However, inconsistencies appear with regard to the effect across gender. Bearman and Bruckner (2001) and Rostosky et al. (2003) found that the protective effect was stronger for females than for males. Further, Bearman and Bruckner (2001) found that when adolescents took a virginity pledge, the length of delay to sexual debut was longer for females than for males. Given the gender differences found in the timing of sexual initiation and the protectiveness of religiosity, this study examined differences among African American male and female adolescents.

## Academic Aspirations

Academic aspiration is defined as adolescents' beliefs about their future, specifically goals for high academic achievement and plans to attend college (e.g., Honora, 2002). Earlier initiation of first sex has been theorized to be associated with poorer academic performance (Dryfoos, 1990) and students with higher educational aspirations are more likely to postpone sexual intercourse (e.g., Dryfoos, 1990). More specifically, initiation of sex was associated with a reduced focus on future academic goals (e.g., Brooke, Balka, Abernathy & Hamburg, 1994). Jessor's (1991) problem behavior theory (PBT) included a construct named "limited perceived chances" for success in life (p. 602) as a risk factor for problem behaviors including risky sex. This construct is similar to the construct used in the current study to measure academic aspirations; the adolescents' beliefs about whether they will attend college. Using PBT as a framework, Costa, Jessor, Donovan, and Fortenberry (1995) examined factors associated with first sex and found that expectation for achievement was associated with a delay in intercourse. Spriggs and Tucker-Halpern (2008) and Frisco (2008) reported that academic goals were associated with delayed intercourse. Additionally, Frisco (2008) used the concept of aligned ambition to demonstrate that adolescents with higher educational goals were expected to understand the consequences of their actions and make smart decisions. Frisco (2008) examined the likelihood of postsecondary enrollment and found that adolescents who initiated sex during high school were less likely to attend college. Schvaneveldt, Miller, Berry, and Thomas (2001) also found that when both adolescents and parents had education goals for the future, sexual debut was delayed. The association was strongest for young black women. Future academic aspirations reflect adolescent beliefs in themselves and it is expected that these factors will be associated with decreased risk for early sexual initiation among African American youth.

## Adolescent Depression and Self-Esteem

Depression and self-esteem are important internalizing factors associated with sexual behavior (e.g., Ritchwood et al., 2014). Depressive symptoms are associated with earlier initiation to first sex. Hallfors, Waller, Bauer, Ford, and Halpern (2005) indicated that sex may be seen as a method to "medicate" or alleviate feelings of depression or isolation. Depression is also expected to diminish cognitive capacity and self-efficacy and results in decreased motivation and confidence in adolescents' ability to resist pressures for sex (Schuster, Mermelstein, & Wakschlag, 2013). For example, using the Add Health data, Harris, Duncan, and Boisjoly (2002) examined the association between "having a nothing to lose attitude" (p. 1029 (including emotional distress) and subsequent risk behaviors, including drug use and early sexual onset. Among adolescents 13-15 years old, emotional distress was associated with early onset of sex. For depressive symptoms, McLeod and Knight (2010) indicated that, among adolescents who initiated sex by age 15, higher levels of depression were observed compared to adolescents who did not initiate by age 15. These findings support the idea that sex might be used to alleviate feelings of depression but do not address these issues specifically among African American adolescents.

There are mixed findings about self-esteem and sexual behavior. Several studies have found that lower levels of self-esteem are associated with earlier initiation of sex (Ethier et al., 2006). In a recent study, Longmore and colleagues (2004) used the Add Health data (similar to the current study) to examine the impact of self-esteem and depression on sexual debut and found that depressive symptoms had a greater impact than self-esteem on sexual onset. Longmore and colleagues (2004) reported that higher self-esteem was associated with sexual debut at older ages for boys and that compared to White girls, depressive symptoms had weaker effects for Black girls. Therefore, higher self-esteem may exert a positive influence for girls leading to a delay in initiation to first sex. Also using the Add Health data, Wheeler (2010) found that higher self-esteem was not significantly correlated with sexual debut one year later. Although the research is inconclusive, it is evident that both self-esteem and depression are associated with first sex, however, there exist differences across gender. Furthermore, when ethnicity was considered there were differences among those of differing ethnicities.

## Family Factors and Sexual Initiation

Studies have consistently shown that various parenting practices such as communication, monitoring, and support are associated negatively with initiation to first sex for adolescents (e.g., Sieving et al., 2000). For this study, two types of parent-adolescent communication are considered: (a) general communication and (b) communication about sex with parents. General communication refers to parent and adolescent discussions of everyday activities, such as school and peer relationships. Communication about sex refers to how frequently parents and adolescents hold discussions about safe sex practices, abstinence, and consequences associated with sexual behavior.

Parent-adolescent communication in regards to sexual activity is generally viewed as important and desirable and is perceived as a means of encouraging adolescents to engage in responsible sexual behavior and delay initiation (Hutchison, 2002; Moore & Rosenthal, 1993). However, Davis and Friel (2001) reported that for both male and female adolescents, discussions with mother about sex were associated with earlier initiation of sex. Similarly, Frederick's cross-sectional study (2008) found that communication was positively associated with sexual behavior It was unclear which occurred first, sex or communication about sex. Current explanations for these contradictory findings include: (a) incongruent reports from parents and adolescents (Lefkowitz, Romo, Corona, Au, & Sigman, 2000); and (b) uncertainty about whether sex occurred before or after communication began (Meschke, Zweig, Barber, & Eccles, 2000). The current study uses parents' reports on communication about sex and adolescent reports on general communication. With the inclusion of only virgins at Wave I for the current study, communication about sex at Wave I preceded first sex.

Apart from specific communication about matters pertaining to communication about sex, Hutchison (2002) found that general communication between parents and adolescents was the greatest predictor of sexual communication. McNeely et al. (2002) indicated that increased mother-adolescent communication was associated with a delay in early intercourse. As well, poor parent-adolescent communication predicted a range of problem behaviors including drug use, delinquency, and early sexual activity (Loeber & Dishion, 1983). Moreover, communication about sex occurred more among parents (mostly mothers) and daughters than among parents and sons (Hutchinson, 2002). These findings suggest that communication about day-to-day activities may foster closeness between parents and adolescents, increase communication about sex, and prevent or delay adolescent problems.

## Family Structure and Family Support

Apart from communication, other family characteristics associated with the timing of sexual intercourse/safe sex practices include family support, family composition, economic status, and parent-child relationships (McNeely et al., 2002; Sieving, Clea, McNeely, & Blum, 2000). Parents transmit their standards of conduct to their children both directly and indirectly (Kotchick, Shaffer, Forehand, & Miller, 2001). Greater parent education predicted older age of first sex among female adolescents

(Miller et al, 1997). In the case of African Americans, Murry (1996) found that African American adolescents ($n$ = 109) who lived in two-parent households that had engaged in conversations with parents about sexual issues, and had greater knowledge about sexual matters were more likely to delay age at first intercourse until 18 years of age and beyond. Although the Murry study looked specifically at a sample of African American adolescents, the sample size was relatively small and the findings could not be generalized to African American populations in general. Using a Dutch sample of adolescents 12-17 years old to examine the association between family cohesiveness and sexual debut, de Graff, de van de Schoot, Woertman, Hawk, and Meeus (2012) reported that family cohesion was associated with a delay in sexual intercourse. In particular, girls who came from families with lower cohesion had their first sexual experiences earlier than girls from families with greater levels of cohesion. On the other hand, studies by Kalina et al. (2013) and Longmore, Manning, and Giordano (2001) indicated that parental monitoring had a stronger impact on delaying intercourse than parental or family support.

## Community Factors and Sexual Initiation

Outside the purview of individual factors and parent factors, there are peers, neighborhood, and school that are associated with age of sexual debut. In a longitudinal study focusing on adolescents between 12 and 15 years old in Chicago, Browning et al. (2004) found that neighborhood collective efficacy delayed sexual onset only for adolescents who experienced greater levels of parental monitoring. Neighborhood collective efficacy was measured, in part, by adolescents' reports about whether there are people in their neighborhoods who they can trust, people who watch out to ensure children are safe, and whether there are adults that children can look up to. The Browning et al. (2004) study is among the few that looks beyond neighborhood disorganization to consider neighborhood relationships and connections. Similarly, Moore and Chase-Lansdale (2001) focused on African American girls living in poor communities: girls who initiated sex or became pregnant perceived less social support from neighbors. Moore and Chase-Lansdale (2001) also concluded that a greater degree of outside the home social support compared to a lower degree of such social support was also protective.

Connectedness to school should also delay sexual onset. *School connectedness* (i.e., "the extent to which students feel accepted, valued, respected, and included in the *school*"; Shochet, Dadds, Ham, & Montague, 2006, p. 170), is associated with positive health outcomes (Shochet et al., 2006) and prosocial behaviors (Markham, et al., 2010; McNeely & Falci,

2004; McNeely, Nonnemaker, & Blum, 2002). Paul, Fitzjohn, Herbison, and Dickson (2000) indicated that, among adolescents in New Zealand, individual and school factors (connectedness to school) appeared to be more important than family composition or socioeconomic status in the decision to have sexual intercourse before age 16. In addition, Mitchell, Rumbaugh-Whitesell, Spicer, and Beals (2007) found that boys who felt more attached to school and reported higher grades were more likely to postpone sexual initiation in contrast to boys who felt less connected to school. The studies reviewed suggest that greater connectedness to school is associated with prosocial behaviors which may include delay in sexual initiation. The current study focuses on how feelings of connectedness to school and neighbors may protect adolescents from engaging in sexual intercourse. This is an important research focus given the limited scholarship on how connectedness outside of the family is linked to African American adolescents' risk behaviors, specifically, early initiation of first sex.

## The Current Study

Weaknesses of previous studies include: lack of theory, lack of longitudinal designs, small sample sizes, limited geographical area, and studying variables in isolation. Informed by a socio-ecological theoretical framework, the purpose of this study is to examine how individual, family, and community connections predict the initiation to sexual initiation among African American adolescents using a large national longitudinal data set. The current study first assesses the extent to which the initiation to first sex is predicted by levels of individual variables (age, gender, religiosity, self-esteem, depression, academic aspirations), family variables (parent education, family structure, family support, parent-adolescent communication, and communication about sex), and community variables (school and neighborhood connectedness). Second, the study examines the extent to which gender moderates the associations between the predictor variables and the outcome (initiation to first sex).

### Study Hypotheses

Given that prior studies have generally indicated that individual/ psychological factors such as greater depression, lower academic aspiration, lower religiosity, and lower self-esteem, are negatively associated with risky behaviors, this study hypothesizes that the lower the (a) academic aspirations, (b) religiosity, (c) self-esteem and (d) the higher the depression, the more likely adolescents will be to initiate sex. As well, gender and age should be predictors, with more boys and those who are older more likely to become nonvirgins at Wave II.

Contradictory findings have been reported for the association between parent communication and adolescent sexual behaviors. Some studies found that parent-adolescent communication about sex was negatively associated with sexual risk behavior including early sex (Moore & Rosenthal, 1993) and others reported that communication was positively related to risky sexual behavior and early sex (e.g., Davis & Friel, 2001). Given measurement of antecedent variables at least 12 months prior to the outcome variable, this study hypothesizes that virgin adolescents exposed to less/lower (a) parent education, (b) two-parent family structure, (c) family support, (d) parental communication, and (e) parental communication about sex, will be more likely to initiate sexual intercourse.

Moore and Chase-Lansdale (2001) posit that adults in the community may provide additional social support for adolescents that may protect against negative outcomes for adolescents. This connection to others in the community or neighborhood has been associated with a delay in sexual intercourse (e.g., Browning et al., 2004; Moore & Chase-Lansdale, 1999). Additionally, feelings of connectedness to school have also been associated with delay in sexual intercourse (e.g., Mitchell, et al., 2007). Associations of school connectedness and neighborhood connectedness with outcomes for African American adolescents are understudied. This study hypothesizes that adolescents exposed to lower (a) neighborhood connectedness and (b) school connectedness will be more likely to initiate into sexual intercourse.

In addition, national data suggest that males tend to initiate sex at younger ages than females (CDC, 2009) and that parents are more likely to discuss issues of sex more with female adolescents than males (Hutchinson, 2002). Therefore, this study examines gender differences as a moderator of the association of variables with initiation to sexual initiation. Because previous studies haven't consistently tested for moderating effects, we look at all the predictors as possibly moderated by gender. However, based on the literature, there should be effects of gender on the associations of specific predictors of first sex. The final hypothesis predicts that the association of familial factors (parent education, general communication, and communication about sex), individual factors (religiosity and future academic aspirations), and extra-familial factors (neighborhood connectedness and school connected) with the outcome are expected to be stronger among girls than boys.

## Method

This study uses data from the National Longitudinal Study on Adolescent Health (Add Health), which measures social contexts (e.g., families, friends, schools, and neighborhoods) and adolescent health and risk behaviors across time. For this study, we use data from Waves I (1994-1995) and II (one year later, 1996). Wave I included a parent questionnaire which measured parent education (most reports came from mothers) and as well as parent-adolescent communication about sexual activity. Overall, there was oversampling for middle and upper class African Americans as well as Hispanics and Asians in order to have more representative samples of youth in the entire US population (Harris et al., 2003).

Adolescents in the in-home sample from both Waves I and II completed an audio computer assisted survey, a method used to capture sensitive topics such as substance use and sexual behavior. For more sensitive topics, the respondent listened through earphones to pre-recorded questions and entered the answers directly. This lessened the potential for interviewer or parental impact on adolescents' reports about their behavior. Lastly, a parent, preferably the resident mother of each adolescent respondent interviewed in Wave I, was asked to complete an interviewer-assisted, optically scanned questionnaire.

## Sample Demographics

For the purpose of this study, the participants included in the analyses were those who answered Black or African American to the question, "Which one category best describes your racial background?" The adolescents' age was calculated from the reported birth date and the year and month of the interview. Adolescents between the ages of 11-15 ($M = 14.36$) who were virgins at Wave 1 were included in the analyses. The rationale for selecting early to middle adolescents stems from previous scholarship which suggests that engaging in sexual activity at age sixteen or older can be considered normative adolescent behavior (Millstein, 2003). Having intercourse in early adolescence is considered risky sexual behavior. At Wave I there were 1205 (51%) African American adolescents who were virgins in the age range 11-15 ($n = 511$ boys, $n = 698$ girls). Parental education (reported mainly by mothers) was based on the following question, "How far did you go in school?" Items were recoded into the following categories: 0 = *no college experience* and 1= *at least some college experience or obtained a college degree and postgraduate*; 14% of the sample did not report on education.

## Dependent Variable

*Sexual initiation.* To determine whether adolescents had engaged in sexual activity the answers to the question: "Have you ever had sexual intercourse?" was 1= *yes*, and 0 = *no*. This variable was used across both waves. At Wave I, the question was used to select virgins and at Wave

II to determine whether participants had initiated sex in the intervening year. Of the 1205 virgins at Wave I, 731 of these participated again (61%) at Wave II. There were 156 nonvirgins at Wave II, 21% of the returnees. To assess potential differences between the participants lost through attrition and those who remained at Wave II, we compared these two groups on the variables of the study with chi-square and MANOVA. Older adolescents, parents with no college degree, and females returned more than did younger adolescents, parents with a college degree, and males. Descriptive statistics on all study variables can be found in Table 1.

**Individual Factors**

*Religiosity.* Previous Add Health users have used the means of three items to measure adolescent religiosity (e.g., Meier, 2003). These Wave I items included the frequency of attendance at religious services, frequency of attendance at religious youth activities, and self-rated importance of religion: "In the past 12 months, how often did you attend religious services?"; "How important is religion to you?"; and "Many churches, synagogues, and other places of worship have special activities for teenagers — such as youth groups, Bible classes, or choir. In the past 12 months, how often did you attend such youth activities?" For the attendance item, participants responded on a 4-point Likert-type scale ranging from 1 = *never* to 4 = *once a week or more*. For the other items responses ranged from 1 = *not at all important* to 4 = *very important*. The 3 items were averaged (alpha = .62).

*Academic aspirations.* At Wave I the mean of two items was used to measure future academic aspirations: "How much do you want to go to college?" and "How likely it is that you will go to college?" Participants responded on a scale of 1 indicating *low* to 5 indicating *high* (alpha = .72).

*Self-esteem* was assessed at Wave I, with four items from the Rosenberg Self-Esteem Scale (Rosenberg, 1965). Sample questions included: "Do you agree or disagree that you have many good qualities" and "Do you agree or disagree that you have a lot to be proud of?" The response scale ranged from 1 = *strongly disagree* to 5 = *strongly agree* (alpha = .81).

*Depression* was measured with a modified version of the Center for Epidemiologic Studies Depression Scale (CESD) which includes twenty items comprising six scales reflecting major facets of depression: depressed mood, feelings of guilt and worthlessness, feelings of helplessness and hopelessness, psychomotor retardation, loss of appetite, and sleep disturbance (Radloff, 1977). Participants in the current study responded to 12 items, such as "In the past 12 months, how often have you laughed a lot" (reverse scored) and "…how often have you cried a lot."

Responses ranged from 0 = *never* to 3 = *most or all of the time* (alpha = .84).

**Familial Factors**

*Parental communication about sex.* The parental communication about sex scale consisted of five items from the parent questionnaire in Wave I: "How much have you and {adolescent} talked about: (his/her) having sexual intercourse and the negative or bad things that would happen if [he got someone/she got] pregnant?; The dangers of getting a sexually transmitted disease?; The negative or bad impact on (his/her) social life because (he/she) would lose the respect of others?; The moral issues of not having sexual intercourse?; and How much have you talked to {adolescent}: about birth control; about sex?" The adolescent's mother (primarily) answered these with 1 = *not at all*, 2 = *somewhat*, 3 = *a moderate amount*, 4 = *a great deal* (alpha = .90). This measure of communication about sex has been used by other Add Health researchers (Majumdar, 2005) with a reported Cronbach's alpha of .93.

*General communication.* Three items measured general communication between adolescents and parents at Wave I. Adolescents were presented with a series of questions regarding things they have done with their parents in the past week. Three items that referred to communication were selected: (1) had a talk about a personal problem; (2) talked about schoolwork or grades; (3) talked about other things they were doing in school. Adolescents answered *yes* = 1 or *no* = 0 to these questions. A sum of these items measured general communication (alpha = .57). Ornelas, Perreira, and Ayala (2007) used these items and reported an alpha of .54.

*Family Structure.* Similar to Lynam et al. (2000), we classified family structure as traditional or nontraditional. Approximately half of the sample (51%) resided in families with *two biological parents* (coded as 1; *others* coded as 0).

*Family support.* Two scales measured adolescents' relationships with their fathers and mothers. Both scales used four items to measure the closeness, warmth, and level of communication within parent-child relationships. Items included "How close do you feel to (name of dad)?" and "Are you satisfied with the way (name of mom) and you communicate with each other?" Responses were on a 5-point scale with reverse coding so that a high score on these items represented high quality relationships with parents. The Father-Relationship and Mother-Relationship scales were averaged, with alphas of .89 and .85, respectively.

**Community Factors**

*Neighborhood connectedness.* Three Wave I items assessed adolescents' connectedness to neighbors: "You know most of the people in your neighborhood"; "In the past month, you have stopped on the street to talk with someone who lives in your neighborhood"; and "People in this neighborhood look out for each other." Adolescents indicated if this was *true* = 1 or *false* = 0. These items were summed (alpha = .53). Danso (2014) used these items to compose a neighborhood social capital scale.

*School connectedness.* Three items from Wave I were used to indicate school connectedness: "You feel close to people at your school"; "You feel like you are part of your school"; and "You are happy to be at your school". These items were reverse coded so that 1 indicated *strongly disagree* and 4 indicated *strongly agree* (alpha = .72). McNeely et al. (2002) also used this measure of school connectedness and reported a Cronbach's alpha of .79.

## Results

The focus of the study was on adolescent initiation to first sex between Waves I and II. Of the 731 participants in Wave II, 156 had sexual intercourse after Wave I. Due to the binary nature of the Wave 2 outcome variable (have sex/not have sex), hierarchical logistic regression was used to test the hypotheses. Main effects and interaction results are reported in Table 2.

| Variables | Wave I All ($n = 2354$) | | Waves I and II Returnees of 1205 Wave I Virgins ($n = 731$) | |
|---|---|---|---|---|
| | Mean or $n$ (%) | SD | Mean or $n$ (%) | SD |
| Parent-adolescent Communication about sex | 3.14 | .82 | 3.08 | .83 |
| General Communication | 1.57 | 1.06 | 1.58 | 1.04 |
| Neighbor Connectedness | 5.30 | .93 | 5.35 | .90 |
| School Connectedness | 3.72 | .87 | 3.85 | .81 |
| Adolescent religiosity | 4.15 | .72 | 4.26 | .70 |
| Academic Aspirations | 4.38 | .91 | 4.57 | .76 |
| Self-Esteem | 4.27 | .56 | 4.35 | .51 |
| Depression | .60 | .39 | .53 | .36 |
| Family Structure | .29 | .46 | .37 | .48 |
| Family Support | 4.32 | .69 | 4.48 | .57 |
| Age | 14.35 | .74 | 14.26 | .77 |
| Males | 1142 (49%) | | 305 (42%) | |
| Females | 1212 (51%) | | 426 (58%) | |
| Parent attended? college | 1135 (48%) | | 331 (45%) | |
| Parent did not attend college | 797 (34%) | | 307 (42%) | |
| Virgin | 1205 (51%) | | 575 (79%) | |
| Nonvirgin | 1149 (49%) | | 156 (21%) | |

Table 1. Descriptives for Waves I and II Sudy Variables of African American Young Adolescents

| Variables | B | SE | OR | CI: LL,UL |
|---|---|---|---|---|
| Age | .48*** | .14 | 1.62 | 1.24, 2.11 |
| Parent Education Status (0 = no college; 1 = some college or more) | .05 | .13 | 1.06 | .82, 1.35 |
| Gender (0 = male; 1 = female) | -.28* | .13 | .76 | .58, .98 |
| Religiosity | -.15 | .12 | .86 | .68, 1.09 |
| Academic Aspirations | .12 | .14 | 1.12 | .86, 1.48 |
| Self-Esteem | -.14 | .14 | .87 | .67, 1.14 |
| Depression | .26* | .13 | 1.30 | 1.01, 1.68 |
| Family Structure | -.28* | .13 | .76 | .59, .98 |
| Family Support | .40 | .14 | 1.04 | .79, 1.37 |
| General Communication | -.01 | .12 | .99 | .28, 1.25 |
| Parent Sex Communication | .02 | .13 | 1.02 | .80, 1.31 |
| Neighbor Connectedness | .06 | .13 | 1.06 | .83, 1.35 |
| School Connectedness | .06 | .13 | 1.07 | .83, 1.36 |
| Gender X Age | .00 | .13 | 1.00 | .77, 1.30 |
| Gender X Parent Education | .34** | .12 | 1.40 | 1.10, 1.79 |
| Gender X Religiosity | -.29* | .12 | .75 | .59, .95 |
| Gender X Academic | .23$^t$ | .13 | 1.26 | .97, 1.63 |
| Gender X Self-Esteem | -.01 | .14 | .99 | .75, 1.30 |
| Gender X Depression | .02 | .13 | 1.02 | .79, 1.31 |
| Gender X Family Structure | -.03 | .13 | .97 | .76, 1.24 |
| Gender X Family Support | -.05 | .14 | .95 | .72, 1.26 |
| Gender X G. Communication | -.11 | .12 | .90 | .71, 1.14 |
| Gender X P. S. Communication | .02 | .12 | 1.02 | .80, 1.29 |
| Gender X Neighborhood | .06 | .13 | 1.07 | .83, 1.36 |
| Gender X School Conn | -.09 | .13 | .92 | .71, 1.18 |
| **Constant** | -1.67*** | .14 | .19 | |

$^t p < .07$. $*p < .05$. $**p < .01$. $***p < .001$. $N = 539$. CI = 95%. Standardized scores were used for all main effect variables in the equation. Interaction terms were computed on standardized scores. Initiation to sex $0 = not$, $1 = have had sex$.

*Table 2. Summary of Logistic Regression for Variables Predicting Initiation to First Sex Between Wave I and Wave II with All Models*

All variables were centered (with standardized scores). In the first model, demographic individual and family variables of age, gender, and parent education were entered first, with individual variables of religiosity, academic aspirations, self-esteem, and depression entered in the second model. In model three, the familial variables (family structure, family support, general communication, communication about sex) were entered, followed by neighborhood connectedness and school connectedness in a fourth step. The interaction terms between gender and all the variables were entered last to test for gender differences in associations of predictors with the outcome. Follow-up of significant interactions involved logistic regressions within gender (see Table 3).

The findings indicated an overall significant model fit in the final model, $X^2$ (25, $N = 539$) 53.95, $p < .001$; the -2 log likelihood was 463.14. As may be seen in Table 2, which provides the results when all models were included in the analysis, the demographic variables of gender and age were significantly associated with initiation to first sex. As expected, boys (B = -.28, OR = .76, $p < .05$) and older adolescents (B = .48, OR = 1.62, $p <$

.001) were more likely to initiate intercourse.

|  | Males ($n = 237$) | | | Females ($n = 336$) | | |
|---|---|---|---|---|---|---|
| Variables | B | SE | OR | B | SE | OR |
| Parent Education Status | -.19 | .15 | .83 | .27[t] | .16 | 1.31 |
| Religiosity | -.01 | .15 | .96 | -.33* | .14 | .72 |
| Academic Aspirations | -.17 | .15 | .84 | .17 | .18 | 1.18 |
| **Constant** | -1.96** | .15 | .35 | -1.85** | .19 | .16 |

Table 3. *Follow-up of Significant Interactions with Gender: Summary of Logistic Regression for Variables Prediciting Initiation to First Sex Between Wave I and Wave II*

## Results of Hypothesis Testing

Hypothesis one predicted that individual factors would be associated with sexual initiation. There was mixed support for this hypothesis. Religiosity, academic aspiration, and self-esteem scores were not significantly related to sexual initiation. As expected, higher depression scores were significantly associated with sexual initiation. Hypothesis two, that adolescents exposed to lower parental communication and parental communication about sex would be more likely to initiate first sex, was not supported. But, as predicted, adolescents in non-two-parent families were more likely to initiate sex. Parent education did not have a direct effect on sexual debut. Hypotheses three and four tested whether adolescents exposed to lower neighborhood connectedness and school connectedness would be more likely to initiate first sex. Contrary to expectations, these community-based hypotheses were not supported. Overall, support for the hypotheses was provided by those who were older, male, had higher depression, and had non-two-parent family structure. These characteristics were all related to higher risk for initiating first sex.

This study also included tests of moderation. More specifically, hypothesis five predicted that gender would moderate the association among predictors and the outcome of sexual initiation. The association of familial connections, individual factors, and community factors were expected to have greater association with outcomes among girls than boys. This hypothesis was partially supported in that there were moderating effects of gender on associations of religiosity, parent education, and academic aspirations with sexual initiation. With respect to religiosity, the interaction effect (B = -.29, OR = .75, $p < .05$) was significant. As follow-up, separate analyses within gender were conducted (see Table 3) in order to examine gender differences among sexual initiation. As predicted, among girls, the first sex initiation was significantly less likely when religiosity (B = -.33, OR = .72, $p < .01$) was higher, whereas there was no significant association for boys (B = -.01, OR = .96, *ns*). Second, gender was a significant moderator for parent education status and sexual initiation. Follow up analyses indicated that higher parent education was more strongly associated with sexual debut among girls (B = .27, OR = 1.31, $p < .08$) than boys (B = -.19, OR = .83, $ns$).

Third, gender moderated the association between academic aspirations and sexual initiation (B = .23, OR = 1.26, $p = .07$). However, follow-up analyses between academic aspiration and sexual initiation showed no significant differences from zero for either boys or girls. The association was negative for boys (B = -.17, OR = .84) and positive for girls (B = .17, OR = 1.18). Contrary to expectations, gender did not moderate the associations of other variables with sexual initiation.

## Discussion

The study used DiClemente et al.'s (2005) socio-ecological model as a framework for examining individual, family, and community factors related to African American adolescents initiation to first sex. All adolescents included in the study indicated that they had not had sex at Wave I. By Wave II, 21% indicated that they had experienced sexual initiation, that is, had first sex. As with previous research, the study found that demographic factors, such as age, gender, and family structure of participants, were related to sexual initiation (Luster & Small, 1994; Majumdar, 2005). Consistent with prior research, boys were more likely to have had sex than girls, and older adolescents were more likely to initiate into sexual intercourse than younger adolescents (Luster & Small, 1994; Mandara, Murray, & Bangi, 2003). Researchers have attributed a greater likelihood for boys to engage in sexual intercourse possibly due to less parental supervision (Mandara et al., 2003). Adolescents living with both parents were less likely to report first sex than adolescents in other family structures. These findings are consistent with Murry (1996) who found that African American adolescents who lived in two-parent households were more likely to delay age at first sex until 18 years of age and beyond. In another study involving eighth grade students, Boislard and Poulin (2011) reported that adolescents who were not in a two-parent family were engaged in earlier intercourse and problem behaviors. Our study did not differentiate between adolescents who were in adoptive two-parent families from those in biological two-parent families. Future studies should consider adoptive children (Grotevant, Ross, Marchel, & McRoy, 1999) and their sexual initiation outcomes. Given the higher rates of single parent families among Black families (Vespa, Lewis & Kreider, 2013), the impact of having two parents or not should be considered when designing programs for Black adolescents. How do single-parent families generate the resources and supervision thought to benefit the children who live in two-parent families? What strengths are present in single-parent families where the children delay sexual debut?

Only partial support was found for the two individual factors examined in this study. Consistent with the literature, greater religiosity was protective against sexual initiation, specifically for girls (Meier, 2003). Having strong religious beliefs may function as a social control mechanism for African American adolescent girls. Only two items measured academic aspiration. They were both related to whether the adolescent expected to go to college. Perhaps also considering their current GPA as well as their academic self-efficacy would have strengthened this measure (Ramirez-Valles, Zimmerman, & Juarez, 2002). The interaction with gender suggested that academic aspirations operated differently for the boys (lower odds) and girls (higher odds), but neither coefficient was significantly different from zero.

In the overall model, depression had a significant direct effect in the predicted direction. For depressive symptoms, McLeod and Knight (2010) found, that among adolescents who initiated sex by age 15, higher levels of depression were observed compared to adolescents who did not initiate by age 15. This study's results were similar in documenting the association of prior depression with sexual initiation. The findings on depression suggest that lowering depression would be an important consideration for lowering the odds of early sexual initiation among African American adolescents.

Contrary to previous research, self-esteem was not significant in the final model. Longmore and colleagues (2004) found that higher self-esteem was associated with sexual debut at older ages for boys and, that compared to Black girls, depressive symptoms had a weaker effect. Using all ethnicities and all ages in the Add Health data (public version), Wheeler (2010) reported that higher self-esteem did not predict sexual debut for virgins one year later. It is possible that an association between self-esteem and depression ($r = -.32, p < .001$) may have meant that depression accounted for the variance in initiation to first sex, leaving less variance for associations between self-esteem and first sex. If so, then including both variables in this study adds important information that studying each variable alone does not provide. Contrary to expectations, the family relationship variables examined were not significantly associated with initiation into first sex. The effect of communication about sex was nonsignificant. Previous studies have found that good lines of communication with parents (Roche, Mekos, & Alexander, 2005) were associated with a delay in sexual intercourse. However, Davis and Friel (2001) reported a positive relationship between communication about sex and early sexual initiation. By using a sample of virgins at Wave I, this study aimed to clarify these discrepant findings. For example, literature reporting no association between conversation about sex and sexual initiation may demonstrate the futility of conversations after initiation has occurred (Davis & Friel, 2001). Earlier cross-sectional results on parent-child communication appear to be better explained as reactive rather than preventive. Other factors not studied that may be associated with a delay in sexual initiation include peer relationships (Kinsman, Romer, Furstenberg, & Schwarz, 1998). Also, the frequency of communication about sex was assessed, but not the level of reciprocity and quality of the communication between adolescents and their parents. Only parents reported on communication about sex. It is possible that parents' rating of communication may be incongruent with adolescents' reports that were not available. Other factors such as parental knowledge and comfort about discussing issues pertaining to sex might help to explain such findings (McNeely et al., 2002).

General communication about sex was not related to first sex. The variable measured communication about life issues and may not reflect association with adolescents' decision to initiate sex. Contrary to expectations, family support was not significantly related to initiation of first sex. De Graaf et al. (2012) reported that family cohesion was associated with a delay in sexual intercourse. Studies by Kalina et al. (2013) and Longmore et al. (2001) indicated that parental monitoring had a stronger impact on delaying intercourse than parental or family support. Going forward, extending the study to parental monitoring measures may be important to more fully understand the effects of family variables on the odds of sexual initiation.

The community connections were not significant for this age group as well. Although studies have found that feeling connected to school and neighborhood may be beneficial for adolescents (Browning et al., 2004; McNeely et al., 2002), with this sample, they were not significant. A possible explanation for this contradictory finding is that these factors may not be salient in early adolescence because familial ties and peer relationships may be valued more in this age group (Steinberg et al., 1994).

This study used gender as a moderator between study variables and initiation to sex. Gender moderated the relationship between religiosity and sexual initiation. Having high religiosity was more protective for girls than it was for boys. Although academic aspiration was not a main effect, and the within-gender associations were not significantly different from zero, the significant interaction results indicated that having higher academic aspirations among boys was somewhat more protective but lower aspirations were a risk factor for early sexual initiation. Among girls the opposite pattern was seen. Such a pattern presents concerns if high aspiring girls are engaging more in first sex, possibly diminishing future success. Perhaps high aspiring girls are more likely to have romantic relationships that could include initiation to first sex. Future research will be useful in explaining the different directions of association for boys and girls.

Prevention strategies should focus on boys with low academic aspirations. More specifically, it might be beneficial if boys with lower academic aspirations are provided with mentors or other resources to increase their academic aspirations. Frisco (2008) found that academic goals were protective against sexual initiation, thus, increasing academic aspirations in boys may result in delayed first intercourse. But the recommendations for low aspiring girls would need to take into account their already somewhat lower likelihood of first sex initiation compared to low aspiring boys or higher aspiring girls. If the interaction by gender found in this study is replicated and follow-up results are similar, then prevention efforts would need to focus on these different patterns for boys and girls.

The study confirms some of the previous research. More specifically, religiosity, academic aspirations, self-esteem, depression, and adolescent age are important considerations either alone or in interactions with gender. Given the protective nature of religiosity in this study, particularly for girls, programs aimed at preventing African American adolescents from early sexual initiation could include church groups and settings. Whether it is having parents who encourage children to engage in religious activities or the activities themselves, parents could be encouraged to have their adolescents participate in religious activities. Adolescent's gender is another important consideration. Efforts at prevention or intervention should consider what works best for boys and girls individually. Factors such as higher academic aspiration may be a greater deterrent for boys than for girls, whereas religiousness was a greater deterrent for girls.

The socio-ecological model was used to guide this research (DiClemente et al., 2005). In support of this theory, gender interacted with academic aspiration, religiosity, and parental education as predictors of sexual initiation. These findings suggest that boys' and girls' behavior is at least partially, but differentially, associated with individual characteristics. Other ecological factors that should be examined to advance understanding of African American adolescents' initiation to first sex include parental monitoring and relationships with romantic partners. Nonetheless, the design of the study helped to address some of the methodological limitations of prior research. First, the sample was drawn from a national data set, which included a large sample of African American adolescents. Data from the CDC and other empirical studies indicate that African Americans have higher rates of teen pregnancy, sexually transmitted infections and diseases, as well as earlier onset of sexual intercourse than any other U.S. ethnic group. Despite a nationwide decrease in early adolescent sex, African American adolescents still have disproportionately higher rates than other ethnic groups. In 1995, 24% of African American adolescents reported having intercourse by age 13 and 73% of high school students reported being currently sexual active; compared to Whites among whom only 5% reported sex by age 13 and 49% of high school students reported being sexual active (CDC, 2007). The 2009 report indicated that 15% of African American adolescents reported intercourse by age 13 compared to 3.4% for Whites reporting sex by 13. Overall, 65% of African American high school students reported being sexually active compared to 42% of Whites (CDC, 2010). Thus, looking at a within ethnic group analysis of early to middle adolescents in a group with higher percentages of at-risk sexual behavior was an important strength of the study.

As a third strength of the study, data were collected from both parents and adolescents. Information about education level and communication about sex was collected from parents whereas information about sexual behavior and individual, family, and community connections were collected from the adolescents. Because this dataset included African American families from all economic strata, it is instructive that parental education was related to adolescent's sexual initiation. More specifically, higher education of parents was associated with lower likelihood of initiation of sex for girls. Nonetheless, other demographic variables might have been considered, such as whether parents of adolescents were themselves teen parents. A fourth strength of this investigation was the use of virgins at time one to examine initiation to intercourse 12 months later, thus controlling for the temporal order of effects. Finally, this research used a multivariate design whereby all study predictors were entered in hierarchical groupings of variables. This design provided greater control for shared variance effects and reduced the likelihood of providing significant findings for variables that might be significant only when tested alone.

There are limitations to this study. First, the study was based on secondary data; therefore, only available items were used to create scales. These items may not necessarily have been the best measure of the constructs identified in the literature and theory. Perhaps a greater limitation of the study was the use of dichotomous items to measure general communication and neighborhood connectedness. Information is lost when variables are measured in such a restrictive manner. Although a longitudinal design constitutes strength of the study, it is also subject to loss of participants through attrition. However, analyses revealed primarily nonsignificant differences between the participants who were in the study at Wave I, and who did not return at Wave II. Furthermore, those not returning (boys, younger, higher parent education) shared only one characteristic associated in the literature with higher risk of sexual initiation of first sex (being male). Another limitation of the study was that differences across sexual orientation were not examined. Initiation into first sex was used as the outcome regardless of the sexual orientation of the adolescent. Research documents lower school performance and higher depression among Dutch early adolescents with same sex attraction (Bos, Sandfort, de Bruyn, & Hakvoort, 2008). As well, Jager and Davis-Kean (2011) note the complexity of coding in the Add Health where participants reported being heterosexual but having same-sex attractions. Future studies should consider differences across sexual orientation. Another weakness is that the data was initially collected over 20 years ago and may not fully reflect the views and behaviors of adolescents today.

Future studies should seek to examine in detail the role that romantic partners and peers play in adolescent sexual decision-making and sexual initiation. Because parental influence tends to decline as adolescents age (Steinberg & Silk 2002) and sexual intercourse may be a "normative" behavior in later adolescence, romantic partners and peers may have greater influence on adolescents' later sexual behavior.

In sum, this study was conducted to examine individual characteristics, familial factors, and community connections as predictors of African American adolescent sexual initiation. Partial support was found for the study hypotheses. Notably, gender, parent education, religiosity, depression, and academic aspirations were associated with the initiation to sexual intercourse as either direct effects or in interaction with gender. Including multiple variables in one longitudinal national study clarified that these predictors of African American sexual debut were present regardless of the presence of other possible predictors.

# References

Boislard P., M., & Poulin, F. (2011). Individual, familial, friends-related and contextual predictors of early sexual intercourse. *Journal of Adolescence*, 34(2), 289-300. doi:10.1016/j.adolescence.2010.05.002

Bearman, P. S, & Bruckner, H. (2001). Promising the future: Virginity pledges and first intercourse. *American Journal of Sociology, 106*, 859–912.

Bos, H. W., Sandfort, T. M., de Bruyn, E. H., & Hakvoort, E. M. (2008). Same-sex attraction, social relationships, psychosocial functioning, and school performance in early adolescence. *Developmental Psychology, 44*(1), 59-68. doi:10.1037/0012-1649.44.1.59

Bronfenbrenner, U. (1989). Ecological systems theory. In R. Vasta (Ed.), *Six theories of child development: Revised formulations and current issues* (pp. 185-246). Greenwich, CT: JAI Press.

Brooke, J. S., Balka, E. B., Abernathy, T., & Hamburg, B. A. (1994). Sequence of sexual behavior and its relationship to other problem behaviors in African American and Puerto Rican adolescents. *Journal of Genetic Psychology, 155*,107–114.

Browning, R. C., Leventhal, T., & Brooks-Gunn, J. (2004). Neighborhood context and racial differences in early adolescent sexual activity. *Demography, 41*, 697-720. doi:10.1353/dem.2004.0029.

Buhi, E. R. & Goodson, P. (2007). Predictors of adolescent sexual behavior and intention: A theory guided systematic review. *Journal of Adolescent Health, 40*, 4-21.

Center for Disease Control and Prevention (CDC). Youth risk behavior surveillance--United States, 2009. *MMWR CDC Surveillance Summaries* 2007; 55 (SS-05). Retrieved from http://www.cdc.gov.

Centers for Disease Control and Prevention (CDC). (2014). 1991-2013 High school youth risk behavior survey data. Available at http://nccd.cdc.gov/youthonline/.

Costa, F. M., Jessor, R., Donovan, J. E., & Fortenberry, J. D. (1995). Early initiation of sexual intercourse: The influence of psychosocial unconventionality. *Journal of Research on Adolescence*, 5, 93-121

Davis, E., & Friel, L. (2001). Adolescent sexuality: Disentangling the effects of family structure and family context. *Journal of Marriage & the Family, 63*(3), 669-681. doi:10.1111/j.1741-3737.2001.00669.x.

de Graaf, H., van de Schoot, R., Woertman, L., Hawk, S. T., & Meeus, W. (2012). Family cohesion and romantic and sexual initiation: A three wave longitudinal study. *Journal of Youth And Adolescence, 41*(5), 583-592. doi:10.1007/s10964-011-9708-9

Danso, K. (2014). Neighborhood social capital and the Health and health risk behavior of adolescent immigrants and non-immigrants. Unpublished Dissertation. Retrieved from: http://conservancy.umn.edu/bitstream/handle/11299/162958/DANSO_umn_0130E_14770.pdf?sequence=1&isAllowed=y

DiClemente, R. J., Salazar, L. F., Crosby, R. A., & Rosenthal, S. L. (2005). Prevention and control of sexually transmitted infections among adolescents: the importance of a socio-ecological perspective--a commentary. *Public Health (Elsevier), 119*(9), 825-836. doi:10.1016/j.puhe.2004.10.015

Dryfoos, J. G. (1990). *Adolescents at risk: Prevalence and prevention.* New York, NY: Oxford University Press.

Ethier, K. A., Kershaw, T. S., Lewis, J. B., Milan, S., Niccolai, L. M., & Ickovics, J. R. (2006). Selfesteem, emotional distress and sexual behavior among adolescent females: Inter-relationships and temporal effects. *Journal of Adolescent Health, 38*(3), 268-274. doi:10.1016/j.jadohealth.2004.12.010

Frederick, H. (2008). *Predictors of risky sexual behaviors among African American adolescents.* Unpublished Thesis. Texas Tech University, Lubbock Texas.

Frisco, M. L. (2008). Adolescents' sexual behavior and academic attainment. *Sociology of Education* 81, 284-311.

Grotevant, H. D., Ross, N. M., Marchel, M. A., & McRoy, R. G. (1999). Adaptive behavior in adopted children: Predictors from early risk, collaboration in relationships within the adoptive kinship network, and openness arrangements. *Journal of Adolescent Research, 14*(2), 231-247. doi:10.1177/0743558499142005.

Hallfors, D., Waller, M. W., Bauer, D, Ford, C. A., & Halpern, C. T. (2005). Which comes first in adolescence - Sex and drugs, or depression? *American Journal of Preventive Medicine, 29*(3), 163-170.

Harris, K. M., Duncan, G. J., & Boisjoly, J. (2002). Evaluating the role of 'Nothing to Lose' attitudes on risky behavior in adolescence. *Social Forces, 80*(3), 1005-1039.

Harris, K. M., Florey, F., Tabor, J., Bearman, P. S., Jones J., & Udry, J. R. (2003). The national longitudinal study of adolescent health: Research design. Retrieved from http://www.cpc.unc.edu/projects/addhealth/design.

Honora, D. (2002). The relationship of gender and achievement to future outlook among African American adolescents. *Adolescence, 37*(146), 301-316.

Hutchinson, M. K. (2002). The influence of sexual risk communication between parents and daughters on sexual risk behaviors. *Family Relations, 51*(3), 238–247. doi: 10.1111/j.1741-3729.2002.00238.x.

Jager, J., & Davis-Kean, P. (2011). Same-sex sexuality and adolescent psychological well-being: The influence of sexual orientation, early reports of same-sex attraction, and gender. *Self and Identity, 10*(4), 417-444. doi:10.1080/15298861003771155

Jessor, R. (1991). Risk behavior in adolescence: A psychosocial framework for understanding and action. *Journal of Adolescent Health, 12*, 597-605.

Jordahl, T., & Lohman, B. J. (2009). A bioecological analysis of risk and protective factors associated with early sexual intercourse of young adolescents, *Children and Youth Services Review, 31*, 1272-1282. doi:10.1016/j.childyouth.2009.05.014.

Kalina, O., Geckova, A. M., Klein, D., Jarcuska, P., Orosova, O., van Dijk, J. P., & Reijneveld, S. A. (2013). Mother's and father's monitoring is more important than parental social support regarding sexual risk behaviour among 15-year-old adolescents. *European Journal of Contraception & Reproductive Health Care, 18*(2), 95-103. doi:10.3109/13625187.2012.752450

Kinsman, S. B., Romer, D., Furstenberg, F. F., & Schwarz, D. F. (1998). Early sexual initiation: The role of peer norms. *Pediatrics, 102,* 1185-1192.

Kotchick, B.A., Shaffer, A., Forehead, R., & Miller, K.S. (2001). Adolescent sexual behavior: Multi system perspective. *Clinical Psychology Review, 21,* 493-519. doi: 10.1016/S0272-7358(99)00070-7.

Lefkowitz, E., Romo, L., Corona, R., Au, T., & Sigman, M. (2000). How Latino American and European American adolescents discuss conflicts, sexuality, and AIDS with their mothers. *Developmental Psychology, 36*(3), 315-325. doi:10.1037/0012-1649.36.3.315.

Loeber, R., & Dishion, T.J. (1983). Early predictors of male delinquency: A review. *Psychological Bulletin, 94,* 68-99. doi:10.1037/0033-2909.94.1.68.

Longmore, M. A., Manning, W. D., Giordano, P. C., & Rudolph, J. L. (2004). Self-esteem, depressive symptoms, and adolescents' sexual onset. *Social Psychology Quarterly, 67*(3), 279-295. doi:10.1177/019027250406700304

Longmore, M. A., Manning, W. D., & Giordano, P. C. (2001). Preadolescent parenting strategies and teens' dating and sexual initiation: A longitudinal analysis. *Journal of Marriage and Family, 63*(2), 322-335. doi:10.1111/j.1741-3737.2001.00322.x

Luster, T., & Small, S.A. (1994). Factors associated with sexual risk taking behaviors among adolescents. *Journal of Marriage and the Family, 56,* 622-632. doi: 10.2307/352873.

Lynam, D. R., Caspi, A., Moffitt, T. E., Wikström, P. H., Loeber, R., & Novak, S. (2000). The interaction between impulsivity and neighborhood context on offending: The effects of impulsivity are stronger in poorer neighborhoods. *Journal of Abnormal Psychology,109,* 563-574.

Majumdar, D. (2005). Explaining adolescent sexual risks by race and ethnicity: importance of individual, familial, and extra familial factors. *International Journal of Sociology of the Family, 31,* 19–37.

Markham, C., Lormand, D., Gloppen, K., Peskin, M., Flores, B., Low, B., & House, L. D. (2010). Connectedness as a predictor of sexual and reproductive health outcomes for youth. *Journal of Adolescent Health, 46,* 23-41. doi:10.1016/j.jadohealth.2009.11.214.

Mandara, J., Murray, C.B., & Bangi, A. K. (2003). Predictors of African American sexuality: an ecological framework. *Journal of Black Psychology, 29,* 337- 356.

Manlove, J. S, Terry- Humen, E., Ikramullah, E. N., & Moore, K. A. (2006). The role of parent religiosity in teens transitions to sex and contraception. *Journal of Adolescent Health, 39,* 578-587. doi:10.1016/j.jadohealth.2006.03.008.

McLeod, J. D., & Knight, S. (2010). The association of socioemotional problems with early sexual initiation. *Perspectives on Sexual & Reproductive Health, 42*(2), 93-101. doi:10.1363/4209310

McNeely, C., & Falci, C. (2004). School connectedness and transition into and out of health risk behavior among adolescents: A comparison of social belonging and teacher support. *Journal of School Health, 74,* 284-292. doi:10.1111/j.1746-1561.2004.

McNeely, C., Shew, M. L., Beuhring, T., Sieving, R., Miller, B. C., & Blum, R. W. M. (2002). Mothers' influence on the timing of first sex among 14- and 15-year-olds. *Journal of Adolescent Health, 31*(3), 256-265. doi:10.1016/S1054-139X(02)00350-6

Meier, A. M. (2003). Adolescents' transitions to first intercourse, religiosity, and attitudes about first sex. *Social Forces, 81,* 1031-1052. doi:10.1353/sof.2003.0039.

Meschke, L., Zweig, J., Barber, B., & Eccles, J. (2000). Demographic, biological, psychological, and social predictors of the timing of first intercourse. *Journal of Research on Adolescence, 10*(3), 315-338. doi:10.1207/SJRA1003_5.

Miller, B. C., Norton, M. C., Curtis, T., Hill, E. J., Schvaneveldt, P., & Young, M. H. (1997). The timing of sexual intercourse among adolescents: Family, peer, and other antecedents. *Youth & Society, 29*(1), 54-83. doi:10.1177/0044118X97029001003

Millstein, S. G. (2003). Risk perception: Construct development, links to theory, correlates and manifestations. In: D. Romer (Ed.) *Reducing adolescent risk: Towards an integrated approach* (pp. 35-43). Thousand Oaks, CA: Sage Publishers.

Mitchell, C. M., Whitesell, N. R., Spicer, P., Beals, J., & Kaufman, C. E. (2007). Cumulative risk for early sexual initiation among American Indian youth: A discrete-time survival analysis. *Journal of Research on Adolescence, 17,* 387-412. doi:*10.1111/j.1532-7795.2007.00527.*

Moore, M., & Chase-Lansdale, P. L. (2001). Sexual intercourse and pregnancy among African American girls in high poverty neighborhoods: the role of family and perceived community environment. *Journal of Marriage and Family, 63,* 1146-1157. doi: 10.1111/j.1741-3737.2001.01146.x.

Moore, S., & Rosenthal, D. (1993). *Sexuality in adolescence.* New York: Routledge.

Murry, V. (1996). An ecological analysis of coital timing among middle-class African American adolescent females. *Journal of Adolescent Research,11,* 261-279. doi:1177/0743554896112006

Paul, C., Fitzjohn, J., Herbison, P., & Dickson, N. (2000). The determinants of sexual intercourse before age 16. *Journal Adolescent Health, 27,* 136-147. doi:10.1016/S1054-139X(99)00095-6.

Ornelas, I. J., Perreira, K. M., & Ayala, G. X. (2007). Parental influences on adolescent physical activity: A longitudinal study. *International Journal of Behavioral Nutrition & Physical Activity, 4,* 1-10. doi:10.1186/1479-5868-4-3.

Radloff, L.S (1977). The CES-D scale: a self-report depression scale for research in the general population. *Applied Psychological Measurement, 1,* 385-401.

Ramirez-Valles, J., Zimmerman, M. A., & Juarez, L. (2002). Gender differences of neighborhood and social control processes: A study of the timing of first intercourse among low achieving, urban, African American youth. *Youth & Society* 33, 418-441.

Ritchwood, T. D., Traylor, A. C., Howell, R. J., Church, W. T., & Bolland, J. M. (2014). Socio-ecological predictors of intercourse frequency and number of sexual partners among male and female African American adolescents. *Journal of Community Psychology,*42(7), 765-781. doi:10.1002/jcop.21651

Roche, K. M., Mekos, D., & Alexander, C. S. (2005). Parenting influences on early sex initiation among adolescents. *Journal of Family Issues, 26,* 32-54. doi:10.1177/0192513X0426594.

Rosenberg, M. (1965). *Society and the adolescent self-image.* Princeton, NJ: Princeton University Press.

Rostosky, S., Regenerus, M. D., & Wright, M. L. (2003). Coital debut: The role of religiosity and sex attitudes in the Add Health survey. *The Journal of Sex Research, 40,* 358-368. doi: 10.1080/00224490209552202.

Sieving, R. W., McNeely, C. S., & Blum, R. W. (2000). Maternal expectations, mother-child connectedness, and adolescent sexual debut. *Archives of Pediatrics & Adolescent Medicine, 154,* 809-816.

Shochet, I., Dadds, M., Ham, D., & Montague, R. (2006). School connectedness is an underemphasized parameter in adolescent mental health: Results of a community prediction study. *Journal of Clinical Child and Adolescent Psychology, 35,* 170-179. doi:10.1207/s15374424jccp3502_1.

Schuster, R., Mermelstein, R., & Wakschlag, L. (2013). Gender-specific relationships between depressive symptoms, marijuana use, parental communication and risky sexual behavior in adolescence. *Journal of Youth & Adolescence, 42*(8), 1194-1209. doi:10.1007/s10964-012-9809-0.

Schvaneveldt, P. L., Miller, B. C., Berry, E. H., & Lee, T. R. (2001). Academic goals, achievement, and age at first sexual intercourse: Longitudinal, bidirectional influences. *Adolescence, 36,* 767–787.

Spriggs, A. L., & Halpern, C. T. (2008). Sexual debut timing and depressive symptoms in emerging adulthood. *Journal of Youth and Adolescence, 37,*1085–1096. doi:10.1007/s10964-008-9303-x.

Steinberg, L., Fletcher, A., & Darling, N. (1994) Parental monitoring and peer influences on adolescent substance use, *Pediatrics, 93(6),* 1060–1064.

Steinberg, L., & Silk, J. S. (2002). Parenting adolescents. In M. H. Bornstein (Ed.), *Handbook of parenting, Volume 1: Children and parenting* (Second Edition) (pp. 103-133). Mahwah, NJ: Lawrence Erlbaum Associates.

Thornton, A., & Camburn, D. (1989). Religious participation and adolescent sexual behavior and attitudes. *Journal of Marriage and the Family, 51,* 641-653. doi: 10.2307/352164.

Vespa, J., Lewis, M., & Kreider, R. ( 2013). America's families and living arrangements: *2012, Current Population Reports, P20-570.*U.S. Census Bureau, Washington, DC.

Wheeler, S. B. (2010). Effects of self-esteem and academic performance on adolescent decision-making: An examination of early sexual intercourse and illegal substance use. *Journal of Adolescent Health, 47(6),* 582-590. doi:10.1016/j.jadohealth.2010.04.009

*Chapter 8*

## Older Transgender Women and Family Relationships

*Martha B. Leighton*

*Plymouth State University*

*Elizabeth M. Dolan*

*University of New Hampshire*

Transgender women face significant challenges throughout the life cycle in comparison to their cisgender sisters (individuals who are assigned female at birth and self-identify as women). Individuals who are trans have been found to face widespread, pervasive discrimination and hostility in multiple areas of their lives and across the lifespan (Langley, 2006; Lombardi, 2010; Yu, 2010). This qualitative study of transgender women aged 55 to 77 examined how: (a) participants experienced a specific challenge, that is, familial disapproval; (b) they developed strengths and resiliencies as a response to that challenge, and (c) they employed coping strategies to counteract the effects of reduced or absent family supports.

Throughout this paper the participants are referred to as *trans women*, or MTF (male to female) individuals. The choice of *trans women* versus *transwomen* is deliberate and akin to the move away from using the term *autistic child* in favor of *child with autism*. In this construction, *trans* becomes an adjective that describes a single aspect of these women's experience–gender identity–rather than making gender identity their sole defining aspect.

### Hobfoll's Conservation of Resources Theory

This paper focuses on resiliency in the face of rejection. Therefore, Hobfoll's Conservation of Resources (COR) theory (1989) is used to examine those individuals who are well-resourced and employ successful coping strategies allowing them to conserve those resources resulting in enhanced well-being. Conversely, individuals who lack resources may employ ineffective coping strategies and experience loss spirals that adversely affect their well-being.

The underlying premise of Hobfoll's theory (1989) is the assumption that individuals are highly motivated to keep, protect, and amass resources. Because the potential, or actual, loss of resources is threatening, individuals may behave in ways that increase their chances of acquiring and maintaining objects, personal characteristics, or conditions that are seen as positive or valuable. To gain resources or to offset losses, individuals may employ resources they have on hand or use resources they can recruit from the environment. When individuals obtain and stockpile resources, they experience positive well-being. When resources are lost or threatened, or when an investment of resources fails to result in additional gain, psychological stress ensues, and the individuals become vulnerable.

Hobfoll (1989) identified four types of resources: objects, conditions, personal characteristics, and energies. *Objects* are considered resources because of their instrumental potential, or because they are difficult to acquire or have monetary value and are closely linked with socioeconomic status. *Conditions* are resources only if they are culturally valued. The condition of being female in a Western society that devalues women is not a resource but being a woman in a matriarchal society would be. Likewise, being a person of size in the United States, where thinness is the standard of beauty, is not a resource, but in other cultures where size is equated with power and wealth, being large would be a conditional resource. The third type of resource, *personal characteristics*, does not refer to attributes such as appearance or intelligence. Instead, Hobfoll used the term specifically to describe an individual's state of mind. In the COR model, personal characteristic refers to an optimistic outlook. An optimistic outlook that conceives of the world as predictable, orderly, and benign is a key resource and aids in resisting stress. The fourth type of resource, *energies*, refers to a variety of intangibles such as time, money, and knowledge. The main utility of energies is in allowing individuals to obtain resources of other types. *Social support*, which can mitigate stress, is not relegated to the four resources, but may be viewed as a resource when it provides other resources and/or facilitates their preservation.

According to Hobfoll (1989), when individuals deploy resources to counteract loss, they often engage in replacement strategies, they replace the original resource with an equivalent or with a symbolic substitute, or indirectly replace the resource with something different that fills the same need. Conservation strategies, on the other hand, do not involve deploying or replacing resources. Instead, individuals conserve resources by reinterpreting the loss as a challenge or a benefit or reevaluating the resource that has been lost and lowering its value, so they no longer experience a feeling of loss.

Because resources are not distributed equally, Hobfoll theorized that individuals with fewer resources would be the most vulnerable to additional losses. Individuals who can stockpile resources are protected by those stockpiles, allowing them to evaluate situations where their resources are threatened and apply resources in an effective manner. Individuals who start with depleted resources, however, have fewer options and may apply strategies that have a lower chance of success and, potentially, a high cost. Over time, individuals who start with fewer resources may apply resources ineffectively and experience multiple net losses, entering what Hobfoll termed a "loss spiral." As their resources become depleted, they lack the ability to offset additional loss, and depletion continues until their well-being is severely affected (Hobfoll, 1989).

Using Hobfoll's COR theory (1989) has important implications for the trans community. Because many trans people face challenges throughout the lifespan that make it difficult to acquire and accumulate resources, COR theory appears to predict that at least some individuals who are trans will experience a loss spiral, meaning they may enter older age with depleted resources. Trans individuals, however, may develop and employ adaptive COR strategies such as replacement and reevaluation that make them more resilient as they grow older. The conservation strategies trans women employed were explored, as well as whether specific resource conservation strategies contributed to strength and resiliency in older age.

### Review of Literature

According to Turner (2009), trans youth commonly experience disapproval and rejection from their parents. Parents may refuse to allow youth to transition, enforcing that refusal with harassment and punishment that penalizes them for dressing and acting in a way that is perceived as "inappropriate." In one study of familial responses to trans youth, 40% of participants described family reactions to their gender identity that were aggressively hostile, including verbal abuse and physical violence (Koken, Bimbi, & Parsons, 2009).

Parental rejection is known to have long-lasting consequences for individuals who are trans, putting them at risk for substance abuse, homelessness, incarceration, suicide, and survival crime such as sex work. Grant et al. (2011) cited figures from the National Transgender Discrimination Survey (NTDS) showing trans individuals who experienced familial rejection were three times more likely to be homeless than individuals whose families were accepting, and nearly twice as likely to become incarcerated or engage in substance abuse as those with accepting families. They also found that rejection increased suicidality dramatically. Fifty-one percent of participants in the NTDS who had experienced familial rejection reported attempting suicide versus 38% of those whose families were affirming.

Later in the life course, rejection by families of origin and intimate partners may result in reduced social supports. Social support from partners, family, and social institutions (such as formal religion) are important to older people because these supports can impact many facets of life, including health, perceived quality of life, and cognitive abilities (Witten, 2009). Cook-Daniels and munson (2010) (sic) suggested that many older trans individuals do not have access to the usual family and friend supports relied on by cisgendered elders because of the alienating effects of transphobia. Spousal support may be particularly at risk and losing a long-term spouse can leave a trans individual without a partner's support at particularly vulnerable times. Witten and Whittler (2004) noted that in some cases, transition may influence relationships with children as well. Children may feel abandoned and angry when a parent transitions, straining intergenerational relationships and further decreasing overall support from family.

Trans elders with diminished family and community supports may experience lower overall well-being and may be more likely to engage in what Witten and Whittler (2004) termed "self-care abuse" (p. 517). Preliminary studies appear to show support for this effect, such as Cook-Daniels and munson's (2010) report that midlife and older trans respondents in their study showed very high levels of self-neglect.

Individuals who are trans may find ways to compensate for lack of family support. Persson (2009) suggested that individuals who are trans may exhibit unique strengths and resiliencies in older age related to their gender identity, including coping skills developed during the coming-out process and a life-time of dealing with discrimination and oppression, lessened sensitivity to ageism since gender-related oppression is perceived as the dominant "ism," strong support from family-of-choice networks, and flexible gender role perceptions.

The purpose of this paper is to reflect on the experiences of a small sample of trans women relative to their families. Specifically, the three research questions concerned: (a) familial disapproval and rejection experienced by the older trans women; (b) strengths and resiliencies developed as a response to familial challenges; and (c) coping strategies employed to counteract lack of family of origin support.

## Methodology

The research design for this study was exploratory and qualitative. The study consisted of a series of interviews that were analyzed using grounded theory techniques. The interview format was semi-structured and was flexible enough to allow for probing questions and elaboration of topics or specific points that arose as the structured questions were answered.

The population for this study was trans individuals who were over the age of 55, lived in the United States, identified as women, and were living as women full-time. Individuals who were female-identified but who had not transitioned were eliminated from the sample frame. The target sample size was 10 to 12 individuals. Older trans women constitute a hidden population that is very difficult, if not impossible, to identify using probability sampling techniques, therefore nonprobability sampling techniques were used. To identify trans women over 55, a combination of convenience sampling and respondent-driven sampling (Icard, 2008) was utilized.

Since trans status is a sensitive issue with the potential to cause harm to participants if confidentiality is breached, particular attention was directed to ethical issues in the areas of informed consent and privacy. To protect the interests of participants, strict confidentiality was observed during data collection and analysis. Each participant was required to complete a consent form meeting the requirements of the Institutional Review Board (IRB), and participants were identified using pseudonyms in all transcriptions, including this chapter.

Data were analyzed and reported in two ways: (a) descriptive demographic analysis of the sample; and (b) grounded analysis of themes identified from the interviews. The interviews were transcribed by the first author and coded using an open coding scheme that allowed themes to develop from the data. Once initial coding had been completed, a second stage of focused coding was performed to identify core concepts and categories to facilitate analysis. Analysis took into account four general categories of phenomena – conditions or causes, interactions among people, strategies and tactics, and consequences (Monette, Sullivan, & DeJong, 2008). Once open coding was completed, and focused coding was applied to identify data categories and key concepts, the data were further analyzed to determine how the concepts and categories that emerged related to the research questions.

The coding scheme was developed by the first author and reviewed and double-coded by the second author. Results of the double coding were analyzed, and interrater reliability was acceptable.

## Findings

### Sample

A total of 11 trans women completed interviews as part of this study, and one trans woman's wife also offered comments. Demographic information gathered from the participants can be helpful in understanding the stories heard. Four participants were from the New England states, and one each from Virginia, Pennsylvania, Indiana, Colorado, Minnesota, Oregon, and Washington. The women who participated in the study ranged in age from 55 to 77 and were racially and ethnically homogenous, with 10 of the 11 participants identifying themselves as White and one participant identifying herself as Native American.

The study participants were generally well educated: All had graduated from high school and completed some form of post-secondary education or training, and nine of the 11 had received a college degree, either an associate's degree or a bachelor's degree. Four of the participants held post-graduate degrees.

Four of the women identified their sexual orientation as bisexual, four as lesbian, three as asexual/none, and one as "bisexual/queer/pansexual." All of the participants had been partnered at some point in their lives – the majority of them with women. Six of the 11 study participants reported they were partnered at the time of the interview, five with women and one with a man. Of the five participants who were not currently partnered, two were widowed after being married to women and three were divorced from women. One of the participants who reported her status as divorced was living platonically with her ex-wife.

### Familial Disapproval and Rejection

During focused coding, experiences with disapproval and rejection by family of origin emerged as a primary theme. Participants also revealed the *consequences* of the disapproval and rejection by their families. Two main concepts arose relating to disapproval and rejection within the participants' families of origin – correction and rejection. The first concept, correction, was a childhood phenomenon. Parents' actions, reactions, and words clearly alerted participants about the unacceptable nature of gender variant behavior. In some cases, the correction was overt. Mary, a 55-year-old scientist who transitioned in her 40s, related one such incident when her "stash" of female clothing was discovered and her parents made their expectations clear that she not engage in feminine behavior: ". . . At one point my stash got found and I kind of, you know, got sat down and, well, you know, 'Boys do this and girls do that.' You know, 'We'd like you to do that.'" Later on, this correction was reinforced when Mary expressed an interest in figure skating and her father insisted that she play a more appropriately "masculine" sport, ice hockey.

Like Mary, Georgette, a 65-year-old former engineer who went on disability to facilitate transition in her late 50s, was caught with female clothing and received a verbal correction from a parent. Georgette interpreted a correction from her mother as a warning to hide her gender-variant behavior if she could not change it.

> There was a coded message that you've just been busted, and you shouldn't be doing this. And if you are going to do this, then here's the protocol. I didn't know what sense to make out of that other than to hide things more carefully.

In other cases, corrections were subtle and sometimes, unspoken, yet participants still got the message – gender variance was wrong and should not be expressed, or it should be hidden. As Wendy, a 77-year-old activist who transitioned in her late 50s, put it: "It wasn't what the rest of my boy friends were doing . . . and I knew that my family probably didn't want to have to deal with it." Kelly, a 66-year-old retired electronics technician who transitioned at age 41, took the covert message to hide her difference to heart:

> The invisible child, that's what I tried be as much as possible. I stayed away from home as often as I could, I didn't have many friends, basically I'd go away and hide or go to the mall or something like that.

The second concept, rejection, was tied to transition and/or coming out to the family and could occur at any time during a participant's life. Participants spoke about rejection by parents, siblings, and children, as well as more distant relatives such as aunts and uncles. Rejection as described by participants could take the form of distancing or termination of a relationship, or it might entail refusing to affirm the participant's gender identity. Most of the participants told of family members who did not affirm their trans identity, although a few spoke of outright relationship termination. Heather, a 58-year-old lawyer on disability who transitioned in her late 40s, noted, "I was banned from coming home" due to rejection on the part of her mother. Isabelle, a 74-year-old former engraver who started transitioning at age 25, spoke of being rejected by her son due to his concerns that her gender identity would confuse his children or jeopardize custody of his stepson:

> I got on the phone and I was, I was asked not to come back any more. That uh, they thought that I was just going to be confusing the [grand]children. But then, ah, then there's the ah, the [grandchild's biological father] that's in the mix as well, and ah they were afraid that if he found out, that he would find some way to use it. Yeah, that some way he'd find a way to cause trouble with it. So that part of it, OK, I understand your issue. One the other side, come on, can't you stand up for me?

Julie, a 77-year-old retiree who transitioned at age 64, also experienced rejection by her son and was estranged from her grandchildren. She said, "My oldest son shut everything off. I am not allowed to come to his house. His children, for sixteen years, did not know their grandfather was a woman."

Georgette told of a more distant relative who terminated their relationship:

> I have an aunt who lives on the East Coast who is near the end of her life and she was my godmother . . . and we've corresponded at birthdays and Christmas for years and occasionally talked on the phone, and when I sent her a letter about my transition I've never heard from her since. And I sent her a couple more cards and no response and they didn't come back as undeliverable. Just no response.

Family members who did not affirm a participant's gender identity responded in a variety of ways. Some did not understand the difference between sexual orientation and gender identity, while others thought it would be easier if the participant were gay. Amanda, a 70-year-old retiree who transitioned at age 49, said of her parents: "They thought I was gay. They had no understanding. They just wanted it to go away. My mother was mostly concerned about what other people would think. And my father just wanted to be left alone." Anna, a 56-year-old musician who was transitioning for a second time, noted, "I had already come out as [gay], so when there was more coming out I think there was stuff like, 'Oh, it would have been easier if you were gay.'"

Others refused to accept the changes that occurred during transition. Isabelle's father told her, "I will tolerate it, but I won't accept it." She said, "He made it known for the rest of his life that I wasn't really his daughter. I was really his son." Beth, a 74-year-old retired engineer who began to transition at age 40, described her children's reaction: "They still love me, but they still want their dad. And I can understand that. They haven't lost me. I'm still here. I still love them as much. But, you know, they want their dad."

Participants reported that disapproval and rejection by families of origin had serious and long-lasting consequences, including mental anguish, depression, substance abuse, and suicidality; suppression of their authentic selves, and delayed transition. Although the negative reaction of loved ones took its toll, the participants also showed an amazing amount of strength and resiliency.

## Strengths and Resiliencies

Participants self-identified numerous strengths and resiliencies developed as a result of their experiences, including honesty, authenticity, positivity, perseverance, self-confidence, resourcefulness, self-sufficiency, decisiveness, self-awareness, giving up gendered expectations in dealing with others, not caring what others thought, seeing both male and female perspectives, combining male and female skill sets, and letting go of male personality attributes such as aggression. An additional strength, self-advocacy, was identified through focused coding.

The participants often saw strengths such as self-sufficiency, positivity, self-reliance, perseverance, resourcefulness, and decision-making as related to one another. Dora linked self-reliance to decision-making:

> I want to be incredibly self-reliant . . . I just don't want to
> impose on people. I think in a way it's a good quality. But
> it's just a side of me. One character of strength I got out
> of this is to a certain level being very, very self-sufficient.
> Making decisions.

Mary correlated decision-making with resourcefulness and self-reliance: "I did have to figure out something for the first time on my own [during transition]. It was actually a good thing to learn self-reliance, resourcefulness . . ." Isabelle saw a relationship between positivity and resiliency: "Resiliency . . . I can get over it pretty quickly . . . I try to find a way around [problems] with a positive resolution rather than just [finding] ways to fight back."

While all the strengths and abilities that were identified appeared to help participants navigate the challenges of daily living, the ability to engage in self-advocacy also appeared to increase participants' optimism about older age. One participant, Isabelle, noted that she no longer feared aging as a trans person, "because of what we're doing here at the [LGBT community center] . . . working to bring more awareness and knowledge to the caregivers and our society that [trans people] are here." Another participant, Wendy, was hopeful that her work with senior-care providers to offer appropriate, respectful care for elder LGBTs would facilitate her own aging as a trans person, and she was also confident in her ability to advocate for herself in older age, if necessary, saying, "I think I'm vocal enough and compelling enough to make a case for myself."

## Coping Strategies/Replacing Supports

Participants were asked to identify support systems, and focused coding was also used to identify coping strategies used by participants to counteract the loss of social support due to disapproval or familial rejection. The trans women interviewed indicated that they found their current partners provided essential support. Similarly, the participants created "families of choice" and were working toward forging relations with their families of origin.

**Relying on Intimate Partners.** When asked to identify their strongest support(s), most participants named their current partners. Ten of the eleven participants were currently partnered with women or had been partnered with women in the past; only one was partnered with a man. Female partners helped provide economic stability by increasing overall income and assets, and they also provided significant social support.

Isabelle explained how she and her ex-wife decided to move in together to conserve financial resources:

> We [decided we could] cast away half of all of our expenses, practically, all of the utilities that we were paying double, etc. etc. etc. . . . I had purchased a townhome and uh, I had room for two, where we would each have our own living spaces and share the common, you know, living room, dining room, uh kitchen, so forth. We'd each have our own suite, basically.

Isabelle acknowledged that entering into a shared living arrangement with her ex-wife made it possible for the two of them to live independently as they aged and avoid the cost of assisted living or nursing home care: "That was part of the original idea, so that we wouldn't be living alone and, uh, getting older as we are, that accidents can happen, falls can happen, but having someone there was an assurance, it was necessary."

Dora also described a shared living arrangement with an ex-partner that combined elements of economic and social support:

> I'm moving in with an old friend. I'm moving out this weekend. Actually, a woman that I had a sexual relationship with years ago. It's more of a friendship relationship, but it may change. We both gone through things. She was married twice, and I was married once - we go back years and years. She owns a house and her daughter and boyfriend live upstairs. The whole first floor is ours. I have my own bedroom and a big living room.

Participants who were doing well financially were clear about the ways in which their female partners contributed to their economic status. Citing her relative financial stability in retirement, Beth said, "I had a good job and my wife had a good job at Harvard . . . we had some savings, not a lot." Judy and Mary, who have been partnered since high school and work as government scientists, said they have been "very lucky" to have two incomes, characterizing their financial situation as "very stable."

Participants were also clear about the ways in which social support from their partners was important to their overall well-being in older age. Mary said bluntly, "I wouldn't be here without her." Beth said of her partner, "She was magnificent support. She had a wonderful heart and she died of lung cancer, but you know she was my true soul mate. We had twenty years together." Kelly described how her partner protected her in a way that others had not:

> I'll give you an example. We were renting at the time, Jeannie's been very protective of me, and the landlord where we were renting was very rude and abrupt to me one day and I mentioned it and she stormed off and gave him what for. Jeannie's a big woman. And she's very outgoing, I'm not. I tend to be on the reserved side. Definitely the reserved side. And she's very outgoing. I think honestly if anyone tried to mess with me and she was around, she'd deck them . . . it wasn't like that most of my life.

Anna's partner specifically affirmed her gender identity:

> All along in the household I am "A" and she is "D." Regardless of how I was presenting outside the house. Actu-

ally, that is a huge thing. I know some people who won't tell their spouse or something like that because ... they are sure that that is the end of the relationship and ... I am in a relationship where my partner knows and affirms who I am. And that is awesome. It's just awesome.

**Fostering Connection with Families of Origin/Families of Choice.** In addition to relying on intimate partners, participants consciously worked to foster relationships with accepting members of their families of origin and/or form new families of choice. Amanda found: "My brother went and had fits and threatened to kill me and all kinds of stuff . . . but, his daughter turned out to be one of my best friends and she's still one of my best friends." Georgette also found a relationship with more distant family of origin members was affirming:

> So I grew up in the Midwest and I had cousins who grew up in the Midwest and a whole branch of that cousin group moved here to the Seattle area so I told them about Georgette and a couple months later I got a call from one of them and they said "We're having Thanksgiving at my place and I'm inviting you and you can come as George or Georgette, it's your choice." So I went as Georgette and it was wonderful. And the younger generation was the second cousins and they were in their late 30s and they got the pronouns like that (snaps fingers) . . . And then after the dinner, I drove his wife, who is five years older than I am, and one of the daughters back to their place and we had, in the 20 minutes on the road, a really good woman-to-woman conversation.

Georgette cited the continuing cultivation of this relationship as a strategy aimed at ensuring she will have adequate social support as she ages in place in the Seattle area.

Forging new connections with family of choice could be as important as, or more important than, connections with family of origin. Beth declined to return to her native England after the death of her wife because her family of choice was so important to her:

> After my wife died, I was suspected of having bone cancer, which turned out to be a false alarm. And at the time I asked a woman if she would be my medical proxy that

was a public health nurse. Just to know she is a director of public health. And her family . . . she and her family took me under their wing. And they become part of my surrogate family here. All the rest of my family is over in England. When my wife died, a number of people said "Well, now you'll be going back to England to be with your family." And I said, "No, my life is here, my home is here, my social structure is here. This is where I belong."

Family of choice relationships were often formed with members of the lesbian and gay communities. Isabelle said:

Most of them have developed from the gay community. Some of my oldest friends that I still am close to, were people that I met early on in my search . . . looking for like minds and people who I could talk to and people who could understand what I am thinking and feeling. So, outside of the gay community I haven't got too many because, well, most people have just moved on anyway.

Dora explained how important the social support was that she gained from her LGBT family of choice:

I played in the women's softball league. If I hadn't done that at that particular point in time to get away and just find myself . . . I would not have had as good of a turnout. I found a new family. I found a new circle. It allowed me to grow into the person I wanted.

Mary's wife, Judy, identified their family of choice as a gay male couple:

We did have Bill and Donald when Donald was still alive. That was a definite second family of choice, a gay couple that we knew, that Donald was my best friend. He died of cancer a few years ago. I ended up moving in with Bill and Donald to help take care of Donald when he was sick . . . we were all very, very close.

### Discussion

Results of the study indicated that participants experienced disapproval and rejection throughout the life course from members of their families of origin and from intimate partners, and that familial disapproval and rejection had negative consequences that often continued to affect them later in life, the most severe of which were mental anguish, delay of transition, and divorce. In response to these familial challenges and other challenges in their lives, participants appeared to develop a number of strengths and resiliencies in older age and employed coping strategies to replace social supports lost due to familial disapproval and rejection. Coping strategies fell into two main categories: (a) relying on intimate partners; and (b) fostering connections with accepting members of their families of origin and/or forming families of choice.

These findings suggest that although family disapproval and rejection are distressing for trans women and have negative consequences throughout the life course, the strengths and resiliencies trans women develop in response to familial challenges and their ability to successfully employ coping strategies to replace social supports lost due to family rejection may mitigate the effects of familial disapproval and rejection and contribute to well-being in older age.

Hobfoll's Conservation of Resources (COR) theory states that individuals may behave in ways that increase their chances of acquiring and maintaining objects, personal characteristics, or conditions that are seen as positive or valuable, and replacing or reevaluating resources that are lost. It also predicts that individuals may conserve resources by reinterpreting loss as a challenge or a benefit or reevaluating a resource that has been lost and lowering its value, so they no longer experience a feeling of loss (Hobfoll, 1989).

Participants in this study demonstrated all types of behaviors predicted by Hobfoll's COR theory. They suppressed their true gender identities to please their families when young. They allied with female partners and maintained family connections to increase their changes of acquiring and increasing conditions (social support) and personal resources (self-esteem). And they conserved resources by reevaluating (reframing) negative experiences.

## Suggestions for Policy and Advocacy

Results of this study indicated that female partners were an important source of security and support for participants. The trans women in this study identified numerous examples of stress-related growth in the form of strengths and resiliencies resulting from the challenges of living as gender-variant individuals. Because social connection appears to foster stress-related growth (Cox, Dewaele, van Houtte, & Vincke,

2011; Tedeschi & McNally, 2011), and because some older trans women may lack social supports due to familial rejection, working to keep trans women connected with family (including family of choice), community, and friends may be effective in increasing their well-being. Mobility issues and lack of access to transportation can impede social connections in older age, so significant others, family members, allies, care providers, and social workers may need to problem-solve to keep older trans women from becoming isolated. Another approach may be to provide trans women with the opportunity to tell their stories and share the entirety of their experiences, including traumatic experiences. One-on-one interactions, family gatherings, support groups, qualitative research studies, classrooms, and oral history projects all provide settings in which trans women might be encouraged to share their experiences. It may also be beneficial to encourage older trans women to engage in activism by volunteering with trans rights organizations or groups with a broader civil rights focus, such as the National Center for Lesbian Rights or the American Civil Liberties Union. Finally, because an accepting social environment appears to encourage stress-related growth (Cox et al., 2011), friends, family members, allies, and providers can monitor their own responses to trans women to ensure they are providing an affirming environment.

## Limitations

This study has limitations. The exploratory nature of the study precludes any possibility of generalized results. The participants in this study were quite homogeneous – primarily White, well-educated, and relatively well-off financially – a direct result of the combination of convenience and respondent-driven sampling. The sample also lacked women of advanced age (age 80 or over), individuals of color, individuals without post-secondary school education, individuals from an urban environment, individuals in assisted living or nursing homes, and individuals of lower socioeconomic status. The sample also lacked participants from the southern United States. In any sample population, diversity helps researchers and practitioners understand the circumstances and resources that might be different from a middle-income sample. Financial and educational resources, as well as where one lives, can, and will, impact an individual's life experiences. A second limitation concerns how transition was addressed.

The study did not capture the experiences of an entire group of older individuals who identified as trans female but who could not transition due to the threat of discrimination. Nor did the study discriminate between individuals who transitioned socially, via the use of hormones, or by undergoing sexual reassignment surgery.

Finally, the study did not differentiate between the experiences of those who transitioned early in life and those who transitioned later. The majority of participants in this study were what could be considered "late transitioners." The differing social contexts and varied intersectionality of these populations suggest that findings might be more divergent if the study had recruited individuals who did not transition, included questions relating to method of transition, or gathered data on how the participants' experiences related to age at transition.

## Future Research

Since research in the field of trans aging is limited, there are multiple opportunities for future research. One suggestion would be to expand this study. Working with a larger sample, focusing on other experiences (such as employment), and using different sampling techniques that produce more diversity, particularly in the areas of advanced age, race/ethnicity, socioeconomic status, educational level, living situation (assisted living/nursing home), and geographical location, would yield additional and potentially more diverse data on the experiences of older trans women. The inquiry could also be expanded to include trans men, whose experiences might be markedly different than those of trans women.

Because social and historical context plays an important role in the experiences of trans women, it will be important to continue gathering data on aging in the trans female community in light of ongoing social and legal changes such as the institution of state and national protections against discrimination related to gender identity and the legalization of same-sex marriage. Ongoing studies can provide important information about how social realities are changing and what the effects of those changes are for the next wave of aging trans women.

## Conclusion

The body of research on trans aging remains limited. This study represents a first step in understanding the lived experiences of trans elders and suggests some directions for future research and legal/policy efforts. It is important to remember that although the results of this study showed the participants faced significant challenges in their family relationships, focusing on strengths as well as deficits revealed some important new information about the ways older trans women adapted to and coped with the challenges of living in a world which is not affirming of gender diversity.

By examining the participants' strengths and resiliencies, as well as their strategies in replacing lost social supports, this study showed the lives of older trans people are defined by more than deficits.  Their life stories are rich, varied, and include successes as well as challenges.  The trans women in this study demonstrated success in maintaining loving relationships with long-time partners and drawing strength from connections with families of origin as well as families of choice.  As researchers, allies, and advocates continue to explore the lives of trans elders, using this technique of focusing on successes as well as challenges can help create a body of work that reflects the diverse experiences of this population and informs efforts to improve their well-being in older age.

## References

Cook-Daniels, L., & munson, m. (2010). Sexual violence, elder abuse, and sexuality of transgender adults, age 50+: Results of three surveys. *Journal of GLBT Family Studies, 6*(2), 142-177. doi:10.1080/15504281003705238

Cox, N., Dewaele, A., van Houtte, M., & Vincke, J. (2011). Stress-related growth, coming out, and internalized homonegativity in lesbian, gay, and bisexual youth. An examination of stress-related growth within the minority stress model. *Journal of Homosexuality, 58*(1), 117-137. doi:10.1080/00918369.2011.533631

Grant, J. M., Mottet, L. A., Tanis, J., Harrison, J., Herman, J. L., & Keisling, M. (2011). *Injustice at every turn: A Report of the National Transgender Discrimination Survey*. Washington, D.C.: National Center for Transgender Equality and National Gay and Lesbian Task Force.

Hobfoll, S. (1989). Conservation of resources: A new attempt at conceptualizing stress. *American Psychologist, 44*(3), 513-524. doi:10.1037/0003-066X.44.3.513

Icard, L. D. (2008). Reaching African-American men on the "down low": Sampling hidden populations: Implications for HIV prevention. *Journal of Homosexuality, 55*(3), 437-449.  doi:10.1080/00918360802345198

Koken, J. A., Bimbi, D. S., & Parsons, J. T. (2009). Experiences of familial acceptance–rejection among transwomen of color. *Journal of Family*

*Psychology, 23*(6), 853-860. doi: 10.1037/a0017198

Langley, L. K. (2006). Self-determination in a gender fundamentalist state: toward legal liberation of transgender identities. *Texas Journal on Civil Liberties & Civil Rights, 12*(1/2), 101-131.

Lombardi, E. (2010). Transgender health: A review and guidance for future research. Proceedings from the Summer Institute at the Center for Research on Health and Sexual Orientation, University of Pittsburgh. *International Journal of Transgenderism, 12*(4), 211-229. doi:10.1080/ 15532739.2010.544232

Monette, D., Sullivan, T., & DeJong, C. (2008). *Applied social research: A tool for the human services*. Belmont, CA: Thomson/Wadsworth.

Persson, D. (2009). Unique challenges of transgender aging: Implications from the literature. *Journal of Gerontological Social Work, 52*(6), 633-646. doi:10.1080/01634370802609056.

Smith, S., Hamon, R., Ingoldsby, B., & Miller, J.E. (2009). *Exploring family theories* (2nd Ed.). New York: Oxford University Press.

Tedeschi, R. G., & McNally, R. J. (2011). Can we facilitate posttraumatic growth in combat veterans? *American Psychologist, 66*(1), 19-24. doi:10.1037/a0021896

Turner, J. (2009). From the inside out: Calling on states to provide medically necessary care to transgender youth in foster care. *Family Court Review, 47*(3), 552-569.

Witten, T. (2009). Graceful exits: Intersection of aging, transgender identities, and the family/community. *Journal of GLBT Family Studies, 5*(1/2), 35-61. doi:10.1080/15504280802595378.

Witten, T., & Whittler, S. (2004). Transpanthers: The greying of transgender and the law. *Deakin Law Review, 9*(2), 503-522.

Yu, V. (2010). Shelter and transitional housing for transgender youth. *Journal of Gay and Lesbian Mental Health, 14*(4), 340-345. doi:10.1080/19359705.2010.504476

Chapter 9

## Themes from Elder Financial Exploitation by

## Family Member Powers of Attorney

*Pamela B. Teaster*
Virgina Tech

*Virginia Vincenti*
Univesity of Wyoming

*Axton Betz-Hamilton*
South Dakota State University

*Cory Bolkan*
Washington State University

*Cynthia Jasper*
University of Wisconsin - Madison

The authors gratefully acknowledge funding from USDA-NIFA through the Wyoming Agriculture Experiment Station, University of Wyoming Social Justice Research Center, Phi Upsilon Omicron and Kappa Omicron Nu FCS honor societies.

Acknowledgements: Lorna Browne, Ph.D., Lecturer, Morgan State University; Ken Gerow, Ph.D., University of Wyoming; Karen Goebel, Ph.D., Professor Emeritus, University of Wisconsin-Madison; Jenna Hotovec, MS, University of Wyoming; Don Rudisuhle, MBA, CFE, Eldertheft Forensics; Yuxin Zhao, B.A., Virginia Tech.

Elder financial exploitation (EFE) of older adults is a widespread and growing problem. In response, the field studying elder mistreatment has grown exponentially, particularly examinations of the subtype area of financial exploitation. Most researchers have focused on identification of the problem. Little work has been conducted on *how* and *why* exploitation occurs, particularly within the family unit. Our exploratory study involving interviews with family members whose older loved ones experienced elder family financial exploitation by person with power of attorney (POA EFFE) is a reaction to the under-reporting and high estimates of EFE occurrence overall, as well as an attempt to understand this unique form of exploitation. Our work adds to the growing body of elder financial exploitation literature because exploiting POA agents (hereafter referred to as power of attorney) are unregulated and their exploitive actions are poorly understood.

## Literature Review

Current demographic trends indicate that the older adult population (aged 65+) is expected to double by 2030 in the United States (Federal Interagency Forum on Aging-Related Statistics, 2012) and that the fastest growing segment of the population is aged 85+. Although there are several ways in which older adults have surrogate decision makers, (e.g., representative payees, bank account signatories, conservatorships, guardianships, quitclaim deeds, and/or trusts), all decision makers are legally bound to act in the best interests of the older person. Older adults with physical and/or cognitive declines in need of increased support or assistance may designate a POA for surrogate decision making for financial, health care, or both. Typically, family members are designated (Gunther, 2011).

Research has been conducted in the areas of elder financial capacity (Sherod et al., 2009), scope of the problem (Acierno et al., 2010; Lifespan Greater Rochester, 2011), outcomes of the problem (Huang & Lawitz, 2016), and types of the problem (Jackson & Hafemeister, 2012). Most studies reveal that family members are chiefly responsible for the perpetration of EFE; moreover, the dollar amounts of the exploitation may be higher than other forms of financial exploitation, such as medical fraud, telemarketing fraud, and other scams (Metlife Mature Market, 2009; 2011). On a national scope, the National Elder Mistreatment Study by Acierno and colleagues (2010) concerned 5,777 community-dwelling adults aged 60 and older and 813 proxies who were interviewed about five types of elder abuse. Findings revealed current financial exploitation by family members at 5.2% and lifetime financial exploitation by a stranger at 6.5%. Spouses or intimate partners were far more likely than were adult children to perpetrate most types of elder abuse.

Similarly, and at the state level, a study by Lifespan of Greater Rochester (2011), another large-scale, population-based, study revealed how infrequently elder abuse situations come to the attention of authorities. The study, which examined self-reported and documented case data on the incidence of elder abuse among elderly New York residents, consisted of 4,156 community-dwelling adults older than age 60 or their proxies and 292 agencies, including Adult Protective Services, Area Agencies on Aging, and law enforcement. Results revealed a self-reported, past-year elder abuse rate of 7.6 percent, led by financial abuse at 4.2 percent.

A study by MetLife Mature Market Institute (2011) revealed that each year elder victims lose a minimum of $2.9 billion, losses that produce an extensive personal and financial impact on both victims and their families. One distinct type of exploitation is that perpetrated by family members appointed as power of attorney (POA EFFE). POA documents, executed for the purposes of respecting wishes concerning health and finances, are easily created and implemented with little oversight. Although these powers have the potential to help an older adult remain autonomous, avoid guardianship, and limit costs to elders in a vulnerable stage of life (Stiegel & Klem, 2008), they also have the potential for exploitation. POA EFFE is rapidly increasing as a function of the growth of the older adult population (Stiegel & Klem, 2008) and because older adults control the lion's share of wealth in the country (Metlife Mature Market Institute, 2009). A lack of reporting to authorities, coupled with the surprisingly high reports by elders experiencing EFE, point to the importance of studying POA EFFE, something about which very little is known (Gunther, 2011).

**Power of Attorney and Elder Financial Exploitation**

Costs associated with financial exploitation are high. A Metlife Mature Market Institute Study (2011, p. 6) found that the annual financial loss to victims of EFE referred to above increased 12% from 2008 to 2010. This figure fails to include estimates in excess of tens of billions of dollars "in health care, social services, investigative and legal costs, and lost income and assets" (MetLife Mature Market Institute, 2009, p. 6). Gunther (2011) reported that the costs of financial exploitation in the State of Utah alone are an estimated $1 million per week.

POA EFFE goes largely unreported and unabated (Acierno et al., 2010; Gunther, 2011; Rabiner, O'Keefe & Brown, 2004). Under-reporting occurs for multiple reasons: elder victims may not recognize behaviors as exploitive; they may remain silent because of shame, self-blame, fear of retaliation and/or further loss of independence; and they may fear loss of the support they receive from the abuser (Hafemeister, 2003; Rabiner, Brown, & O'Keeffe, 2006). Victims may also feel sympathetic and protective of the exploiter, especially when family loyalties, codependency, substance abuse, and mental illness are involved (Capezuti, Brush, & Lawson, 1997).

Extant data lack uniformity and exist only at the state level (Stiegel & Klem, 2008). Of the EFE cases reported, a national survey of state Adult Protective Services (APS) agencies found that only 14.7 percent were substantiated (Teaster, Dugar, Mendiondo, Abner, & Cecil, 2006). Because EFE often goes unreported, it remains a secret within many families. Estimates of the incidence of elder financial exploitation range from as low as 10 (Thomas, 2014) to as high as 44 (Lifespan of Greater Rochester, 2011) unreported cases for every one reported to authorities.

From data provided in reported cases, family members appointed as POA by elderly relatives are frequent perpetrators of EFE (MetLife Mature Market Institute, 2011). The MetLife Mature Market Institute studies (2009; 2011) are widely cited in connection with this concern; however, these studies relied solely upon secondary press accounts of EFE because firsthand accounts are extremely difficult to obtain. Rabiner, O'Keeffe, and Brown (2004) emphasized that it is important to learn about characteristics, causes, and consequences of EFE and that the family system represents a critical place to examine these factors. Understanding the characteristics of those who experience EFE, its antecedents, and consequences is crucial to prevention and intervention efforts. Being able to understand family systems where POA EFFE occurred adds to an understanding of risk and protective factors related to EFE.

## Characteristics of EFFE Perpetrators and Victims

Data on reported cases of POA EFFE indicates that those who have responsibility for both caregiving and financial management are more likely to exploit (Stiegel & Klem, 2008) than those without both responsibilities. Stress caused by time, energy, and emotional demands of caring for someone with increasing needs and the demands of financial management responsibilities may be intensified by the lack of understanding of physical/mental changes that can occur with aging (James, 1994).

Prior researchers report that older (>75) White women who live alone are a high-risk group for financial abuse (Tueth, 2000). There are a number of explanations for this finding. For example, because women live longer than men, more women are available to be financially exploited. Furthermore, societal gender stereotypes that portray women as weak and vulnerable may also contribute to victimization. Cohort effects associated with gender role expectations can also play a role in financial exploitation; many widowed older women may not have experience handling household finances, opening the door for perpetrators to step in under the guise of helping. Few researchers have specifically examined gender differences and gender roles in elder abuse in general. Among those that have examined gender as a significant factor in elder abuse, the results have been mixed with some studies finding no gender differences in prevalence (Yon, et al., 2014; 2017). These mixed results underscore an empirical need for more focused attention on understanding gender within the context of elder abuse in general, and elder financial exploitation in particular.

**Theoretical Frameworks and Concepts**

Because there are multiple levels of opportunities and barriers that people experience in maintaining financial well-being in later life and victims of EFE are embedded within a system of hierarchical contexts (e.g., individual, family, community, society), a socio-ecological approach is useful for understanding the problem. As an organizing framework for intervention and its sustainability, Bronfenbrenner's (1979; 1986) Ecological Systems Theory provides a focus on the elder victim and four influencing systems (see Figure 1):

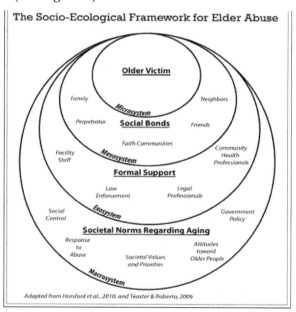

*Figure 1. The Socio-Ecological Framework for Elder Financial Exploitation*

(a) the *microsystem* is the elder victim within his or her environment, (b) the *mesosystem* represents the relationship between the victim and relatives and friends; (c) the *exosystem* represents environments external to the victim (e.g., community services) that may affect his or her well-being; and (d) the *macrosystem* includes broad ideological values, norms, and cultural and institutional patterns (e.g., state/federal programs and regulations/policies) (Horsford, Parra-Cardona, Post, & Schiamberg, 2010; Parra-Cardona, Meyer, Schiamberg, & Post, 2007).

It is important to examine EFE within the family system because the etiology of EFE and the variables that influence a perpetrator's decision to engage in exploitative behaviors are highly complex. People experiencing EFE are not isolated agents but rather are embedded within and influenced by intricate social and environmental networks. A broad perspective increases our understanding of these complicated issues.

## Research Design and Methods

Because so little research is available on POA EFFE, we used a qualitative approach (Patton, 2014) to investigate how and why trusted POA family members use their authority to perpetrate EFE. We decided after a few interviews that we needed to explore different family member perspectives within the same family. When possible, we interviewed two or three family members within the 10 individual family cases.

### Participant Recruitment

Using a convenience sample, we recruited 14 participants from nine states by distributing flyers, contacting staff members at senior centers, word-of-mouth, email, and sharing information about the study at professional conferences. Participants were 18 years of age or older who believed that their loved one age 60 or older was a victim of POA EFFE. The study was approved by the University of Wyoming Institutional Review Board.

### Study Instrument and Data Collection

The interview guide was developed by members of the research team and included semi-structured interview questions adapted from Siedman's (1998) phenomenological approach involving three separate, in-depth interviews. Questions focused on family systems as the primary social systems in POA EFFE. The inquiry explored characteristics of older adults that made them vulnerable to perpetrators, relationship types, power and exchange dynamics, social networks of the victims and perpetrators, and the dynamics of the financial abuse itself. Questions for Interview I explored significant experiences that the interview participant perceived to be foundational to the EFE. Probing questions included exploring relationships between elders, perpetrators, and other family members. Questions for Interview II concerned details related to the exploitation, including who was involved and how was it handled by perpetrators, other family members, lawyers, Adult Protective Services, mediators, guardians and any others who were involved. Interview III focused on short- and long-term impacts on participants, elders, and family members.

## Data Collection

Data were gathered through recorded interviews conducted by three co-investigators on the research team. Most participants were interviewed in-person (eight); however, four interviews were conducted by telephone due to issues of distance, and one interview was conducted both in person and via telephone, again due to distance. According to Novick (2008), telephone interviews are an adequate alternative to in-person interviews. Each of the three interviews was between 60 and 90 minutes in duration. Some interviews were separated by a couple of days, and others combined into one interview session depending on schedules and accessibility. During each interview, sketching a genogram, or a graphic representation of at least three generations in a family system (Chrazstowsi, 2011), for each family which helped the interviewer to remain clear about who family members were and their relationship to each other during the interview process. The genogram proved helpful in later analyses.

## Data Analysis

Prior to analysis of the interview transcripts, pseudonyms were assigned to ensure confidentiality for the participants, victims, and other individuals. During the coding process using NVivo 11, investigators thoroughly read and analyzed each transcript to code salient excerpts. Discussions among researchers addressed differences in order to achieve consensus on incongruent coding of particular excerpts to aid the team's interpretation of participants' experiences. Subsequently, team members reviewed codes and grouped them into categories until consensus was achieved. They then used the same procedure to identify broader themes. The current analysis focused on the theme of risk factors within families for EFE as well as explored its gendered aspects.

# Results

## Participants

Data were gathered between 2011 and 2013 concerning eight female and five male victims aged 60+. Fourteen study participants aged 18+ (11 females and 3 males) were recruited via snowball sampling and were assigned pseudonyms by the study team. Among the participants from the 10 families, there were 10 daughters or step-daughters, one granddaughter, two sons, and one son-in law (Table 1). Three couples were victims; the rest were either widows or widowers. Study participants described POA EFFE by nine female and four male perpetrators.

| Families | Participants | Victims | Perpetrators | Victim Marital Status |
|---|---|---|---|---|
| Tyler | Three stepdaughters | Alyssa | nephew and girlfriend (fictive daughter) | widowed |
| Jefferson | Marilyn and Rod (daughter and son-in -law of victim) | Holly | Noah & Morris (husband) (son) | married, then widowed |
| Hunter | Shauna (daughter & co-POA) | Parents | Middle daughter (Hilary) & son-in-law (Eddie) | married |
| Peterson | Bryce (son) | mother | daughter | |
| Marks | Joyce (granddaughter) | grandmother | Karla (daughter) Chris (husband) | divorced |
| Matthews | Opal & Adrian (son & daughter) | mother | Erin (daughter) | widowed with partner |
| Quinn | Susie (daughter) | father | son and granddaughter | widowed |

Table 1. Summary of Particpants, Victims, and Perpetrators

## Family Risk Factors for Exploitation

For this monograph, we report on the entire sample and themes that emerged from transcripts that revealed gender issues. Below, we discuss three major themes emanating from coding the interviews. One theme dealt directly with family dynamics, particularly when one or more family members became dominant or dominating as well as coercive of the parent and/or other family member. Another theme was family communication, or the lack thereof, influenced by: (a) family cultural communication patterns, (b) family members' reactions to authority shifting to the POA agent(s) from parent(s), (c) geographic proximity, and/or (d) the time period and stages of the life course of relatives. A third theme was family members' inability to recognize that POA EFFE was occurring, including factors, either individual, systemic, or in combination, that thwarted attempts to remedy the exploitive situation. We conclude with a discussion on the gendered aspects of EFE that emerged from the participants' experiences.

## Theme I: Family Dynamics *(Micro and Mesosystem Levels)*

**Risks Inherent in Power Dynamics among Family Members.**
One risk factor that arose in our coding was that of a dominant family
member. In some cases, there was a dominant parent, who, in addition to
controlling a spouse and children, not surprisingly, controlled the family's finances. This typology reflects an earlier time in the mid-twentieth
century when control by a paternal head of the household was normative.
However, as the controlling parent aged, the practice that involved not
sharing the family financial decisions with a spouse or other members of
the family became an opportunity for POA EFFE. Such was the case of
Shawna's father and mother.

> ...because my father took care of everything... I got the impression
> that he didn't consult with her [the mother] on almost anything
> and maybe that got worse as they aged, maybe it wasn't quite that
> way when their younger years but when I became aware that she
> didn't know what was going on, he didn't ask her, he just did
> things....

Because Shawna's mother knew little of the family finances, she
was willing to respond to the requests of her other daughter, Hilary. One
of two trusted daughters she and her husband had named as POA, Hilary
lived nearby. The other agent, Shawna, lived 2,000 miles away, but vis-
ited her mother frequently. Because of the controlling relationship modeled by her parents, Hilary was submissive to her controlling father, and
later, to her own spouse, Eddie. Again, Shawna explained that her mother
*would have signed anything Hilary asked her to sign because she trusted Hilary.*
This dependency opened the door for eventual exploitation by Hilary and
her husband.

In another example of family domination, Rod remarked that
his father-in-law, Noah, wanted his wife Holly to obtain money that her
parents had put in a trust for her in order to support his failing business.
He coerced Holly into giving him money from her trust, which was established to protect her from her husband's poor financial management.
This type of acquiescence is not uncommon among this generation of
women, as mentioned in Shauna's case above.

The experience of Bryce provides yet another example of power
dynamics within the family. In this situation, Bryce believed his sister's
power and control over their mother enabled POA EFFE:

> I think she may have misled my mom in some other ways just to
> keep my mom's emotions happy, and I certainly understand, I'd
> be willing to do the same thing to not be totally self-disclosing to

somebody who was going to be easily agitated etc. But, I don't believe . . . the primary thing was this. . . . I don't think that she dared let my mom know . . . what my mom was signing or she would have never signed it.

**Risks of Coercion and Control Through Entitlement and Guilt.** A typical scenario of POA EFFE is one in which children who cannot seem to survive on their own, due to personality traits and sometimes in concert with mental health issues, physical health issues, drugs, or alcohol, become highly dependent upon the older parent. According to Tueth (2000), some perpetrators are career criminals who lack a history of long-term and stable relationships. The infirmity of the elder becomes the occasion to provide "help," but the offer of assistance is really an opportunity to move into the elder's home and control him or her, especially the finances. Joyce described such a situation in which her Aunt Karla had experienced financial problems for a long time.

> . . . Grandma started having these strokes, . . . Karla and Chris moved in with her . . . because Karla couldn't afford an apartment . . . she didn't have power of attorney at the time, but she would take Grandma to the bank and withdraw sums of money.

A second example is exemplified in Bryce's family, where the sister became even more controlling after becoming a single parent of four children.

> ... my sister was, uh was divorced and a single mom with four kids and I think her way of coping with her single status... was to be a real type-A kind of controlling person. Uh, a couple times when I would drop my mom off, I literally would leave early because I just, quite frankly, couldn't stand being around my sister and her attitude. My mom could put up with that and indeed they, I think, benefited from each other's company um for a couple of months and then she would get fed up... with my sister and want to come back to her home.

Bryce's sister later exerted power and control to coerce their mother into signing legal documents and maintained little communication with Bryce about the well-being of their mother.

**Risk of Control Through Deception and Threats.** Some instances of POA EFFE are accomplished through deception, which was often facilitated by other family members.  Below is an example of a deceptive situation.  Again, Bryce explained.

> ...[I]t was done in my sister's lawyer's office who my mom was led to believe, and correctly so,[that] this is a woman who makes her living in dealing with senior issues, who writes powers of attorney all the time, so she had a collaborator. The collaborator in this... collusion, in this little deception, was this big heavy-hitting player who's considered one of the best senior-oriented attorneys in Maryland....The document had to be as nitty-gritty detailed about ...all of the financial but all the other health [matters]. The document was so extensive it basically let my sister run my mom.

Deception by family members and by collaterals enabling the deception isolates the elder. Family members who seek to gain access are thwarted by the deception, which draws the noose of isolation tighter, with the elder complicit with the deceptive acts because she is unaware of the actual situation.

In some instances, family members controlled each other through threats regarding persons or the disposal of the estate, as in the case of Marilyn, who was actually afraid of her brother, Morris.

> I know he's my brother, and, I mean, we're not close. As children um, well he had behavioral problems and, and so basically, I was afraid of him a lot when I was a little kid, you know, like he'd say, "do this for me". [And raise his fist in the air].

Morris became POA for their mother, Holly, who, like his deceased father, also coerced  his mother into giving him her trust funds.

In another example of a family member's threatening behavior, Bryce recounted that his sister

> ...threatened to sell the house out from under me [laughs] because . . . she saw it as an encumbrance[.] . . . by that time I had paid . . . [the mortgage down to] about twelve thousand, my place is worth about two hundred thousand. But she had control of it and she basically threatened, she threatened to sell my place out from under me, which is my retirement income, those four units, I'm living in one of my four units. Um, you know, that's pretty, that's pretty bizarre.

Threats had the double effect of endangering the elder and family members. Consequently, as shown below, communication between and among family members diminished or stopped altogether.

## Theme II: Family Communication *(Micro and Mesosystem Levels)*
**Risks Inherent in Family Structure, Communication, and Culture.** A second risk factor was that of family structure, particularly its unique culture and communication style. In the family of Bryce, early traumatic events significantly affected the family culture:

> …my brothers were one and a half and two and a half years old when my father was killed in a house fire. They ended up spending nine to fifteen months in a hospital because of their second and third degree burns, it was really traumatic…I was at the dentist so I wasn't involved with the fire, I said my sister was in the womb, uh, at the time that that happened so she was isolated from that tragedy, from the stress and trauma of that.

As a result of the tragedy that Bryce's sister was born into, Bryce and his sister never felt close to their two older brothers, who dealt with lifelong, lingering trauma. Bryce's sister may have suffered from inadequate attachment to her caregivers due to the attention her older siblings required during their recovery. The eldest brothers were distanced from their younger siblings and were uninvolved in the later care of their mother.

In the experience of Adrian, the family culture centered around values of rugged individualism, which resulted in distanced family relationships. In addition, birth order and age differences between siblings contributed to ambivalent adult sibling relationships. According to Adrian,

> …[Y]ou know, by the time I . . . came around, my older brother and sister were off in school and then by the time uh my younger brother, or sisters came around, I was in school so you know, we were um actually … three separate groups.

Adrian stressed that one of his siblings thought that their mother should just take care of herself, a mindset that led to POA EFFE later.

> …you know, um his comment to me was that well you know, mom's very capable of handling her own affairs and, you know, it's none of our business, um, and uh you know, he told me that, you know, she's an adult, she's still . . . under Wyoming law . . . she's perfectly capable of making her own decisions.

Alternately, Adrian was quick to point out that his mom was becoming quite frail and unable to care for herself.

> And she had a bladder infection and we didn't know, . . . there was all kinds of issues but because of both medical and, you know, confidentialities we have no idea what my mother's true medical condition is. To this day, we don't know. Because we, we have no access to that information because of the way the law is set up…And we're not getting it from my sister who will not tell us anything. She, she won't communicate with us at all. And my mom, … at this point, …we don't know if she's … has dementia, or Alzheimer's.

The lack of communication reflected the lack of family closeness, which also created a risk factor for POA EFFE later. Family closeness was diminished by distance, age, and family culture. As another example of lack of family closeness, Bryce observed, "we just moved in different circles and, you know, if we'd been in an adjacent town, in an adjacent block it might have been different, but literally we were a family in name only."

## Theme III: Attempts to Intervene in the Exploitive Situation (*Meso and Exosystem Levels*)

At some point, family members realized that exploitation was occurring, and they tried to confront the problem themselves. Their early efforts were often greeted with roadblocks. For example, Opal remarked, "We've offered along the way to all pick up the slack and divide the responsibilities and um help however we could, but we get, you know, we get just a blank stare."

Similarly, when family members tried to extract information from the elder, their efforts were unsuccessful, Adrian, Opal's brother, tried to assist, but to no avail:

> …we tried to give her a, like I said, we had an estate planning type book to where we could sit down and say, "okay, mom, you know uh if something were to happen how, you know, how would we know where anything is? What. . . are your wishes, you know? Where do you want to buried, what are your . . . wants, needs, desires?" And she, she just blew us off . . .

It was very unclear whether their sister, Erin, had POA. Adrian had many questions. He felt like he was unable to get information, stressing that he was shut out by his mother and sister and hindered from getting information from professionals by the Health Insurance Portability and Accountability Act (HIPAA). Also, apparent in the interviews was how stressful and difficult it is for family members to determine who actually has the POA designation and the powers extended to him or her. Not knowing whether his sister had POA authority, Adrian, questioned:

> . . . if uh my sister does have power of attorney, how would you officially or unofficially, … find these kind[s] of things out? …..What are my mother's wishes in all of this[?] You know, … what steps and actions have been taken? We don't know.

**Gendered Aspects of EFE** *(Micro, Meso, Exo, and Macrosystem Levels)*

We also observed how gender played a role in POA EFFE. For example, elements of power dynamics, control, and coercion that were exemplified in the themes described above can also be interpreted as representative of stereotypical masculine gender roles. In research on intimate partner violence, masculinity and gender roles have been used as a predictor for potential violent behavior; although more evidence is needed to understand the potential link between gender roles and abuse (Anderson, 2005), especially regarding elder financial exploitation.

Another example of how gender potentially plays a role in POA EFFE is when an elder's choice of POA is based on gender biases, with the most obvious example illustrated by Susie's story:

> my father comes from the old school that males always understand financial situations better. Unfortunately, in my own family, it turns out that my brother doesn't have a clue and [Laughs] I have a background in personal [and] family [finance]. So, I would relate the information to my brother to relate it back to my father, and then it would have to become my father's idea. I was very clever at that. [Laughs] But, finally when he, my father, realized that some things didn't seem right and my husband took all the records that he had and made some sense out of them, and this involved hundreds and hundreds of hours of work, and we set up spreadsheets and sent this information to my father, my father finally realized who was the expert in finance. [Laughs] So, then he started to rely on me for double checking and we found situations where bills had been paid two or three times, and then other bills had not been paid at all, into the point of adding additional liability in this, um, apartment complex [that my father owned].

Due to gendered caregiver roles, choice of POA was selected, in many instances, because the caregiver was proximal to the elder and already providing him or her some help. Thus, the primary caregiver, regardless of competency to manage the elder's funds, became the elder's designee for POA. An example of this gendered choice is evident in the case of Bryce and his sister:

> My sister, she really cared about family. For example, twice in my mom's last year she called me, once in print and twice on the phone, and … said, "Bryce, you more than any of my other brothers call and talk to mom, thank you for that, I really appreciate that." So, she was sensitive to my mom's needs and she appreciated me, although when I went there, heaven help me, after the first feel-good twenty-four hours, it was really difficult being in her household. But, you know, we're all a mixed bag.

With a rise in gender fluidity and the changing landscape of gender identity, societal understanding of gender roles may evolve significantly for future cohorts. It will remain an important empirical question to explore how gender roles may play as a risk or protective factor for elder financial exploitation.

## Discussion

From the interviews, we identified several risk factors for exploitation by a family member POA. The major themes that emerged from the families' experiences can be best understood from a socio-ecological systems framework. Although our focus was on the context of family dynamics, we noted several individual, *microsystem level* risk factors that appeared to put elder victims at risk. In multiple incidents, for example, the declining health status of the elder victim was associated with POA EFFE.

At the *mesosystem level* (comprising the relationship between elder victim and family members), the three-interview sequence revealed risk factors associated with family dynamics and family communication. For example, the inappropriate exercise of power and control was a common problem emanating in both the *micro and mesosystem levels* of interaction. Some exploiting family members simply continued patterns of parental financial rescue behaviors that past generations had already modeled for them, although it was not apparent from the interviews that the earlier paternal behaviors were necessarily exploitive. The activation of a POA document and the concomitant health decline of the elder in the families appeared to change the family power structure. Often, the family member most proximal to the elder was designated as the POA, which became a problem only when he or she used the power over other family members in a self-serving manner. In some cases, the POA was further influenced to exploit due to power and control exerted by others, such as the agent's spouse.

Under the theme of power and control, and occurring at both *micro and mesosystem levels*, is coercion through entitlement and guilt induction. In the literature on abusive relationships, it is widely accepted that power and control are methods that abusers use to gain and maintain control over a victim (Lehmann, Catherine, & Simmons, 2012; Policastro, & Finn, 2015). In these cases, financial exploitation is perpetrated for the personal gain of the POA. Other strategies used to facilitate power and control are via isolation or gaslighting (i.e., a form of manipulation used to make others doubt their own perceptions or memory). In the cases of Bryce and Adrian, the exploiter curtailed communication with other key family members, which left them concerned yet uninformed about the elder victim's finances as well as health and well-being.

Further examples of the significant influence of power and control dynamics occurred when certain family members took advantage of an elder with declining mental and/or physical health under the guise of "helping" (whether intentional from the beginning or as it altered over time). In exchange for his or her mere presence, the family caregiver may determine that she needs to be remunerated from the older adult's assets. Thus, taking money from the older adult becomes justified in the mind of the perpetrator because, first, he or she deserves it for taking care of the elder, and second, because the older adult would eventually give it to him or her anyway. Further, the perpetrator justifies that other family members choose not to be or cannot be proximal to the older family member and consequently are not entitled to the elder's money, regardless of what a trust or will says about the remainder of an estate when the principal dies. This justification of exploitation by a POA is discussed by Rabiner and colleagues (2004; 2006), who proposed that the social (or family) network of the perpetrator may actually enable the perpetrator to financially abuse. This was true in the case of Joyce's aunt Karla, because her social network encouraged exploitation of the grandmother by repeatedly giving Karla money upon request. Alternately, the social or family network may serve as a protective factor for the elder victim when the network attempts to intervene to stop the abuse or to enlist the aid of critical others. An example of protection was the family network of Shauna, who attempted to intervene in the suspected exploitation of her parents.

At the level of the exo- and mesosystem were mechanisms that served to thwart the intervention by family members who suspected that financial exploitation was occurring. Family members Adrian and Opal were stymied for at least two reasons. First, their mother and their sister blocked efforts to ascertain whether their mother had actually designated their sister as her POA, let alone the parameters of the authority she had designated. Second, they were unable to recover information that might help their mother due to the protections of health-related information under HIPAA. Consequently, state and federal laws intended to protect individuals may actually work to their detriment when exploitation is discovered.

Finally, the role of gender appeared to play a part in POA EFFE. Because most caregivers are women, and at least one of the family caregivers remained very near the older adult and tended to be chosen as the POA, regardless of fitness to serve in that capacity. Further, in some instances, the female POA exhibited the learned behavior of her parents, which involved secrecy as well as power and control. When, in some instances, the POA was "left behind" or remained in the hometown as the elder's caregiver, the occasion for perpetrating exploitation presented itself, and the POA simply acted in what she perceived as behavior that was both normative within the family and warranted so that she could continue caregiving.

It is important to emphasize that those who provide care to older family members do not do so without costs (e.g., money, time, emotional support). Inherent costs of care provision should be understood as much as possible by the elder care recipient as well as involved family members. It is crucial to avoid exploitation of the elder as well as of the family member providing direct care and oversight. A solution is to involve the older adult and the caregiving and care-involved children in open, honest, and periodic discussions about what is expected and what is fair to the sibling directly responsible for care provision.

## Limitations

This study and its findings are not without limitations. First, the findings are based on a small sample and are not intended to be representative of all cases of POA EFFE. Second, the POA EFFE upon which our analysis was conducted was typically not reported to or confirmed by authorities with power to act. Third, elders in our study who executed POAs were born in the 1920s and 1930s, persons who came of age in the years preceding and during World War II. Their children are likely Baby Boomers, persons born between the years of 1946 and 1964. As a result, it was societally normative for many women of the earlier age cohort to become homemakers. Thus, many women were unable to hold a mortgage or credit card in their own name. Unless a woman challenged these expectations, many were dissuaded from involvement in family finances, with the consequence that many rarely, if ever, were involved with financial matters. Moreover, many were left were ill equipped to address them when life circumstances (e.g., death or divorce of a spouse) changed, even more so when confronted with their own chronic illness and cognitive decline.

Our examination of POA exploitation by a family member contributes to an area of exploitation about which little is currently known. These data and their findings illuminate a body of knowledge on POA EFFE that was heretofore largely anecdotal in nature.

## Conclusion

In conclusion, POA EFFE has the potential to impoverish elders and fracture social and family networks. POA EFFE can reduce the quality of life for present and future generations as well as the communities in which they live. It can even result in the premature death of the elder as well as mental and physical health problems for the family members affected by the exploitation. This exploratory project investigating POA EFFE provides clues into ways that family members exploit elder relatives, and by extension, other members of the same family. Understanding pathways of POA EFFE suggests ways to enable individuals, families, and communities to prevent and intervene. With an understanding of risk and protective factors, it is possible for health providers, family financial planners, and attorneys to help older adults make the best possible selection(s) of a POA, to prepare families for their loved one's potential needs in old age, as well as to intervene, as early as possible, when POA EFFE is suspected.

## References

Acierno, R., Hernandez, M. A., Amstadter, A. B., Resnick, H. S., Steve, K., Muzzy, W., & Kilpatrick, D. G. (2010). Prevalence and correlates of emotional, physical, sexual, and financial abuse and potential neglect in the United States: The national elder mistreatment study. *American Journal of Public Health, 100*(2), 292-297. doi:10.2105/AJPH.2009.163089

Anderson K. L. (2005). Theorizing gender in intimate partner violence research. *Sex Roles52*, 853–865.

Bogdan, R. C., & Biklen, S. K. (1998). *Qualitative research in education. An introduction to theory and methods.* Needham Heights, MA: Allyn & Bacon.

Bronfenbrenner, U. (1986). Ecology of the family as a context for human development: Research perspectives. *Developmental Psychology, 22,* 723-742.

Bronfenbrenner, U. (1979). *The ecology of human development: Experiments by nature and design.* USA: President and Fellows of Harvard College.

Capezuti, E., Brush, B., & Lawson, W. (1997). Reporting elder mistreatment. *Journal of Gerontological Nursing, 23*(7), 24-32.

Centers for Disease Control (2014). *The social-ecological model: A framework for prevention.* Retrieved from http://www.cdc.gov/violenceprevention/overview/social-ecologicalmodel.html

Chrzastowski, S. K. (2011). A narrative perspective on genograms: Revisiting classical family therapy methods. *Clinical Child Psychology and Psychiatry, 16*(4), 635-644.

Fattah, E., & Sacco, V. (1989). Crime and victimization of the elderly. *New York, NY Springer-Verlag Publishing.* doi:10.1007/978-1-4613-8888-3.

Federal Interagency Forum on Aging-Related Statistics. (2012). *Older Americans 2012: Key indicators of well-being.* Retrieved from https://agingstats.gov/docs/PastReports/2012/OA2012.pdf

Glesne, C. (2006). *Becoming qualitative researchers: An introduction* (2nd ed.). Boston, MA: Pearson Education.

Gunther, J. (2011). *The Utah cost of financial exploitation.* (No. 32). Washington, D.C.: American Bar Association.

Hafemeister, T. L. (2003). Financial abuse of the elderly in domestic settings. In R.J. Bonnie, & R.B. Wallace (Eds.), *Elder mistreatment: Abuse, neglect, and exploitation in an aging America* (pp. 382-445). Washington, D.C.: National Academies Press.

Horsford, S. R., Parra-Cardona, J. R., Post, L. A., & Schiamberg, L. (2010). Elder abuse and neglect in African American families: Informing practice based on ecological and cultural frameworks. *Journal of El-*

*der Abuse & Neglect, 23*(1), 75-88. doi:10.1080/08946566.2011.534709

Huang, Y., & Lawitz, A. (2016). *The New York state cost of financial exploitation study.* New York State Office of Children and Family Services.

Jackson, S.L., & Hafemeister, T.L. (2012). Pure financial exploitation vs. hybrid financial exploitation co-occurring with physical abuse and/or neglect of elderly persons. *Psychology of Violence, 2*(3), 285-296. doi:10.1037/a0027273

James, M. (1994). Abuse and neglect of older people. *Family Matters, 37,* 94-97. Retrieved from https://aifs.gov.au/publications/family-matters/issue-37/abuse-and-neglect-older-people

Lehmann, P., Simmons, C. A., & Pillai, V. K. (2012). The validation of the checklist of controlling behaviors (CCB) assessing coercive control in abusive relationships. *Violence Against Women, 18*(8), 913-933.

Lifespan of Greater Rochester, (2011). *Under the radar: New York state elder abuse prevalence study - Self-reported prevalence and documented case surveys.* Retrieved from http://www.lifespan-roch.org/documents/UndertheRadar051211.pdf

McDonald, L., & Thomas, C. (2013). Elder abuse through a life course lens. *International Psychogeriatrics, 25*(08), 1235-1243.

MetLife Mature Market Institute, National Committee for the Prevention of Elder Abuse, & Center for Gerontology at Virginia Polytechnic Institute and State University. (2009). *Broken trust: Elders, family, and finances.* New York, NY: MetLife Mature Market Institute.

MetLife Mature Market Institute, National Committee for the Prevention of Elder Abuse, & Center for Gerontology at Virginia Polytechnic Institute and State University. (2011). *The MetLife study of elder financial abuse: Crimes of occasion, desperation, and predation against America's elders.* New York, NY: MetLife Mature Market Institute.

Novick, G. (2008). Is there a bias against telephone interviews in qualitative research? *Research in Nursing & Health, 31*(4), 391-398.

Parra-Cardona, J. R., Meyer, E., Schiamberg, L., & Post, L. (2007). Elder abuse and neglect in Latino families: An ecological and culturally relevant theoretical framework for clinical practice. *Family Process,* *46*(4), 451-470. doi:10.1111/j.1545-5300.2007.00225.x

Patton, M.Q. (2015). *Qualitative research and evaluation methods: Integrating theory and practice.* (4th ed.). Thousand Oaks, CA: Sage Publications.

Policastro, C., & Finn, M. A. (2015). Coercive control and physical violence in older adults: Analysis using data from the National Elder Mistreatment Study. *Journal of Interpersonal Violence, 32* (2) 311-330. DOI: 0886260515585545.

Rabiner, D. J., O'Keeffe, J., & Brown, D. (2006). Financial exploitation of older persons: Challenges and opportunities to identify, prevent, and address it in the United States. *Journal of Aging & Social Policy, 18*(2), 47-68.

Rabiner, D. J., O'Keeffe, J., & Brown, D. (2004). A conceptual framework of financial exploitation of older persons. *Journal of Elder Abuse & Neglect, 16*(2), 53.

Seidman, I. (1998). *Interview as qualitative research. A guide for researchers in education and social sciences,* New York, NY: Teachers College Press.

Setterlund, D., Tilse, C., Wilson, J., McCawley, A., & Rosenman, L. (2007). Understanding financial elder abuse in families: The potential of routine activities theory. *Ageing & Society, 27*(4), 599-614.

Sherod, M. G., Griffith, H. R., Copeland, J., Belue, K., Krzywanski, S., Zamrini, E. Y., ... & Marson, D. C. (2009). Neurocognitive predictors of financial capacity across the dementia spectrum: normal aging, mild cognitive impairment, and Alzheimer's disease. *Journal of the International Neuropsychological Society, 15*(02), 258-267.

Stiegel, L. A., & Klem, E. V. (2008). *Power of attorney abuse: What states can do about it.* Washington, DC: AARP Public Policy Institute.

Strauss, A., & Corbin, J. M. (1990). *Basics of qualitative research: Grounded theory procedures and techniques.* Thousand Oaks, CA: Sage Publications, Inc.

Teaster, P., Dugar, T., Mendiondo, M., Abner, E., & Cecil, K. (2006). The 2004 survey of state adult protective services: Abuse of adults 60 years of age and older. Washington, D.C., *National Center on Elder Abuse.*

Thomas, D. (2014). *The Wyoming cost of financial exploitation 2011, 2012 and 2013.* Cheyenne, WY: Department of Family Services.

Tueth, M. J. (2000). Exposing financial exploitation of impaired elderly persons. *The American Journal of Geriatric Psychiatry, 8(2)*, 104-111.

University of Wyoming (2016). *About us: WyGEC.* Retrieved from http://www.uwyo.edu/geriatrics/about/

University of Wyoming (2016). *Agricultural experiment station: College of Agriculture and Natural Resources.* Retrieved from http://www.uwyo.edu/uwexpstn/

Vincenti, V., Browne, L., Betz-Hamilton, A., & Jasper, C. R. (2014). Clues to the power of attorney-based elder financial abuse within the family system. *Journal of Consumer Education, 30*, 45-58.

University of Wyoming Extension. (2013). *Planning ahead: Difficult decisions.* Series of bulletins B-1250.1 through B-1250.11.

Yon, Y., Mikton, C., Gassoumis, Z., & Wilber, K. (2017). Elder abuse prevalence in community settings: A systematic review and meta-analysis. *The Lancet, 5(2)*, e147 – e156.

Yon Y., Wister A, Gutman G, & Mitchell B. (2014). A comparison of spousal abuse in mid-and-old aged: is elder abuse simply a case of spousal abuse grown old? *Journal of Elder Abuse & Neglect, 26*, 80–105.

## Chapter 10

# Politicizing the personal and personalizing the political through dance: Audience resonance, reflexivity, and response to a dance performance created from qualitative data

## Elizabeth Sharp

## Genevieve Durham DeCesaro

*Texas Tech University*

### Introduction

A basic principal of feminist theorizing is that the *personal is political*, meaning that personal biographies and choices are embedded in a wider political landscape (Lloyd, Few, & Allen, 2009). A classic example to illustrate this concept is sexual harassment. Many women think that they did something to invite the harassment–they believe their individual actions (e.g., what they chose to wear or what they said) led them to being harassed by a man (Connell, 2014). Challenging this de-contextualized (individualized) analysis, feminist thought points to wider contextual patterns of sexual harassment, showcasing sexual harassment of men against women as a manifestation of political power structures. The incredibly high rates of men sexually harassing women provide evidence that this is not an individual issue, but a reflection of a politicized pattern of gendered power.

Building on the premise that the personal is political, the purpose of our dance project, *Ordinary Wars*, was to bring into focus the wider political landscape of expectations of conventional femininity and how such expectations are embodied in "ordinary" women. The project foregrounds powerful cultural ideologies affecting women's individual choices about their identities, relationships, and families. In this chapter, as a way to politicize the personal, we share our analysis of audience members' individual reactions to this politically charged dance performance.

### *Ordinary Wars* Project and Concert: A Brief Description

Before sharing our audience data, we offer a brief description of our work together. Our project, titled *Ordinary Wars*, is a product of our shared identities as feminist scholars and our goal to publicize women's "ordinary" narratives in innovative and provocative ways. We sought to create a dance performance based on social science qualitative data. Toward this end, in 2011, we submitted an institutional grant proposal, titled *Toward Innovative and Transdisciplinary Methodologies: Re-presenting Social Science Data Through Dance*. The proposal featured a transdisciplinary collaboration between a social scientist (Elizabeth) and a choreographer and dancer (Genevieve). Our proposal, as well as two subsequent proposals extending the project, was funded.

The culmination of our work together is an evening-length dance concert, created by choreographers' analyses of two of Elizabeth's qualitative datasets. The concert comprises six dances and is performed by members of Flatlands Dance Theatre, a professional, not-for-profit dance company (www.flatlandsdance.org). Prior to each dance, actors perform dialogues from the qualitative datasets. To view the performance, see http://www.ordinarywars.org. As of this writing, the concert has been commissioned four times and performed six times in Texas, Colorado, Virginia, and Michigan.

The data anchoring this project are from a dataset on brides/new wives and another dataset on single women. One dataset is from a constructivist grounded theory study examining 18 young white women's weddings and their first year of wifehood. Data were collected through focus groups and individual interviews in a midsize, southwestern town in the United States (for more information about the methodology, see Durham DeCesaro & Sharp, 2016). The other data is from a constructivist grounded theory study examining 35 single women in seven cities in the United States. For both projects, interviews were audio recorded and transcribed verbatim. The data included more than 1000 double-spaced pages of transcripts and 45 hours of audio recordings, which Elizabeth gave *all* of it to Genevieve.

As we have written about previously, we were deliberate in our decision to re-present data of women's experiences in ordinary (largely overlooked, daily) conditions (e.g., transitioning to marriage, thinking about being single, thinking about motherhood) in a dance concert. Our decision hinged on three important considerations:

1. The topics in Elizabeth's studies are rarely discussed in com-

munity dialogues—in other words, there is little public discourse about the routine and pervasive expectations of contemporary femininity for women in their 20's and 30's;

2. Contemporary (or historical) dance rarely features ordinary women's experiences as subject matter;

3. Compared to other topics, academic researchers tend to gloss over single women, weddings, and transitions to wifehood.

Drawing on our feminist training and grounding, we argue that the lack of attention to ordinary women's lives is a missed opportunity. As a corrective, our vision of our work together was to affect change in our respective fields and in our communities through making visible the extraordinary *ordinary* internal struggles and tensions women face in contemporary society.

The fully-realized concert comprises six distinct dances. (See appendix A for a brief description of the dances.) The concert was developed and arranged to engage and challenge the audience. From her two decades of experience in dance, Genevieve understood that audiences without a background in dance might disconnect from the concert if the performance was too abstract. Being mindful of this, we decided to include in the concert "performance of the data as spoken word narrative and several dances with linear narrative or clearly structured storylines. Affording audiences a level of familiarity with what they are viewing is helpful in encouraging those audiences to engage with, interpret, and dialogue about what they are seeing" (Durham DeCesaro & Sharp, 2016, p. 5).

We also created interactive opportunities for our audiences. When audience members entered the lobby prior to a performance, they were able to read about the concert and its larger research agenda on signage posted on the lobby walls. In addition, during intermission, audience members were offered a cupcake served on a napkin; the napkins were printed with statistics, for example: "44% of U.S. adults are single. 1,138 benefits are given to married people." Our intention here was to encourage audiences to question what they were "biting into" when consuming products typically associated with marriage as a largely heteronormative institution.

## Data Collection from the Audiences

After the conclusion of each concert, we asked audience members to provide feedback about the concert. While our early attempts at data collection were unsuccessful, our attempts to be more transdisciplinary in our data collection efforts, particularly at our last two performances, generated much more data.

We sought audience data from each of our performances, including our pilot performance. We tried a variety of data collection strategies, including long (multiple-page) paper surveys, brief (front/back only) paper surveys, online surveys, text messaging, focus groups, and hybrid focus group/talkback sessions. The strategies with the greatest success (i.e., receiving responses from the most audience members) were brief paper surveys (accompanied by payment) and hybrid focus group/talkback sessions. The last two performances yielded 45 paper surveys (out of an audience of approximately 100 people) and 100 brief paper surveys (out of an audience of 140 people), respectively; this was a considerable improvement over the rate of return for the online surveys (a total of 10 for three performances, with more than 300 audience members combined) and the longer, paper surveys. Additionally, we had between 20 and 45 people at each of the hybrid focus groups/talkback sessions at our last two performances. Prior to that, we had six people participating in focus groups at the first performance, seven at the second performance, and none at the third performance.

## Politicizing the Personal and Personalizing the Political: Resonance, Reflexivity, and Response

How might we determine if audience members understood and enacted the feminist tenet that "personal is political"? We suggest that there are at least three indicators that offer evidence that the performance fostered a sense of personal engagement with the political material. The indicators include: (a) whether the performance resonated with them; (b) whether the performance encouraged the audience members to reflect in deep and meaningful ways; and (c) whether the performance engendered a sense of response or a call to action for audience members. By sharing data from our audiences, we support our claim that the performance served as a catalyst for simultaneously personalizing the political *and* politicizing the personal.

### Resonance

As we described in our book, "Resonance is the gut reaction, the emotional connection, the sensory experience that viewers describe. Resonance can be positive, but also deeply painful, or rooted in anger, fear, or frustration" (Durham DeCesaro & Sharp, 2016, p. 51). Below, we share selected audience data signifying *resonance*. The reader will notice several dimensions of connection manifested in audience members' descriptions.

1. "I felt a feeling of guilt, in a way…of my own station."
2. "Love it. Very emotional for me as a single woman who has expressed a lot of the doubts about marriage."
3. "…So to me it was very powerful to hear and know I'm not the only one and that it's ok if I don't want kids."
4. "Positive and pleasurable. I laughed, connected, had an emotional response with the performance on different levels."
5. "Tonight was beautiful, and I am genuinely content and happy that these topics were spoken."
6. "Touched me, brought at my own emotions about the struggle of being single and being judged provoked a lot of emotion for me."
7. "'Brave' makes me cry, y'all. As a lesbian, I felt both moved and also a teensy bit underrepresented, but, like, I get it."

As the above data showcase, audience members described a variety of sensory reactions, such as guilt, pleasure, contentment, affirmation, joy, and sadness. In quote #3, the participant described the concert as "powerful," clarifying that her feeling of power came from realizing she was not alone in her thinking. She indicated that the concert gave her affirmation in that, "It's ok if I don't want kids." Excerpt #5 also expressed her gratitude that the "topics" (i.e., conventional expectations of femininity) were being spotlighted ("spoken"). Her comments provide evidence for our initial claims that topics of ordinary femininity are not part of the public dialogue. Issues of struggle, judgment, and underrepresentation are all evident in the aforementioned data and reflect the core of feminist theorizing. Moreover, the excerpts featured above belie the beginnings of connections between data, personal response, and sociopolitical positioning. In other words, making the personal political cannot happen, at least in our concert, without resonance. We contend that is a key point of consideration for researchers as we consider how and why we are using certain media, venues, and methods to engage our audiences.

## Reflexivity

We believe that in order for our work to function as an instigator of transformative cultural, social, and political change, it must encourage the viewer to reflect on the ways in which the issues presented on stage interface with the viewer's own lived experiences. According to feminist scholars, reflexivity is a critical engagement and personal scrutiny of the issue at hand (see Sharp & Weaver, 2015). Typically, reflexivity is enacted by scholars or students, that is, individuals studying or interacting with the concept itself. We would argue, though, that the *Ordinary Wars* performance served as a catalyst for a wide variety of audience members to be reflexive.

Maxine Greene (1978) offers a definition of reflexivity as being "wide-awake." The viewer is encouraged to move from resonance into a space of deliberately making connections between personal experience and social positioning. Such connections are described in the comments of some of our viewers, which we have excerpted in our book (Durham DeCesaro & Sharp, 2016, pp. 51-52) and below:

> 1. "I really loved the concert. I think it portrays ideas that aren't normally discussed, it lets me think about different ideas opposite to how I was raised."
> 2. "As a whole I don't really know how to interpret it. Coming from a divorced family, my father failing twice at it and being predominately raised by my mother, my thoughts on women and the need to get married have always been that it is not supposed to be happy."
> 3. "I felt like I could relate for my mother raising me to be a housewife because of my culture."
> 4. "I loved the performance. My family has always been supportive of my choices – but there has been an underlying theme of traditional expectation."
> 5. "I'm 35 – I, too, have thought I better get after having babies, time's almost up/what's wrong with me?"
> 6. "I've found myself thinking and even saying some of the things from the text."
> 7. "This concert was really relatable to my current experiences."
> 8. "From a male perspective, very illuminating. Many common issues that bear discussion as a culture."
> 9. "Very similar to what we are going through as a soon to be married couple. Almost every bit of dialogue in the performance have been observed by my fiancé in the previous few months."

Of interest in the responses above is the tendency of viewers to connect what they viewed and felt to how they were raised and/or to their current social position. This is an essential component of politicizing the personal; in our post-concert focus group/talkback sessions, viewers analyzed their emotional reactions to a theatrical presentation and then connected those reactions to specific sociocultural expectations. The result of that process is an increased awareness, for our audience members, of the ways in which those expectations directly affect them, daily.

### Responding: Embodying Political Issues and Taking Action

The manifestation of feminist theorizing is, of course, praxis—putting theory into action (Stanley, 2013). In Critical Pedagogy: Notes from the Real World, Joan Wink (2005) highlighted action as integral to the cycle of critical pedagogy. She argued that the cycle includes: naming, critically reflecting, and engaging in action. We created the dance and offered the data collection immediately afterwards Below are some data excerpts underscoring audience members' expressed commitment to taking action, as a result of viewing the concert:

> 1. "I feel an immediate desire to discuss this with women I am close to like my sister, mother, and girlfriends. And any men willing to discuss topics explored."
> 2. "My favorite dance was "To Find My Voice." It made me realize that I can have all of the things that I want, regardless of what they are if I find my voice to say all that I want."
> 3. "I wish I knew how to get involved with the project."

Response #1 above indicates that the concert stimulated a need, for one audience member, to discuss the issues presented with her friends and family members. Similar to data in the resonance section of the paper, this statement also reflects the scarcity of public dialogue about the ordinary experiences of women. Response #2 illustrates one audience member's realization that finding and using her own voice is central to realizing her goals.

This is a fundamental principle of feminism and of critical pedagogy, yet women who do use their voices to articulate and achieve their goals continue to be marginalized as outliers who abandon or betray traditional notions of femininity. In terms of Response #2, this point is crucial to completing the journey from personal to political; the responder, in making a choice to take action (or, at least to contemplate taking action) must also understand the social implications of that choice. One of the ways that we work, in our project, to encourage an understanding of those implications is through dialogue, described in more detail in the section below.

### Integration of Resonance, Reflexivity, and Response

In several instances when we were able to conduct focus groups, we encountered audience members who articulated their integration of all three indicators of engagement: resonance, reflexivity and response. This was especially likely to happen when an audience member was living in the social position illuminated in the dance (e.g., either: bride, new wife, or single woman) and/or a graduate student studying the same topics. Because the focus group in Blacksburg, Virginia consisted primarily of graduate students in the Human Development and Family Studies department, some participants were not only living experiences presented onstage, but were also studying those experiences. performing the bridal role. As cited in our book (Durham DeCesaro & Sharp, 2016, p. 60), one participant explained:

> It is a very ambivalent situation to be a social scientist who studies this [topic] but also, you know, be performing the [bridal role] at the same time so I am aware. So one of my favorite scenes was when she is like "ahh… ooh… look at my precious [ring] and she gets tricked into signing this, you know, marriage contract and, you know, gets a baby thrown at her. The stork absolutely my favorite [laugher]… absolutely my favorite part. But it did a really good job of capturing the ambivalence, you know, like, we have sparkles of our very own but they come with costs and… I am aware of the costs and I am aware of, …, the meaning that is ascribed to this event but, at the same time, I am still buying into and performing it, maybe because I am not brave enough, I don't know… just kind of like…what can we do?. It seems like the alternative of not doing it is not really an alternative so just kind of play the role but I am conscious of the role that I am playing at the same time and how preposterous things are and I'm just really trying to not be that bride because I am aware of it, I am like "no, we are not doing that" – not doing this, not doing that, no favors, … not buying into that crap, not impressing people, so I am trying to keep it reeled in, … so it can be like small scale and, you know, reasonable…

The participant noted that she was "aware of the costs" associated with traditional notions of marriage and expectations of femininity associated with being a bride. She then subsequently indicated that she was "buying into it and performing it." Here, we can see that she realized that femininity is a performance. She mused whether or not she was "brave" enough to challenge social expectations for brides – a compelling and nuanced question. She refused to flatten the complexity of the issues or to dismiss the power of conventional expectations. She finished her statement by listing some specific (albeit small, as she says) actions that she will take.

In addition to this audience members' complex and thoughtful engagement with the performance, we have also have several critical responses from graduate and undergraduate students who viewed a videotaped version of the performance in their courses. We were encouraged to show the video in our classes because several Virginia Tech graduate students had approached Elizabeth to ask about the possibility of showing the dances in the undergraduate classes they teach as way to highlight course concepts. As a response to their request, we created an overview curriculum to accompany guided viewing the performances for college (and high school) students. Please see chapter seven in Durham DeCesaro and Sharp (2016) for a curriculum for sex/gender courses and qualitative methodologies.

## Conclusion

Our feminist scholarly identities are the crux of our *Ordinary Wars* project—our feminist training helped us create the idea for the project and to remain steadfast in our goals to ignite transformation within our disciplines and our communities. Through our extraordinary journey of examining and showcasing ordinary women's stories in an innovative way, we think that we have encouraged audience members to politicize the personal and to personalize the political. We describe our innovative use of secondary qualitative datasets and our unique approaches to audience data collection to encourage other researchers to take risks and to experiment with new ways of thinking about, analyzing, and collecting data. Our concert creates opportunities for audiences to meaningfully engage with content that is unquestionably personal and undeniably political–and in so doing, reinforces the idea that our (women's) ordinary lives are anything but.

# References

Connell, R. W. (2014). *Gender and power: Society, the person and sexual politics.* Hoboken, NJ: John Wiley & Sons.

Durham DeCesaro, G., & Sharp. E. A: (2016). *Ordinary Wars: Toward Innovative and Transdisciplinary Methodologies.* Champaign, IL: Common Ground Publishing.

Greene, M. (1978). *Landscapes of Learning.* New York, NY: Teachers College Press

Lloyd, S. A., Few, A. L., & Allen, K. R. (Eds.) (2009). *Handbook of feminist family studies.* Thousand Oaks, CA: Sage.

Sharp, E. A., & Durham DeCesaro, G. (2015). Modeling innovative methodological practices in a dance/family studies transdisciplinary project. *Journal of Family Theory & Review, 7,* 367–380. doi:10.1111/jftr.12109

Sharp, E. A., & Weaver, S. E. (2015). Feeling like feminist frauds: Theorizing feminist accountability in feminist family studies research in a neoliberal, postfeminist context. *Journal of Family Theory & Review, 7*(3), 299-32. doi:10.1111/jftr.12080

Stanley, L. (Ed.). (2013). *Feminist praxis (RLE feminist theory): Research, theory and epistemology in feminist sociology.* New York, NY: Routledge.

Wink, J. (2005). *Critical pedagogy: Notes from the real world.* New York, NY: Pearson/Allyn & Bacon.

## Appendix A: Choreographer's Descriptions of Dances and Sound Scores (as available)

Note: Unless otherwise indicated, the term "choreographer" refers to the lead choreographer. Two additional choreographers, both affiliated with Flatlands Dance Theatre, created a total of three dances out of the six included in the final concert structure.

"*I Was Happy in the Pictures;*" Choreographer's statement: This trio used as its stimulus six statements excerpted from the data. The statements are not connected in a linear way, but each contains particular imagery that, as the choreographer, I found striking in terms of communicative potential. The dancers contributed to creating movement motifs using the statements as prompts; parts of those motifs are all used within the frame of the larger dance. Taken as a whole, this particular work represents, abstractly, different ideas about a wedding day, none of them particularly joyful. I would suggest that this trio questions commonly publicized ideas about the way a woman "should" be on her wedding day. The statements pulled from the data used as stimuli for this work were: *'It's a lot harder than what I thought it was going to be'; 'The yellow roses were gorgeous;' 'So I wasn't like giddy or blissful or anything like that and I'm not sure why exactly I just wasn't'; 'You can tell that I was happy in the pictures, you know it's not a fake smile'; 'As soon as we were married my love for him increased greatly and I don't know why I guess'; 'And I kinda felt like I had an identity crisis a little bit '(laughing). 'I mean not really by any means but it kinda felt like I got lost in what he wanted.'*

Sound score:
Broderick, P. (2011). We Enjoyed Life Together. [Recorded by Peter Broderick]. On Music for Confluence. London, England: Erased Tapes Records.
Hooson, C. (2009). A Quietly Gathering Tragedy. [Recorded by Dakota Suite]. On The End of Trying. Cologne, Germany: Karaoke Kalk.

Choreographer's statement: This sound score is minimalist in nature, giving an unobtrusive backdrop to the choreography. I selected the two pieces, which are edited to play back to back, because they are both abstract, reinforcing the approach to the choreography. Additionally, they are uncommon enough to generally not trigger particular audience member connections, meaning that the audiences can focus in on the dance as it is danced.

"*A Thin Line;*" Choreographer's (secondary choreographer 1) statement: Prior to reading interview transcripts, I had notions of my own about marriage and family, and I think those ideas influenced my choreography as much as the information and opinions gathered from the interview data. It seemed as if many women interviewed had similar negotiations or struggles with maintaining balance in their lives, and I have experienced that myself. This idea served as the nucleus of this duet, and I explored and expanded beyond this initial idea of losing and regaining balance to develop the work.

"*Dressed (Parts 1 and 2);*" Choreographer's statement: This is a comedic dance. It is heavily influenced by the inescapable presence of a wedding dress, complete with all of the symbolism and meaning said dress embodies. The character of the bride re-presents many of the emotions discussed by the women in the interviews; I chose to highlight these by drawing attention to them using humor and exaggeration. While the quintet does poke a bit of fun (as did some of the study participants) at all of the drama of a wedding day, the choreography retains a central humanity expressed through the female dancers' care of and concern for the "bride.

Sound score:
Giachinno, M. (2009). Married Life. [Recorded by Michael Giachinno]. On *Up*. Burbank, CA: Walt Disney Records.
Bacharach, B. (1963). Wishin' and Hopin'. [Recorded by Ani DiFranco]. On *My Best Friend's Wedding: Soundtrack from the Motion Picture*. New York, NY: Sony BMG Music Entertainment.

Choreographer's statement: This sound score is meant to trigger audience connections and to provoke audience response. The first piece of music is taken from the animated film *Up*, which begins with a story about the expectations associated with a woman who is a new wife. The score is fairly well known due to the overall popularity of the film. Besides providing a secondary reference for some audience members, this particular piece of music also provides a light, airy, and anticipatory "feel" to the first part of the choreography, which underscores the nature of the story being told in this section. The second piece of music is a tongue-in-cheek reference to the social expectations new wives still experience. The song, "Wishin' and Hopin,'" was popularized by Dusty Springfield in 1964. The recording that I use in *Ordinary Wars*, though, is performed by Ani DiFranco, a contemporary feminist singer-songwriter.

*"With Doubt;"* Choreographer's (secondary choreographer 2) Statement: In making this work, I found the dialogue from the interviews quite compelling, serving as a springboard for the movement I created. The participants had varied stances about children, from traditional to what might be viewed as less conventional. I took those viewpoints, as well as my own, and created movement to represent women who were either strongly for, against and apathetic to bearing children. Circular movement and pathways were used as themes to represent cycles in life, indecisiveness and all things maternal.

*"The Cowboy, the Lawyer, and the Stork;"* Choreographer's (secondary choreographer1) Statement This satirical duet uses humor and props to dramatize some components of marriage (e.g., the contract, expectations for married women) that, though normalized in our social fabric, are startling to watch unfold.

*"To Find My Voice;"* Choreographer's statement: This ensemble emerged from an observation that, largely, singlehood was being marginalized in our concert. Because there are numerous accessible and recognizable symbols associated with marriage and motherhood, we'd capitalized on those to create a number of dances. *"To Find My Voice"* builds singlehood into the choreography by featuring portions of the transcripted data recorded into the sound score and by prominently positioning the work at the end of the concert.

Sound score: "Fjögur Píanó," by Sigur Rós.

Choreographer's statement: I selected this piece of music because of its ambient quality and its lack of what I would term "climactic" moments. I knew that I wanted to include recorded voice-overs on top of this piece's sound score, so selecting an even, minimalist, and sparse composition was critical. In "To Find My Voice," recorded performances (verbatim) of interview data are integrated into the selected musical accompaniment so that the audience hears the vocal performances as part of, rather than separate from, the backdrop of sound. This choice allowed me to guide, through non-linear narrative, the audience's understanding of this particular dancework.

After the final dance, *"To Find My Voice,"* the dancers participate in a performance piece, *"Brave."* *"Brave"* is a movement statement that includes oral and written presentation of language excerpted from the data.

Chapter 11

# Interesting Journeys: Administration, Gender, and Diversity

*Judith L. Fischer*

Texas Tech University

*Kevin P. Lyness*

Antioch University of New England

*Maresa J. Murray*

Indiana University

*Jean Pearson Scott*

Texas Tech University

*Donna Sollie*

Auburn University

*Anisa Zvonkovic*

East Carolina University

The attention paid to sexuality, gender, and family diversity has been both explicit and implicit in many Groves conferences. The study of these subjects often unfolds and exposes the most personal and intimate details and characteristics of its members. Such an examination is a difficult challenge and, at times, a painful process. Issues of privacy exploitation, morality, ethics, legality, personal belief, and self-judgment are among the obstacles to be overcome. (Roger Rubin, 2012, p. 241)

## Introduction

This chapter began as a panel discussion at the Groves Conference meeting in Denver, 2016. The panelists/authors are uniquely qualified to comment on the issues of gender and diversity as they have experienced these in their multiple roles in institutions and organizations. In this chapter, the authors discuss their personal journeys as administrators and/or institutional representatives. We each contributed a section and provided commentary on sections. Through the mutual sharing in this chapter, the personal becomes political. Authors appear alphabetically.
Across authors, topics include:

- How they came to their positions (including their academic "ah-ha" moments)

- What they hoped to accomplish

- What they were able to accomplish

- Supports and encouragements

- Roadblocks and challenges

- Recommendations for the future of the field and of higher education.

### From Judith Fischer

What is an academic "ah-ha" moment? In my own journey, the first salient experience was in my initial academic job hunt in the fall of 1971 and spring of 1972. There were some interesting reactions to my application. At the time of my job hunt, I lived in Boulder, CO, where I was finishing my doctorate. My then husband and I had a preschool-aged son. One institution wrote me back stating that they weren't looking for anyone in hippie attire or Bolshevik beards (yes, they said that). Representing a different institution, a phone interviewer stated that they were concerned about what I would do with my small child. In the next paragraphs I unpack these moments as I see them now.

Forty years — and more — later, these experiences are still with me. And there are a number assumptions at work that reflect more than the seemingly micro-aggressions of the men of those times who were in positions to hire faculty. An overarching aspect that is obvious is the patriarchal assumption that men are rightfully in positions of power in a capitalist society and they rightly represent and rule the institution of the academy. From this position of power men were gatekeepers who chose to let in men similar to themselves. Thus, the man who wrote the letter seemed to reject emerging expressions of masculinity that challenged their own views. The letter called up an interesting mash-up of insecurities: hippie attire was loose and free, in contrast to the traditional jacket and tie attire expected of men of that time; Bolshevik beards invoked the specter of communist sympathizing, a threat to capitalist economic and social structures. Women were rejected without even having to say so, because patriarchal privilege failed to "see" women. Women were not imagined as even being interested in broaching the gates of that academy. Another important aspect of this long-ago letter is the assumption of cis-gendered people. Even if the letter writer did recognize that a woman might apply, by writing what they did, they rejected any applications from those who were trans*. In those times, I suspect they didn't have a vocabulary of such concepts, but that blindness to possible varieties of human expression limits advancements of people. Understating the case, I did write back that I didn't think my family would be comfortable there.

With respect to the second example, the phone call, again assumptions rooted in patriarchy were present. It didn't seem to occur to the callers that I had had that small child all through my doctoral work and we had somehow figured it out. As well, the question seemed to suggest that married women with children shouldn't work for advanced degrees or work in academia once graduated. In that same call, the interviewer said something along the lines that they had had a woman once. Given the patronizing tone of that description of their past experiences, I suspect it wasn't just women with children with whom they experienced uncertainty, but women in general. They were gatekeeping their department's academic ranks.

So how did I get my start in academia? I was fortunate to be offered a position in a small department where a feminist woman had pioneered before me. She had educated the men in the department that women didn't automatically make the coffee or take the minutes at faculty meetings. And she had children. In my years there, I found some of the men working on issues of white, male, heterosexual privilege.

But to back up a bit, how did I get to a position where I could earn a doctorate? Men in my undergraduate institution encouraged me to continue my studies. Based on the comments I heard, the one woman on the faculty (a research associate) who was a potential role model was held in low regard. I worried I would become like her. But I also realized I would be me regardless of what degrees I had or did not have. And I realized she faced so much sexism that it must have been very difficult for her. There is a class privilege component to my story as well. I received an NIH stipend to attend graduate school with no strings attached (other than to make progress toward my degrees) as to how to spend the stipend or conditions about who I could live with. Other women received government stipends with restrictions on what could be purchased and how (they handed in coupons to purchase food at the grocery store). And they couldn't be living with a man. It was called "welfare". We both received stipends but were treated very differently. In addition to class privilege, I also benefit from white privilege. In the 1960s and 1970s I doubt I would have been granted admission, received fellowships, gotten job offers if I had been otherwise.

Yes, times have changed. Women make up half or more of graduate students in social science disciplines. They hold professorships and are department chairpersons, deans, and hold positions of power in academic institutions and organizations. But we remain in a society that continues to reflect patriarchal assumptions and arrangements, that uses diversity to divide, and that shames those who do not conform. "Ah-ha" moments are not a thing of the past. To me the US presidential election of 2016 afforded one such moment after another. I am discouraged now but I have hope for the future because I believe white male privilege is unsustainable. The old departmental gatekeepers have been replaced, although work remains at the highest levels of academia and the boards that govern these institutions. The next sections describe the work and lives of people who are working toward a future of diversity and equality.

**From Kevin Lyness**

I have been fortunate to teach in two academic programs that are fully committed to social justice and gender equality — in the Marriage and Family Therapy training programs at Antioch University New England and Colorado State University. I received my PhD from a program that was working on issues of gender and power and I was fortunate to get feedback on my privileged position (though I know at the time I was sometimes defensive, and at other times clueless), and I've later been able to reflect on the privileges that I enjoyed then and continue to benefit from as a cis-gender white male. I also had the advantage of being raised with a feminist mother and to have worked throughout my life with and for women.

To me, some of the current dialogue (that we're still having to have) about women's rights being human rights, as well as the human rights of LGBTQ+ individuals, has really struck a chord with me. I had an experience when I was younger of living with a partner (but not being married), and when she passed away, I was not able to use funeral leave at work because we weren't married. During this very traumatic time for me, I also realized that so many people live in relationships that aren't recognized as legitimate (and that for the longest time could not be legally recognized) and that everyone deserves to be treated with dignity and justice. Since that time, I have continually learned more about the role of gender and gender role socialization in relationships (as a couple and family therapist, these are issues that are vital to understand), as well as the role of power and oppression across social locations, and the intersectionality of these issues of access to power. I continue to work in settings that encourage me to explore my own privilege and exercise of power, and I choose relationship partners that help push me in this area as well.

So, what have I been able to accomplish? I was part of the team that developed the PhD program in Marriage and Family Therapy at Antioch University New England, where social justice is the primary mission of the program. We are one of a very few doctoral programs in MFT that has such an emphasis, and I'm proud of our program and the work we've done in this area. One area that I'd like to highlight about our program is the diverse nature of our student body. Having a direct mission of social justice means that we draw a very diverse group of students, and that diversity includes racial and ethnic, gender and gender expression, sexuality and sexual orientation, religion, national background, and age.

I have also tried to take an active role in national service, serving on the Commission on Accreditation for Marriage and Family Therapy Education (COAMFTE) and on the COAMFTE standards review committee that recently drafted new accreditation standards that significantly bolstered content and expectations regarding issues of culture, gender, sexual diversity, and power.

In both of these settings (at my university and in national service), I have tried to pay attention to and to use my privilege in ways that empower others, and to learn from my missteps. I have also had the freedom to be able to choose to work in settings that promote social justice, and I think I work at one of the best universities in this regard! Of course, there has also been backlash and barriers, most notably when I was working on revising accreditation standards where we tried to expand the language used to be more inclusive. This led to a national campaign to rein in what others saw as an overreach of the Commission and we ultimately had to roll back some of the changes we proposed. One lesson from this, though, is that we got a conversation started and opened the door for later changes. This is one thing I've learned in administration — sometimes your first efforts only pay off later, and doors that are closed now can be opened again.

**From Maresa Murray**

One of my most profound "a-ha" moments happened when I embraced the privilege of unapologetically saying "thank you for the invitation to serve, but at this time, I'm going to decline the invitation." In simple terms, this boils down to the positive power of saying no, and the pivotal key was not just saying no, but refusing the guilt of turning down a few very important administrative service opportunities. It merits mention that my rank is Associate Clinical Professor, which is a non-tenured position. The implicit risk involved in my firm, but gentle, refusal of these administrative service invitations is that I might have been potentially at risk for professional scrutiny.

One particular instance of my refusal to serve on a committee happened a few years ago when I served as the elected Secretary for the Bloomington Faculty Council (BFC), which is the operational faculty senate body on the campus of Indiana University-Bloomington. It was the first time that a non-tenured African American female faculty member had been elected to serve on the BFC Board, which also meant that I was in the forefront more often than previously, which in turn meant that my invitations to serve on committees exponentially increased. One of those invitations came from our campus Provost, as she thought I would be an excellent fit for a campus initiative. Since I sat directly next to the Provost at all of the BFC business meetings, although I was nervous about doing so, I kindly informed her of my decision to decline the invitation, explaining my appreciation for being considered but decided that the committee would not be a positive move to make at that time in my career trajectory. The Provost proceeded to cover the microphone with her hand, since all of our business meetings were open to the public and meticulously transcripted, and told me a story about which she recently heard.

She described an article she read of an African American Clinical faculty member at another university who was inundated with administrative obligations, an experience that was markedly increased for her because there were very few retained African American faculty on her campus with her level of institutional memory, since minority faculty members were being avidly recruited, yet not retained and quickly leaving her campus after short periods of time. The Provost went on to finish the story by telling me that the woman eventually came to an enlightened understanding of her role on the campus, and that the very fact that she is an outstanding and enduring African American faculty member on that campus was, in fact, an act of service within itself. Therefore, she became more selective about serving on the committees that would best fit her own professional goals. After the Provost shared that story with me, I told her how much I appreciated her gracious acceptance of my "no." Right before she lifted her hand from the microphone to start the BFC meeting, she encouraged me to continue practicing that level of professional discernment and said it will serve me well in the higher-level administrative roles taken in the future.

## From Jean Pearson Scott

My earliest "ah ha" moment in the professional world came at the time of hire in my first tenure track position. I assumed that the salary I earned would be the same as my male colleagues who were also new assistant professors. I received a reality check when the Dean told me matter-of-fact (with no pretense of apology), "Of course, you won't be making the same salary as _____ because he has a family and needs the extra income." I had not encountered this kind of blatant discrimination in my graduate program. My academic mentors were traditional women in many ways, yet highly accomplished trailblazers. They had worked hard and had learned how to choose their battles and mostly how to work toward goals within the academic system of the day without making waves. I remember that my academic advisor would clean house or wash clothes, drop her children off at school and be sitting at her desk at 8:00 a.m. Before her retirement, she was awarded one of the highest awards the academic system bestows. It did not take long for me to realize that the world of academics was a male dominated system. My mentors had worked extremely hard to make it to the top. When I had my two children, I learned that no full-time woman faculty member in the College had had children before, at least in any one's memory, and there was no protocol or policy for maternity leave. I must note, however, that the College and Department worked with me to make sure that my classes were covered and students' progress on research was not interrupted. At that time, there was enough flexibility in the system that a new situation could be accommodated. This was a time when I appreciated that being in a Department of Human Development and Family Studies gave me advantages that other employed women did not have (access to quality childcare, flexibility in research and teaching responsibilities).

One thing that I have learned is that, as human beings, we have wounds that can go deep especially as a result of harassment and discrimination. In the late 1990s, I served as the faculty advisor to the LBGT student group on campus. I decided to serve in this capacity because I was a white, middle aged, heterosexual, female with tenure. I had several gay/lesbian colleagues who were untenured and not out to the academic community; they knew that sexual orientation was a sensitive, volatile issue on a conservative campus. I made the decision to serve as the faculty advisor because I saw that I was at the right place and right time to be an ally. Although the organization carried out several successful projects, I saw firsthand how personal issues can sabotage programmatic goals of an organization. One officer of the student group was coercive and abusive to other members and resented my position as a heterosexual advisor. Turmoil among the officers prompted the unfair response of, "What did you expect?" from those who were fearful of students with LBGT identities. Progress may come as one step forward two steps back when leaders of social justice issues set themselves up as gatekeepers, put personal needs or approval above program goals, or contribute to divisiveness that poisons an initiative or brings condemnation by others. Also, I am reminded from this experience that social justice does not come as smoothly, respectably, and cleanly as the history books might suggest.

Over my career, I have served as an Associate Chair and Chair of a department. Presently, I serve as the Faculty Ombudsperson for a large, comprehensive university. As I have worked with faculty and administrators to resolve disputes, I become more resolute that the best we can do to preserve academic freedom and shared governance in the academy is to have a strong infrastructure (faculty senate, College faculty councils) to give voice to faculty perspectives. Having a voice is vitally important as the terrain of higher education is changing rapidly and innovations have a short shelf life. My hope is that the academy will continue to be a place where diversity is valued and all voices are heard.

### From Donna Sollie

My coming-of-age experiences as a high school student and undergraduate in the late 1960s through the early 1970s in the state of Mississippi were influenced by the social issues and related activism that was sweeping our county, and my increasing understanding of the racial and gender oppression in my state and our country. It was an exciting time in many ways, as well as a challenging time, and the enlightening readings in my sociology courses combined with the social activism on campus contributed to my commitment to social justice, and my interest in continuing my studies.

Certainly both of my parents were supportive of my interest in graduate school, but my determination was strengthened by my mother's defense of my goals, in her sharp retort to a chauvinist male sociology professor who told her that I should focus on finding a husband and having children rather than pursuing graduate degrees—as the saying goes, she did not suffer fools gladly, and also did not hesitate to state her opinions. The strong and fiercely supportive women in my family were excellent role models!

Throughout my academic career, my interest in gender and

women's issues intensified, and I remain fascinated by the ways that gender influences individual identities, opportunities, and relationships. The Feminism and Family Studies Section in the National Council on Family Relations has provided rewarding and stimulating collaborative opportunities throughout my career, not to mention life-long friendships. My experiences in Women's Studies, as an affiliate professor and as Director of Women's Studies for 8 years at Auburn University, have been thought-provoking and gratifying. And I have been most fortunate to have wonderful departmental colleagues throughout my career.

However, although my interest in gender and women's issues was supported by wonderful departmental colleagues, that interest has not always been viewed so positively across campus. One of these colleagues let me know, fairly early in my career at Auburn, that my activities attracted attention and provided a topic of conversation at the noontime pick-up basketball games where male faculty gathered for exercise and gossip. Apparently my HDFS colleague was often questioned about what "the Femi-Nazi" — that would be me! — was up to.
And before I submitted my materials for evaluation for promotion to the rank of Full Professor, a caring colleague was concerned that the title of the book, which I co-edited with Leigh Leslie, might be detrimental to my review due to the word feminist in the title. These experiences exemplify the ongoing challenges and negative perceptions that we face as we iden-tify as feminist academics as we work toward addressing inequities.

For the last 10 years of my career, I served as the Assistant Provost for Women's Initiatives at Auburn University in the Office of Inclusion and Diversity. Being a feminist and being an administrator at a university brought unique challenges as well as opportunities. Holding a university leadership position provides an avenue for working with engaged people who share the goal of creating an environment that values women and men equally and offers men and women the same opportunities. The work of Fine and Buzzell (2000) that re-visions feminist leadership as service that challenges the gendered organizational beliefs of institutions has been instrumental in my administrative work. As a feminist adminis-trator, my goal was to develop and implement programs for students and faculty members that are creative, connected, focused on the communities within and outside the university, and committed to change. There have certainly been challenges along the way, however----and often these chal-lenges reflect the persistence of subtle and often not-so-subtle academic climate issues that are still pervasive in the academy.

One of the challenges that academia faces is attracting and re-taining a diverse faculty, which will enrich instruction and bring dif-ferent abilities, thought patterns, and approaches to discovery and problem-solving. Ensuring that these faculty members advance through professorial ranks is critically important. Other challenges center on addressing work-life and climate issues that can negatively impact all faculty members, but that are more likely to impact female and minority faculty members. In order to effectively address these challenges, we developed a number of low-cost, high impact initiatives at Auburn University. These initiatives included mentoring programs, networking opportunities, facilitating scholarly development, facilitating leadership development, and addressing family-friendly and work-life policies. These initiatives reflect a "small wins" approach to altering ongoing practices that reflect gender bias by focusing on "fixing the organization, not the women who work for it" (Meyerson & Fletcher, p. 136). Our Pathways to Full Professor Initiative focuses on increasing the number of women who advance to Full Professor Rank and into institutional leadership positions, and includes workshops, dossier reviews, and mentoring programs.

It is critical that universities facilitate the development of female students and address their concerns. With that goal in mind, we started the Women's Center at Auburn University (AUWC) in 2006. Our tagline is "Actualizing the Potential of All Women," and we promote and support women's leadership and personal and professional growth through education, advocacy, and outreach. The AUWC provides resources, expertise, and mentorship to empower and encourage Auburn University to overcome gender inequity and gender-based violence on campus. Our student group, the AUWC Leadership and Advocacy Council, is an avenue for student leadership and advocacy. Our Advisory Board, composed of university and community members, plays an important role as we develop programs and strategic plans.

We have a Women in Science and Engineering Institute (WISE) which includes programs for K-20 and faculty members. The mission of the WISE Institute is to encourage, promote, and enhance the entry, retention, and success of females in the fields of science, technology, engineering, and mathematics (STEM) at all levels. Student programs include a WISE Learning Community and an active Graduate Women in Science organization; these programs provide mentoring and networking opportunities as well as support for women students in areas that typically have low female representation. Our WISE Steering Committee, with faculty representatives from 10 academic colleges, provides guidance for our mentoring and networking programs, our Speakers Series, and the new TESS (Together Embracing Successful Scholars) talks which highlight outstanding female scholars at Auburn University.

Throughout my career, I have been very fortunate to have faculty colleagues who made my daily life engaging and encouraged me to pursue administrative positions, supportive department heads, opportunities to be involved in leadership positions in professional organizations, especially the National Council on Family Relations, and long-term collegial relationships within the discipline of family studies (including those with several of my co-authors on this paper). I have found it very helpful to learn from my colleagues at other universities, and in academic departments throughout the university, as we share ideas about successful programs and strategies for addressing university climate issues.

Some of the roadblocks and challenges that are ongoing include subtle and pervasive sexism, funding for programs, and recognizing that change takes time and it is imperative to be persistent. One effective way to address challenges is through building collaborations with individuals across the institution. As we look to the future of our disciplines and of higher education, and the continuing challenges to address inclusion and diversity, there are several actions we can all take at our institutions. Be an active voice in lobbying for more women in higher administration positions. Utilize institutional data and COACHE (Collaborative on Academic Careers in Higher Education) data in developing rationales for developing programs and initiatives to address gender inequities and climate issues at all levels of the university. Volunteer to be on your institution's Commission on the Status of Women, or similar committee; if one doesn't exist, develop a proposal, and submit it to the Provost at your university. Cultivate collaborative relationships across the institution. Articulate the importance of units such as Women's Centers and Women's or Gender Studies Programs.

I have often commented that in my 30 years at Auburn University, and particularly in the administrative and leadership positions that I've held, it has been necessary to continue working toward goals of inclusion and equity, particularly in the face of challenges and setbacks. I wrote the last paragraph about a month ago, before the quote that has now become part of our national consciousness says: "Nevertheless, she persisted." It was interesting to see my observation about the necessity of persistence.

Undoubtedly, our ongoing challenge is to persist. Luckily, we have so many more people who are persisting together. Our combined voices and efforts do make a difference.

### From Anisa Zvonkovic:

Having been an administrator at one level or another nearly consistently since receiving tenure, I reflect back on why and how I got into administration. Given that the audience for this volume is family scientists, I will say that we could look to our family experiences for answers to these questions. In my case, I was one of four children, and the only girl. I think I grew up solving interpersonal squabbles, thinking about how to manage household workload since my mother worked outside of the home, intervening from time to time with larger social and bureaucratic systems, and generally being the one person at home that everyone, no matter who they were fighting with, could talk to. I leave it to my readers as to whether these activities became part of my management skill set and my philosophy.

I suppose in my pre-tenure days, I very often felt like I could do a better job than my supervisors, if only because my philosophy and instinct are always to communicate. Having had five department heads before I was tenured, I experienced a lack of coordination, communication, and consistency, and I knew I could do better. My first administrative gig was directing the graduate program. In that role, my orientation as a systems thinker was important. I made decisions that included long-range trajectories of student training, programmatic concerns, and explanations of all of these forces to students and faculty. I still think of those students as "my" students.

I will also say that I have always been aware of how my gender and my ambiguous ethnicity have affected my work as an administrator. On the negative side of the ledger, as business literature and stereotypes have told us, people expect women to be warm and approachable and people have a hard time accepting women's authority. On the positive side, I do feel that my staff, faculty, and students enjoy talking to me and that I am able to get my finger on the pulse of what is happening here. I cannot say for sure if my ethnic background in a culture that was more communal and less individualistic can take credit for my systems orientation toward change and problems, but I do know that I think systemically and that really helps me to think about how to improve work practices and ensure everyone feels valued.

I hoped to accomplish a system in which everyone felt heard and valued – because they could see and express how their work contributed toward a greater whole. Of course, this is an impossible goal. Nevertheless, I do think I come closer to this goal every year and there is some evidence of my success. I can write about the high teaching evaluations in my units and the steps we take to ensure that our curriculum remains relevant and lively. I can write about programs I've initiated to support faculty in writing grants and the success rate they have achieved with externally funded grants. More to the point, I remember a university wide evaluation of administrators at Texas Tech in which my faculty's very high ratings of my performance were even mentioned in the summary Institutional Effectiveness report. Similarly, at Virginia Tech, I have won the College of Liberal Arts and Human Sciences' Administrator of the Year

Award.

What is increasingly important to me now is building social and human capital so that other faculty can become the great administrators too. All of my departmental advisory committee members are women, currently with rank of Associate and some in non-tenure track appointments. I'm concerned with how I cultivate their talent, help them to preserve their work life balance (since that is my area of research, after all!), and expose them to my philosophy without burdening them with the preoccupations I have that make my work more difficult than it needs to be, arguably. I want to share how rewarding administration can be, rather than the frustrations. In particular, I have a messianic zeal for the work of administering programs which train students to improve human lives and relationships across the lifespan. To me, training students and future leaders in this work is important for the future of higher education and also for the future of a civil society.

## Introduction to Commentary

Authors/panelists were invited to comment on each other's observations. This section of the chapter contains the thoughts of the authors concerning cross-cutting themes. There were a number of themes, including: the degree to which personal experiences were framed in ways that went beyond the personal, persistence, power in intentionality, power in collaboration, change and the power of relationships. Several authors noted wider issues of diversity. Below are the authors' comments.

### From Judy Fischer: Personal Experiences Framed Beyond the Personal

Each author identified personal experiences: Judy described the subtle and not-so-subtle discrimination against women in her first job search. She placed this discrimination in the context of patriarchal (white) gatekeeping. Kevin touched on a deeply personal loss that contributed to a deepening of empathy towards those with less privilege. Maresa identified the ways in which occupying a niche not well populated can result in others' seemingly trying to fill out a balance sheet by enlisting her service and how important it can be for one's own well-being to say no. Jean relayed hurtful interactions with others early in her career that demeaned her as a professional based on her gender. Her sense of fair play and justice are manifested in many ways, one of which is her role as a university Ombudsperson. Donna's moving ahead with her own career goals and working to advance women in academia were facilitated by the unwavering support of her mother. And Anisa's early family life and cultural background helped her in a number of ways to negotiate with others within systems, especially taking a more communal orientation within those systems. In professional settings she learned to discern how things could be done better and, as department head at more than one university, she strives to empower others.

The experiences of these panelists were not simply held tightly within themselves, but seemed to form catalysts to personal and professional growth. In some sense, the new gatekeepers are blowing up the gates of injustice, discrimination, and invisibility.

## From Kevin Lyness: The Value of Persistence and Taking a Long View

One theme that stood out for me across these stories was persistence, exemplified in the quote Donna highlighted. Each of these panelists has persisted through varying levels of adversity, discrimination, and backlash, and has been able to have strong positive influences as a result. It would be interesting to hear more about what enabled each of us to persevere. It seems that it has been a mix of external supports and internal strength, optimism, and commitment. Related to the notion of persistence is taking a long view, which includes choosing one's battles, working for incremental change, and taking care of one's self.

## From Maresa Murray: Power and Intentionality

After hearing the specific details expressed by the panelists, I was struck by the absolute intentionality of being strategic with the power we were each privileged to wield. There is a Bible scripture that comes to mind from Luke 12:36 which states that much is required of the person to whom much is given. It was quite clear that we, on the panel, had been given very much and that we cared to use that administrative power to help those without a seat at decision-making tables.

It seems that each panelist was very cognizant of an area dealing with gender roles in their respective administrative post, with Anisa and I doing the same, with an additional layer of negotiation needed for ethnicity. Being quite familiar with the sociological theories that espouse the importance of racial identity being more important than gender identity in African-American women, I was neither surprised that our panel colleagues were extremely aware of gender barriers and stereotypes, nor was I shocked to find myself primarily communicating about racial barriers and stereotypes.

And as we shared the details of our respective experiences in administration, a subtle question of hope emerged for me.....What if the panelists could actually work together from our respectively strategic vantage points to create positive administrative change? So often these power dynamics are negotiated in silence and darkness out of necessity, so that the strategic initiatives won't be undermined. But I was awestruck by the amount of thought and intention that went into the management of each step along the way for the panelist, and it made me want to congratulate each person on negotiating a strategy that was "custom made" for each person, taking into account one's own personality, race, gender, sexual orientation, etc. Enjoying the beautiful mosaic of strategy enacted by each person within their own professional context was absolutely beautiful, and it left me with a smile of admiration for each panelist.

Beyond a shadow of a doubt, I felt that each panelist understood the gravity of the power with which they were entrusted, and they maximized the penetration of positive influence behind closed doors, where folks would never guess the depth of brokerage invested in creating opportunities for social justice in the academy.

## From Jean Scott: Power of Collaboration

A theme that catches my eye is the power of collaboration at multiple levels. Donna noted that building collaborations across the academic institution is one strategy for dealing with challenges to improvements in university culture and climate. Collaboration has been helpful in my work as a university faculty ombudsperson; bringing together persons and unit representatives who can problem solve together. Anisa observed that her systems orientation naturally framed her approach to highly successful administration; being able to see the larger picture and the importance of listening to all person's voices. In Kevin's experience, professional service collaborations get difficult conversations on the table. In a cautionary sense, Maresa's "ah ha" story reveals a strength in discerning when a gracious "no" is the better option. Collaborative work empowers when it brings together persons with the right alignment of personal and professional motivation and social responsibility for fairness and justice. Finally, Judy's idea of a panel discussion at the 2016 Groves Conference on Marriage and Family opens a rich treasure of stories, which with their telling, empower both speakers and listeners.

## From Anisa Zvonkovic: Change and Relationships

As I re-read the comments, I am struck with what my colleagues had to say about making changes. Jean wrote "social justice does not come as smoothly, respectably, and cleanly as the history books might suggest" and I think each story addressed how social change can occur. Donna wrote about how, in her role as Assistant Provost, she focused on low-cost, high-impact activities, partly because of budget issues and partly because her focus was on fixing the system, not the people whose lives were made difficult by engaging in the system. This perspective reminds me of one of my critiques of the self-help work-life literature, which often tells women they need to manage their time better rather than recognizing that the system that sets them up to perform more tasks than is possible to perform in a 24-hour period is really what needs to change! Kevin wrote about his work with the COAMFTE and how some of their recommendations needed to be rolled back, demonstrating the rocky paths to enact social change. Both Judy and Maresa wrote about their experiences as the only woman or only African-American woman faculty member, and how they enacted social change by being visible, being productive, showing what can be accomplished. In sum, the only way to work toward social justice and to enact change is through relationships. Luckily, those relationships, forged under fire, are also nourishing and sustaining.

## Closing Thoughts

The opening quote situated the chapter in the pioneering and often self-revealing history of members of the Groves Conference on Marriage and Families as they met on topics of sexuality, gender, and diversity. The contributors to this chapter carried forward these Groves traditions. Importantly, they affirmed the stake all human beings have in fairness and opportunity and justice for people of all genders and ethnicities and class. Higher education was our common situation, but as writers of sections of this chapter, we began with a keen awareness that our personal experiences reflect membership in groups defined by gender and ethnicity and their intersection. Just as our stories exist in the wider realm of experiences that we share as human beings, our goals embrace a future that builds on and transcends these experiences. Politicization of personal experiences invites others to resonate with them and to take action. In the view of many of us, American society in 2017 seemed to have lurched backward to a more unjust past. There is a larger societal debate about identity and politics that goes beyond the more modest goals of the chapter. As long as gender and ethnicity and class are used to privilege one group over another, then social justice in academia and elsewhere remains elusive. Marian Wright Edelman, of the Children's Defense Fund, provided an aspirational message about an American future that embraces social justice:

> Remember and help America remember that the fellowship of human beings is more important than the fellowship of race and class and gender in a democratic society. (Marian Wright Edel man, 1993, p. 54)

# References

Edelman, M. E. (1993). *The measure of our success: Letter to my children and yours.* New York, NY: Harper Collins.

Fine, M. G., & Buzzanell, P. M. (2000). Walking the high wire: Leadership theorizing, daily acts and tensions. In P. M. Buzzanell (Ed.), *Rethinking organizational and managerial communication from feminist perspectives* (pp. 138-156). Thousand Oaks, CA: Sage.

Meyerson, D. E., & Fletcher, J. K. (2000). A modest manifesto for shattering the glass ceiling. *Harvard Business Review, 78(1),* 127-136.

Rubin, R. R. (2012). Chapter 9. Sexuality, gender, and family diversity. In R. R. Rubin & B. H. Settles (Eds.) *The Groves Conference on Marriage and Family: History and impact on family science* (pp. 195 – 247). Ann Arbor, MI: MPublishing, University of Michigan Library.

**Contact Information for Authors (authorship is in alphabetical order):**

**Judith Fischer,** past Department Chair, Texas Tech; past President Groves Conference
        judith.fischer@ttu.edu
        Professor Emeritus
        Department of Human Development and Family Studies
        Texas Tech University
        Lubbock, TX

**Kevin Lyness**, Department Chair, Applied Psychology; Program Director of Ph.D. in MFT; past member and past Chair of the Commission on Accreditation for Marriage and Family Therapy Education (COAMFTE); past member of Standards Review Committee for COAMFTE
        klyness@antioch.edu
        Professor
        Department of Applied Psychology
        Antioch University New England
        Keene, NH

**Maresa J. Murray**, past Co-chair, NCFR Inclusion & Diversity Committee; Liaison, Office of Strategic Hiring & Support, Indiana University
        marjmurr@indiana.edu
        Clinical Associate Professor and Director of Undergraduate Education
        Applied Health Science
        School of Public Health
        Indiana University
        Bloomington, IN

**Jean Pearson Scott**, Ombudsperson, Texas Tech University; President, Groves Conference; past Department Chair, HDFS, Texas Tech University
        jean.scott@ttu.edu
        Professor
        Department of Human Development and Family Studies
        Texas Tech University
        Lubbock, TX

**Donna Sollie**, Past Assistant Provost for Women's Initiatives, Office of Diversity & Multicultural Affairs, Auburn University
        sollidl@auburn.edu

Professor Emeritus
Human Development and Family Studies
Auburn University
Auburn, AL

**Anisa Zvonkovic**, Dean, College of Health and Human Performance;
President NCFR
zvonkovica18@ecu.edu
Dean
Health and Human Performance
East Carolina University
Greenville, NC

*Chapter 12*

## Beyond bathrooms: A primer on gender and sexuality

*Meg Bolger*

*Perry Cohen*

*The Venture Out Project*

Gender is an incredibly complex topic and something that continually and constantly evolves and changes. While we gave our best effort to answer the questions, no information should be taken as fact for the entire transgender community. If we were to write about what it means to be a woman, many of the women reading the piece would have agreements and disagreements, tweaks and changes, and other identities that would impact their experiences. This is also true here. We share this information in the hopes that it will lead to deeper understanding, empathy, and connection, both for the transgender community and for our own relationships with gender.

We offer a number of suggested links and resources throughout the article. All of the references to these resources can be found at: www.ventureoutproject.com/personal-is-political.

### What are differences between sex and gender identity?

Sex (sometimes referred to biological sex/anatomical sex) refers to the physical aspects of our bodies, more specifically to characteristics that we associate with "sex" i.e. chromosomes, hormones, and anatomical characteristics. These may include primary sex characteristics (ones we are born with) and secondary sex characteristics (ones we develop during our lifespans).

The Safe Zone Project (2017) provides an easy to understand explanation of gender identity being "who we know ourselves to be, based on what we understand to be the options for gender, and how much we align (or don't align) with one of those options." The difference between biological sex and gender is that sex is referring to the physical make-up of our bodies and gender identity is referring to our understanding of self. In simple terms we can say, "gender is what's in our heads and sex is what's in our pants."

## What does it mean to be transgender? What are some of the important terms and concepts to know?

Just as there are so many ways to be a man or a woman, there are myriad ways to be transgender, no one definition would satisfy or accurately represent the entire community. Let's start again with the connection between assigned sex at birth and gender. Our culture has led us to expect that anyone who is assigned male at birth must identify as a man and anyone assigned female at birth must identify as a woman. For the sake of explanation, a person who is transgender does not experience that alignment between their assigned sex and their gender identity. In other words, their assigned sex at birth and their gender identity doesn't match.

Susan Stryker, a leading trans scholar, defines transgender people as those who challenge gender norms by "mov(ing) away from the gender they were assigned at birth, people who cross over (trans--) the boundaries constructed by their culture to define and constrain that gender" (2008, p.1).

There are lots of ways that might manifest, and here's where it can get complicated. First let's start by talking about the gender binary. In the simplest terms the gender binary refers to the notion that there are only two genders, male and female, and that these genders exist on opposite poles. Some members of the trans community transition from male to female, or from female to male. Example: Cynthia was assigned male at birth (M) and now identifies/is a woman/female (F). There are lots of different terms Cynthia might use to describe herself and her identify. Cynthia may label herself as a woman, a transwoman, and/or as MtF (male-to-female).

There are also people who were assigned either female or male at birth and who identify with a non-binary gender identity. Unlike the binary trans experience we discussed above, where a person transitions from male to female or vice versa, some people identify as non-binary. In other words, they do not identify with the sex they were assigned at birth, and also don't identify as the "opposite" of that sex. Example: Charlie was assigned male at birth and identifies as non-binary. That means when someone asks, "Ok so is Charlie a man or a woman?" Charlie's friends reply, "Nope."

It is important to know that transitioning looks different for every trans person and medical transition is not a requirement for being trans. Some folks identify as transgender and do not medically transition. This can be for many reasons, including lack of desire, lack of access, safety, etc. When we think about trans people, there is a tendency to focus primarily on medical transition and surgery more specifically. A common question trans people get is, "Have you had the surgery yet?" This question is important to unpack.

There is no single surgery related to a person's status as transgender. There are a number of different types of surgeries that someone may seek out (and again some may not). These include top surgery (chest reconstruction), bottom surgery (construction of vagina or penis), plastic surgeries (facial feminization or masculinization) to name a few. These surgeries may be cost prohibitive, are rarely covered by insurance, and are major surgeries. For these reasons, and many others, a trans person may seek out these surgeries or they may not.

Surgery is not the only type of medical transition someone may seek out or consider and medical transition is not the only type of transitioning that is important to understand. Someone may transition socially, by coming out to themselves, their friends/family, to co-workers, to specific communities they are involved in. They may come out in different spaces, work, home, church, sports teams, etc. Asking people to use a new name or pronouns are key aspects to a social transition.

There is also the legal aspect of transitioning, changing your name and gender marker on legal documents. This can include travel documents, IDs, licenses for your business/marriage, diplomas, health insurance, etc.

A lot of times there are thresholds established, by systems and also by individuals, that communicate, "you'll be transitioned enough *at this point* for me to recognize your identity." That could be a friend saying, "well they haven't had surgery yet so I'm not going to use their new name." That could be a medical professional being unwilling to prescribe hormone therapy because someone isn't living openly with their family and friends. It could be that an employer won't change an employee name in the system without their driver's license being changed. These barriers are incredibly invalidating for a trans person. It is important to consider, as those who want to validate trans identity, what thresholds we establish, why, and what ways that might negatively affect the trans people we work with, love, and serve. If someone says they are trans, they are trans. There is no amount of surgery, hormones, or other processes that determine if someone is trans. Referring back to the discussion of gender identity, it is an internal sense of self. It's something a person knows and may be independent of their physical body.

**What does it mean to be gender non-binary or nonconforming? What are the important terms and concepts to know?**

As we mentioned above, some people identify as non-binary, meaning that they don't identify as men or women, but something beyond that binary. What it means to be affirming of trans people like Cynthia who do identify within the binary and what it means to be affirming and inclusive of non-binary people can sometimes look very different. Many of our systems, bathrooms, sports teams, resource groups, etc. are set up along binary gender lines. Men over here and women over here. If you do not identify within those two categories, as a man or a woman, often times there is no clear place for you to go or way for you to access what you need.

The trans community faces significant discrimination and risk factors across many different areas of life, this risk is increased for non-binary individuals. If we look to the Trans Discrimination survey (Harrison, et. al., 2012) we see, "As compared to transgender-identified survey respondents, genderqueer were people more likely to: Suffer physical assaults (32% compared to 25%), survive sexual assault in K-12 education (16% compared to 11%), face police harassment (31% compared to 21%), be unemployed (76% compared to 56%), avoid healthcare treatment for fear of discrimination (36% compared to 27%)". We highlight these statistics to demonstrate the critical difference affirming a non-binary person can make upon a broad array of health, wellness and social measures. It is common today for schools and organizations to create policies that are inclusive of transwomen and transmen, i.e., if you identify as a man you can participate in "men's groups", but less common is to create policies that expand beyond the binary to help ensure that non-binary folks are included in the conversation. It is important not only to ask the question of "when we say this is a women's group, are we inclusive of all women, including trans women? But also to ask questions like, "If someone identified as non-binary, would we have appropriate resources and support systems for them?"

## How are gender identity and sexual orientation related?

If gender identity could be summarized as how you understand yourself, sexual orientation might be summarized as who you find yourself attracted to. I once heard a friend say, "gender is who you go to bed as, sexual orientation is who you go to bed with."

The reason these come up together is because we use gender as the main means by which we describe who we are attracted to. Our gender and the gender of people we are attracted to often equals the sexual orientation label we might use. For instance, if I identify as a woman (my gender) and am primarily attracted to other women (gender of people I'm attracted to) I might label my sexual orientation with the label gay or lesbian. It's important to remember that although gender is used to describe our sexual orientation, our sexual orientation and gender are two distinct and different parts of our identity.

### What do these letters mean, and how many should I use? (LGBTQAI)

There are lots of letters you might have seen. LGBTQQIATSP... the list goes on.

**L**esbian **G**ay **B**isexual **T**ransgender **Q**ueer **Q**uestioning **I**ntersex **A**sexual **T**wo-spirit **P**ansexual.
LGBTQ+ is the acronym that we use (the + indicates that this acronym continues). Typically, we recommend using whatever acronym is being used by the LGBTQ+ community in your area. If GLBT is what is more commonly used, use that. If LGBT is used, use that.

It is important to note that LGBTQ+ is used to describe a group of people or a set of identities, not to describe a single individual. We'd recommend replacing the phrase, "I have an LGBTQ person in my family," with, "someone in my family identifies as part of the LGBTQ community," or "I have a sister who is queer."

### There seem to be a lot of different pronouns now. How can I be most respectful?

There are lots of different sets of pronouns. The most popular ones you already know; he/him/his, she/her/hers, they/them/theirs. They/them/theirs has more recently been adopted for use by people as a singular pronoun, "My friend Marcus is coming over later, **they** are awesome I think you'll really like **them**." Use of they as a singular pronoun has also been approved by many different sources including the Washington Post and AP as well as APA.

If you want to be respectful of people's pronouns, learn what they are and then use them. The best way to learn what pronouns you should use for someone is to ask them. "Hey I'm Stan, my pronouns are he/him, what's your name and pronouns?" If someone doesn't share their pronouns with you, you can always just use their name.

### What other terms should I know?

Whatever terms are being used in your community that you are unfamiliar with. We have a link on our resource page to a handy hand-out of some do's and don'ts when it comes to language, but otherwise when you don't know a term inquire, learn, or write it down and do some research.

## What are some helpful resources to help me keep current?

Concepts around trans issues are growing and evolving. Keeping up with what is current can seem overwhelming, but it doesn't have to be. The first thing you can do is talk to people about gender. Whether that's someone who identifies as trans or with your cisgender friends and colleagues. We find that a fear of saying the wrong thing or appearing uneducated is a tremendous deterrent to having important conversations around gender and one way to get more educated and practice these words is to talk.

Many college campus and communities have LGBTQ+ resource centers. Most are staffed with people to help you work through your questions, provide you with reading lists and resources, and connect you with community events, lectures and talks. Many of these centers also have a speakers' bureau and can connect you to trans and gender noncon-forming folks who will come speak or who provide educational opportu-nities. .

There are also numerous conferences that take place across the country where you can go much more in depth about trans health care, mental health, education, wellness and more. The longest standing are: The Philadelphia Trans Wellness Conference, Gender East, Gender Odys-sey, First Event, PFLAG (Parents and Friends of Lesbians and Gays), and Out in the Open. There are also many more regional conferences, many of which are free to attend.

If you can't get to a resource center or conference, here are some great stand-alone websites with links to them in the references:

- GLAAD - general primer on gender and trans rights
- GLSEN - resources for educators
- National Center for Transgender Equality - primer on trans rights and links to resources
- Gender Spectrum - specifically for K-12 educators and their "Guide for Schools"
- PFLAG - great catchall for resources
- Transgender Law Center - legal resources
- The Venture Out Project - outdoor adventure programs for trans youth and families & trans-inclusive educational programming

- The Safe Zone Project - resources for LGBTQ/ally trainings educators
- Teaching Transgender - for educators wanting to teach/train about trans issues

If you are specifically looking for glossaries or vocab lists try these:

- Transgender Terminology - National Center for Trans Equality (NCTE)
- Glossary of Terms - Gay & Lesbian Alliance Against Defamation (GLAAD)
- LGBTQ+ Vocab List - The Safe Zone Project

Many trans and gender non-conforming folks have youtube channels. Try searching your topic within youtube. We also have favorite videos and video series on gender which is linked at our website: www.venture-outproject.com/personal-is-political.

In sum, there are a lot of resources available to keep track of the shifting landscape of language. The most important thing is to be open and keep talking to people.

### References

Gender Spectrum. (n.d.) *Resources.* Retrieved from https://www.gender-spectrum.org/resources/

GLAAD. (n.d.) *Media reference guide - transgender.* Retrieved from https://www.glaad.org/reference/transgender

GLSEN. (n.d.) *GLSEN resources for educators.* Retrieved from https://www.glsen.org/educate/resources?gclid=CKC-gdL6-9ICFQhLDQodz-CADiA

Harrison, J., Grant, J., & Herman, J. L. (2012). A gender not listed here: Genderqueers, gender rebels, and otherwise in the National Transgender Discrimination Survey. *LGBTQ Public Policy Journal at the Harvard Kennedy, 2*(1), 11–24.

National Center for Trans Equality. (n.d.) *Issues.* Retrieved from http://www.transequality.org/issues/resources/transgender-terminology.

PFLAG. (n.d.) Retrieved from https://www.pflag.org/

Safe Zone Project. *Safe Zone Project Curriculum V4.0, page 31.*(2017) Retrieved from www.thesafezoneproject.com

Stryker, S. (2008). *Transgender history.* Berkeley, CA: Seal Press..

Teaching Transgender. (n.d.) Retrieved from http://www.teachingtransgender.org/

The Safe Zone Project. (n.d.) *Vocabulary extravaganza. Retreived from http://thesafezoneproject.com/wp-content/uploads/2014/09/Vocabulary-Extravaganza-Facilitator-Guide.pdf*

The Venture Out Project. (n.d.) Retrieved from http://www.ventureoutproject.com/

Transgender Law Center. (n.d.) Retrieved from https://transgenderlawcenter.org/